THE STIRLING ANTIQUARY.

THE STIRLING ANTIQUARY.

REPRINTED FROM

"THE STIRLING SENTINEL,"

1888-1893.

EDITED BY W. B. COOK

VOLUME 1

PRINTED FOR PRIVATE CIRCULATION

KALPAZ

ISBN: 978-93-5128-793-3(HB)

First Published in 1893
Indian Reprint in 2017

Published by

Kalpaz Publications
C-30, Satyawati Nagar,
Delhi – 110052
E-mail: kalpaz@hotmail.com
Website: kalpazpublications.com
Ph.: +91-9212142040

Cataloging in Publication Data—DK
Courtesy: D.K. Agencies (P) Ltd. <docinfo@dkagencies.com>

The Stirling antiquary : reprinted from "The Stirling sentinel" 1888-1893 / edited by W.B. Cook.
volumes cm
"First published in 1893"—Title page verso.
ISBN 9789351287933

1. Stirling (Stirling, Scotland)—History. I. Cook, W. B. (William B.), -1912, editor. II. Stirling sentinel.

DA890.S8S75 2017 DDC 941.312 23

INDEX.

The Stirling Antiquary.

MUNICIPAL ANECDOTE OF PRE-REFORM TIMES.

The following interesting local anecdote is from the inexhaustible fund possessed by our esteemed townsman, Mr George Mouat:—In September 1827, the Stirling Guildry, who had the power to elect four members of the Town Council, sent as their representatives the following gentlemen:—Alexander Mouat (Dean of the Guildry), William Forbes, Peter Stoddart, and William Wright, all men of advanced views and independent opinions. In the course of the year 1827-28 these members of the Council formed a party for reforming the close Corporation, and they soon obtained a number of adherents. The Convener of the Seven Incorporated Trades—William Miller, baker—having died, the Reform and anti-Reform parties in the Council stood equal, there being ten on either side. Provost Buchan threw in his lot with the reformers, but it was necessary, before any action could be taken, to secure a majority, and by some means or other the Deacon of the Tailors was gained over from the other side. Unfortunately, however, the deacon got involved in business difficulties, and was obliged to take refuge in the Sanctuary of Holyrood. Here he was maintained for several months at the cost of the Reform party, and his affairs were arranged in time to allow him to take part in the election at Michaelmas 1828. On the morning of the Council meeting the "young party" breakfasted together in the Provost's house in Lower Castlehill—the house occupied by the late Mr Dawson, and now untenanted—and afterwards marched to the Town House in Broad Street. The first business was to fill the vacancy in the Council caused by the death of Convener Miller, and the Reform party succeeded in carrying John Stewart, hammerman, a victory which enabled them to eject all their opponents from office. There was great rejoicing in the burgh over the defeat of the anti-Reformers, the bells being rung and a procession taking place, in which a pole was carried with a flesher's apron fixed half-mast high, the fleshers at that time being the predominating incorporation of the Seven Trades, and their deacon the leader of the anti-Reform party.

ED.

THE LEGEND OF THE WOLF.

About the end of the 9th century, when Donald V. reigned in Scotland, Stirling was taken by Osbrecht and Ella and defended against the Danes. The sentinel at the South Port of the town had been overcome with fatigue and fallen asleep, when he was awoke by the howling of a wolf which had climbed a crag in the neighbourhood. The moment was a critical one, as the Danes were at hand, but the garrison being alarmed, the invaders were soon put to flight. In commemoration of the incident which saved the town from a surprise, a wolf recumbent on a rock was adopted as the amorial bearings of the burgh.—[The above was contributed by the late Mr James Shirra to *Northern Notes and Queries*, a valuable periodical, now very scarce.]

BIBLIOTHECA STIRLINENSIS.

The following notes are supplementary to those which appear in "Stirling Notes and Queries," two volumes printed for private circulation, 1883-1886:—

Stirling, a Satirical Poem, in three cantos, by a Gentleman of Stirling. Edinburgh: Printed and sold by Robert Menzies, Brodie's Close, Lawnmarket. Sold also by W. M'William, Bookseller, Edinburgh; and by James M'Laren, Bookseller, Stirling. 1809. (Price 2s 6d). 37 pp. 8vo.

[The first canto is devoted to a description of the lounging shops, as the author calls them, of Stirling, the Coffee-House, and the Ball-Room. The lounging shops are the places where

"Stirling's sons in various parties meet
Hands in their breeches, lounging in the street;
Or one by one in sneaking progress drop,
To damn mankind in Elgin's idle shop."

The Coffee-Room does not seem to have been either clean or comfortable, as the poet says:—

"Like fishing nets, suspended cobwebs spread
From the black ceiling, almost touched my head;
Placards, advertisements, defil'd and torn
And filthy maps the greasy walls adorn."

The bright surroundings of the Ball-Room are more congenial to the author's tastes.

"The gay assembly claims my willing song,
Where youth and beauty grace the sprightly throng;
All Stirling *fashionables* here are found,
And rustic *beau monde* from the country round."

The second canto is a Prayer to Hymen in behalf of

the Old Maids, in a rather amorous strain. The following is "A worthy sample of the maiden list."

"No cash, 'tis true, the lover here will find,
But amply stocked indeed her liberal mind;
And furnish'd well with self-spun sheets her home,
The Holy Bible, and a small toothcomb."

Another is thus described—

"Her hair in partial locks adorn her head,
And, soft as oakum, beautifully red;
Straight hanging, graceful, and in front divides,
And falls nine inches down her temples' sides;
Her face is scarlet, unadorn'd by art,
But large carbuncles blaze on every part:
And bursting from their sockets seem to rise,
Her goggling, large, and dull, unmeaning eyes,
Each forth projecting from its usual place,
And rolling, far outshoots her burning face.
Smooth as a lemon-peel her nose divine,
That, tip't with crimson, upward tapers fine.
Round massy lips her heav'nly mouth adorn,
And one smart bore-tooth, crooked as a horn."

And so on. His old maids one by one are clothed with all the uglinesses, and adorned with all the graces, or disgraces, that ever pertained to the sex, till the description palls, and by reiteration ceases to be even amusing. The third canto is the said Old Maids' Tea Party, in much the same strain, in which their dress, character, and conversation are remorselessly and satirically criticised, with great vigour and a little coarseness. The pamphlet is published anonymously, but was written, I believe, by Mr H. P. Paget. It is interesting chiefly, apart from its style, as affording a glimpse of Stirling society about the beginning of the century, and some of the personal allusions must have been pretty obvious at the time, when the various blanks and dashes could more readily be filled up than they could be now.]

Extracts from a Poem on The Prospect from Stirling Castle.

I. The Vision.
II. Carmore and Orma, a Love Tale.
III. The Garden.
IV. The King's Knot.
V. Three Hymns, Morning, Noon, and Evening.

By David Doig, LL.D.
[Quotation from Horace here.]
Stirling:
Printed by C. Randall.
MDCCXCVI.

[The above is a small quarto of 36 pages. The author in the advertisement says that near 40 years ago he was so much struck with the beauties of the prospect, that he was surprised no Native of the place had ever attempted to celebrate them in *descriptive poetry*. He then formed the resolution, and actually commenced to write the poem, which, upon the publication of the above as a specimen, he says "is now upon the point of being finished," and promises if the Public relish the Sample he will furnish the Stock, and that such a circumstance might possibly accelerate the publication of the whole Poem. The author, David Doig, was a learned philologist, the son of a small farmer in Forfarshire, and was born in 1719. He was educated at the University of St Andrews, where he took his degree of B.A., became teacher of Monifieth parish school, and subsequently of that of Kennoway and Falkland. Afterwards the Magistrates of Stirling appointed him Rector of the Grammar School. The University of Glasgow conferred on him the degree of LL.D. upon the same day that he received from St Andrews his diploma as M.A. He was an eminent Oriental scholar, with a thorough knowledge of the history, languages, and literature of the East, wrote many dissertations for the Encyclopædia Britannica, and crossed a lance with Lord Kames when he propounded his theory regarding the original state of the human race. Dr Doig died on the 16th March 1800, and the Magistrates of Stirling erected a marble monument to his memory.]

The Whole Prophecies of Scotland, England, Ireland, France, and Denmark, Prophesied by Thomas Rymer, Marvellous Merling, Beid, Berlington, Waldhane, Elirain, Banestar, and Sybilla. Containing many strange and marvellous matters, which has happened, and will be known for times to come, from the year of our Lord 1622 to 1822.

From 1622 to 1745, Good was expected,
But from '45 to 1822, Ill was done and good neglected.

To the Four Corners of the World.

Asia, Africa, Ignorant and Leal,
Europe and America with broils will prevail.

Falkirk: Printed and Sold by Daniel Reid, at the Stirling-shire Printing-Office, 1782. (Price Threepence. (48 pages, 12mo.

The Gentle Shepherd, a Scots Pastoral Comedy. With all the Songs, by Allan Ramsay. Falkirk: Printed and sold by P. Mair. MDCCXC.

[This is in the usual chap-book style, with a small crook cut on the title page, but with a fairly well-designed border, indifferently printed. 60 pages 12mo.]

Elcho Castle; or, Edmund & Velina: a Tale.

Descend from thy wall, harp of Cona, with thy voices three! Come with that which kindles the past: Rear the forms of old, on their own dark brown years!

Ossian.

Stirling: Printed and sold by C. Randall. 1796.

[A poem, 12 pages 12mo, beautifully printed, containing about 300 lines.]

The Cottage in the Glen, a Tale of the Seventeenth Century; Old Brown, a humorous sketch; and The Knight of Jed, a Border Ballad. By Robert Wighton.

Falkirk: Archibald Johnston, High Street. 115 pages 12mo. (No date.)

An Analytical Statement of the case of Alexander, Earl of Stirling and Dovan, &c., &c., &c., Containing an Explanation of His Official Dignities, and Peculiar Territorial Rights and Privileges in the British Colonies of Nova Scotia and Canada, &c., &c. And also shewing the Descent of the Stirling Peerage Honours, supported by Legal Evidence, and the law and usage of Scotland appertaining thereto. With a variety of incidental notes and observations. By Sir Thomas C. Banks, Bart., N.S. "Fiat Justitia, ruat cœlum." London: James Cochrane and Co., 11 Waterloo Place, Pall Mall. 1832. Pp. xlix. and 124, together with two genealogical tables.

[The following manuscript note is on the title page of the copy described above, "*Title ought to be*, 'A production intended to prove by groundless assumption—gross fabrications—perversions and misapplications of alleged facts, that black is white.']

Rural Poetry. By Andrew Buchanan.

"Grant me, indulgent Gods! with mind serene,
And guiltless heart to range the sylvan scene.
There pleasing objects useful thoughts suggest;
The sense is ravish'd, and the soul is bless'd.
On every thorn delightful wisdom grows;
In every rill a sweet instruction flows."

Young.

Stirling: Printed for the Author, by J. Fraser. Sold by J. Forman, Stirling; J. Peddie, Perth; W. M'Donald and J. Laird, Crieff. 1817. 12mo. pp. vi. and 144.

[The author, like most of our minor poets, seems to have been a working man, on which account he craves the leniency of the learned critics, and hopes they will not demand of him the pure diction of the classical scholar. The preface is dated from Crieff. Can any correspondent give any facts or dates regarding this author?]

Sovereign Goodness Display'd; In a Brief Relation of Some of the most Remarkable Dispensations of Divine Providence, in the Spiritual Exercises of Ann M'Nicol, Parishioner in Killern. Glasgow: Printed and Sold by Will. Bell. Sold also by John Bryce and Robert Farie, Booksellers, Saltmarket; and by the Author's Relations in Strathblane and Killern. M.DCC.LXXXI. 28 pp., 8vo.

[Printed from a manuscript, after the death of the authoress, which occurred in 1752. In recounting "some of the general occurrences of her younger years," the authoress says, "I was conceived in sin, every faculty of my soul being stained with original guilt; and born in Bucklyvie, in the parish of Kippen, in the year of our Lord 1720."]

Report as to Improving the Navigation of the Rivers Forth, &c., and the Advantages of small Canals demonstrated. By Alexander M'Gibbon, Stirling. Edinburgh: Printed and Sold by R. Menzies, Lawnmarket; and by James Forman, Bookseller, Stirling; and by the Author, at his Writing Office, Broad Street, Stirling. 100 pages octavo. 1810.

[An elaborate report, in which the author claims to have made what he calls really a great discovery, that for the mere trifle of £1060 10s Stirling could be made a foreign port, open to navigation from Alloa, for vessels of 300 tons, which would certainly encourage trade, and save much land carriage. The writings of Smeaton and Watt he finds nothing to the purpose, being loose conjectures, and the result of mere eye surveys, while much of his information was got from conversation with long experienced fishers and skippers. He measured the loops and necks of land, and sounded the whole tide way, and from these facts formed his calculations. He proposes branch canals, or arms, along the level, not only to every farm, but to every field of the farms, just by widening one of the ditches. Altogether, it is a curious and entertaining piece of literature, in which are embedded some valuable facts of contemporary local history.]

Glasgow. J. I.

THE OLD STYLE OF CELEBRATING THE KING'S BIRTHDAY IN STIRLING.

On the occasion of the King's birthday, the members of the Stirling Guildry, the Trades, and others, used to turn out in Broad Street at the invitation of the Town Council for the purpose of drinking His Majesty's health. They formed three sides of a square in front of the Town House, with a military band in the centre and a firing party from the Castle outside. The Magistrates and Council assembled in the Council Chamber (now the Parochial Board-room) and afterwards came down stairs to take part in the demonstration. Glasses were served out and a round of wine allowed for each of the three toasts usually drunk, a *feu de joie* accompanying the cheering. After the last toast the glasses were tossed up in the air, that is to say, if they were not seized by some one in the outside crowd who thought it was a pity to waste the crystal. The expense of the entertainment was borne by the Common Good. The custom was discontinued in the reign of William IV.

THE STIRLING TRADES "BLUE BLANKET."

The Blue Blanket of the Stirling Trades is about 2⅞ yards square, and is made up of ribbons and silk 8 inches broad sewed together, of a dingy flesh-colour and faded sky-blue, with a St. Andrew's Cross in white silk from corner to corner. It is attached to a piece of wood, the ends of which are fixed to poles for carrying. The Convener is provided with a sash of rich white silk 2⅞ yards long, having a fringe 8 inches deep, and he wears an ancient sword on great occasions. He walks under the banner, the floating ends of which are held by ribbons the blanket requiring four craftsmen to bear it aloft. The tradition is that when Mary Queen of Scots granted the charter of privilege on 16th April, 1556, to the Stirling Trades, she presented them with a banner made by herself and her maids of honour. When the banner was unfurled at the Cross in High Street it was the signal for the Trades to fly to arms and rally round the Convener, each burgess being required to bring along with him two pecks of meal and a bag of onions for his subsistence while his services were required. The blanket was kept in a strong oak box furnished with seven locks. Each deacon had a key, so that all had to be present before the box could be opened. The "airings" were considered notable occasions for "a guzzle and a spate" at the expense of the Incorporation. The blanket was held up by the corners by four persons standing on chairs, while the deacons danced the Reel of Hoolachan below it. Sometimes it was fixed to the ceiling of the room.—[J. S. (James Shirra) in *Northern Notes and Queries*].

A TAX FOR PROTECTION IN STIRLING.

From Robert Heron's "Journey through the Western Counties of Scotland," Edinburgh, 1793:—

"In the times when this country was frequently ravaged, either in consequence of feuds among its native inhabitants, or by the incursions of enemies, the peasantry of the circumjacent country depended for their protection upon the Governor, or Constable, of Stirling and the garrison of Stirling Castle. For this protection they paid a certain annual tax. They no longer have occasion to flee within the bounds of the castle, or to call upon the garrison for their defences; but the tax, or duty, continues still, agreeably to the ordinary laws of inheritance, to be levied, and serves as a memorial of the unsettled manners, and the insecure condition of our ancestors."—Vol. II., p. 446.

CURIOUS EXTRACTS FROM THE *SCOTS MAGAZINE.*

In the lists of deaths given in each month's issue of the Magazine are the following:—(Jan. 1739) Mr Horne, an eminent banker, and Chief Lamplighter to His Majesty, a place of about £600 per annum. (April 1739) Edward Ridder, the famous pastry-man, who had taught near 6000 ladies the art of pastry. (June 1839) In St. Margaret's Workhouse, Westminster, in the 138th year of her age, Margaret Paton, born near Paisley. (Sept. 1739) In Wicklow County, Josias Parsley, in the 107th year of his age. (Feb. 1740) In the parish of Bize, in the diocese of Comminges in France on the 19th Jan. last, N.S., John Roger Gaston, aged 129. He was never sick, never took physick, and was a brisk man till within a fortnight of his death. The Sieur Valade, Parson of St. Michael, one of the parishes of Vienne in France, aged 119. He was ordained a priest in 1652, said mass until his sight failed about a year ago, was sensible to the last, and subject to no aliment but the weight of years. In the parish of Wooten, near Barcham downs, South Britain, Widow Roust, aged 105. (April 1740) aged 110, Mr Davies, who lately kept Harry's coffee house, Fleet street, London. He retained all his senses till his death, and would read the smallest print without spectacles. (June, 1740) Charles Thomson, Esq., aged 104, who had command of the Boyne man-of-war in Queen Anne's reign. (Sept., 1740) George Austin, aged 120, who was clerk to the parish of Carlow, 80 years. (Oct., 1740), aged 109, Margaret Fytch, called at London, Queen of the Gipsies. (Nov. 1740) In the isle of Leon, aged 121 years and 4 months, Bernard Salunt, born at Narbonne. He retained his judgement till the last. In the list of marriages for June 1840 is that of Thomas Ashburnham, an ale-house keeper in Fleet

Street, aged 85, married to his eighth wife, aged 45. In the list of new books for Feb. 1740 is noted what would prove a very handy compendium in these days to distracted householders hunting for a new house—a list of houses in and about Edinburgh, to be let or sold, showing the conveniences of each house, where it is, the yearly rent, and of whom to enquire. 1d. Appendix to ditto, 1d. A very irreverent custom—which we would hardly have expected to find in Scotland—is disclosed in a letter to the Editor in the number for July 1740. It is dated from Edinburgh, and is signed G. P. "Sir, I was very well pleased some *Sundays* ago, to observe the zeal shown by the clergy in their late act for the more strict observance of the Lord's Day; and was in hopes, when I heard it read from the pulpit, that some notice would have been taken therein of an indecency (to give it no worse name) which I daresay must to every person of piety and good manners be offensive; and that is, a custom which I see is pretty universal among our lower sort of folks, of cocking on their hats whenever the sermon begins."

Glasgow. T. M.

THE BEREANS IN STIRLING.

The Bereans were a sect of Christians now extinct, who originated in Scotland in the 18th century. Their name was derived from the circumstance that the inhabitants of Berea "received the word with all readiness of mind, and searched the Scriptures daily."—Acts xvii. 11. The founder of the Bereans was the Rev. John Barclay, a native of Perthshire, from whom the sect also received the name of Barclayans. The peculiarities of their creed were that the knowledge of God's existence and character is derived from the Bible alone and not from reason or nature; that the Psalms of David do not relate to David at all, but exclusively to Christ; that assurance is the essence of faith; and that unbelief is the unpardonable sin.

The adherents of the sect in Stirling usually met in Allan's School, Spittal Street, but on special occasions they assembled in the building on the opposite side of the street, at present occupied by Mr Crocket, leather merchant. Mr George Mouat tells a story, that at one of the services conducted by an Edinburgh shoemaker, named Donaldson, a popular preacher among the Bereans, a dog belonging to William Lockhart, publican, which had followed its master to the meeting-house, became excited by the preacher's vigorous delivery and rushed out at the door, overturning the plate with the collection, to the great consternation of the elder or deacon in charge, and the no small amusement of the passers-by. Ed.

BLIND ALICK AS A SCRIPTURE CONCORDANCE.

The following anecdote of Blind Alick was obtained by us from the late Mr George Chalmers, builder :—Thomas Chalmers, the town bellman, when a youth, attended the Rev. Mr Gilfillan's Bible class in Viewfield Church, and on one occasion a verse of Scripture was given out by the minister for proof, without any reference to where it was to be found. Chalmers searched the Bible for the passage for several days, but failed tofind it. At last he bethought himself of applying for assistance to Blind Alick, whom he found as usual in the Back Walk. The following conversation ensued :—

Chalmers—Eh, man, Alick, I'm in an awfu' strait.

Alick—Hoo that, Tammy?

C—I've a verse to prove for the minister, an' I dinna ken where it is.

A—It'll be i' the Buik.

C—Ou, ay, it's i' the Buik, but I canna fin't.

A—What is it?

Chalmers then repeated the words, and Alick in an instant gave chapter and verse, which were verified by the boy on the spot by a reference to the Bible which he carried in his pocket. Ed.

THE BURGH BUILDINGS OF STIRLING.

In the beginning of the century the site of the Burgh Buildings in King Street was occupied by the Mealmarket, a stone wall, with a large red-painted gate, facing what was then called Quality Street. When the question of doing away with the Mealmarket came up in the Town Council in 1815, it divided the members into two parties, viz., the Broad Street party, headed by Provost Anderson, and the Low-Town party, headed by Bailie, afterwards Provost Gillies. On the vote being taken, the proposal to abolish the Mealmarket was carried by the narrow majority of 1, and it was resolved to build an "Athenæum." It was originally intended to give the first floor of the building for a County Hall, but the county people refusing to subscribe towards the cost of erection, this intention was departed from. The foundation stone was laid with masonic honours in presence of a large assemblage. The prayer on the occasion was offered up by the Rev. John Russel (Burns' "Black Russel"), one of the ministers of the East Church. The opening took place on 17th January, 1818. The shops on the ground floor were sold to Patrick Connal, merchant, and the shop to the right hand, or east, was first occupied by Miss Fletcher, haberdasher, the shop facing the Corn Exchange being taken by Messrs Drummond & Sons, seedsmen. The premises were afterwards purchased by Messrs A. & J. Mouat, drapers, who opened the shops right through and carried on business there for many years. The first floor was let to the Stirling Subscription Reading Room, and the top flat to the Stirling Library. In 1873 the Council resolved to occupy the building themselves, and the reading-room was converted into the Town Clerk's office, while the place occupied by the Library was fitted up as the Council Chamber. The statue of Wallace, for which the arched portico was built in 1859, was executed by Mr Handasyde Ritchie, and was presented to the town by the late Mr William Drummond. ED.

EXTRACT FROM PRIVY COUNCIL RECORDS RELATING TO ABERFOYLE.

The Earl of Airth (Menteith) had procured letters of caption against his relative, John Graham of Duchrae, and Thomas Graham, his son. There being considerable difficulty in having this served, he took advantage of the fact that Thomas Graham was to have a child baptised at the Kirk of Aberfoil, and judging that the whole family might be found together, he proceeded thither (February 13, 1671) with Alex. Muschet, messenger, and a strong party of his friends and dependents, all well armed. Duchrae, though he considered himself in possession of a sufficient protection from the King, deemed it necessary that his christening party should also be well armed. At the Bridge of Aberfoyle, the Duchrae party—including the minister and elders of the parish—met Alex. Muschet, who had come forward with a few attendants to execute the writ, while the Earl of Airth remained, with some others of his party, at a little distance. When Muschet told Duchrae to consider himself as his prisoner, the latter took out a protection, which he held forth with words of scornful defiance, calling out, "What dar ye do? This is all your master"—the truth being that the paper was not a protection from civil debt, but merely bore reference to another question regarding the removal from certain lands. Meanwhile the baby was set down upon the ground, and the Duchrae party prepared their swords, guns, and pistols for a conflict, avowing to Muschet and his friends that they would kill the one-half of them and drown the other. They did, accordingly, press first upon Muschet, and then upon the Earl and his friends, who quickly gave way, but rallied and stood upon their defence. It was alleged that the Earl was narrowly missed by several bullets, and it was certain that some of his servants were wounded, one Robert M'Farlane losing two of his fingers. With great difficulty, they were allowed to get off with their lives. Duchrae, notwithstanding an attempt at counter-action, was condemned to go in Edinburgh Tolbooth, and give ample caution that he would keep the peace towards the Earl of Airth and his tenants.

A. C.

THE CHAPLAINRY OF CAMBUSBARRON.

The late Mr James Lucas, writer, Stirling, in examining the titles of Jane Athol Duthie, wife of Captain James Galloway, of the Royal Navy, found that she had inherited the right of patronage in the Chaplainry of Cambusbarron. She held her lands blench under the Earl of Mar, the charter containing the following clause:—

"All and whole the half lands of Cambusbarron lying in the parish of St Ninians, and Sheriffdom of Stirling, with the advocation, donation, and right of patronage in the chaplainry of Cambusbarron, which formerly pertained to the deceased William Lesslie, of Balquhain; together also with the parsonage, teinds, and teind bolls of all and sundry the foresaid lands."

Can any of our readers tell who now enjoys the right of Mrs Galloway?

Ed.

THE OLD NAME OF KING STREET.

When the Mealmarket occupied the site of the present Burgh Buildings, King Street was sometimes called the Mealmarket and sometimes the foot of the town. It was very uneven and badly paved, and was almost entirely occupied by brewers of small ale called "pundy," and public-houses with "louping-on stones" in front. Among those who lived in this quarter of the town was a man called Alexander Robertson, a somewhat affected and pompous-speaking individual. In the course of a conversation with a residenter in the upper part of the burgh, Robertson remarked, "We are people of quality who live here, and we call it 'Quality Street!'" This name stuck to the street until 1820, in which year the Town Council re-christened several streets, Quality Street being called King Street in honour of the accession of George IV.

Ed.

NAMES OF STIRLING STREETS.

At the Town Council meeting on 20th November, 1843, Bailie Rankin stated that there were two places in town that had no name—from the foot of King Street to the foot of Queen Street—and there were two county gentlemen who took a deep interest in the prosperity of the town—one of them, it was well-known, was the cause of the thoroughfare being made. He would therefore submit that the space from the foot of King Street to the Royal Hotel be called "Murray Street" (after William Murray, Esq. of Polmaise), from the Royal Hotel to the foot of Queen Street be called "Ramsay Street" (after Mr Ramsay of Barnton), and from the Royal Hotel down to Mr Henderson's building at the top of Forth Place, be named "Maxwell Street"—the latter after Mrs Murray. This was agreed to, and it was also agreed to name two places in Dumbarton Road, Albert Place and Victoria Place respectively, after the Prince-Consort and Queen Victoria. Drummond Place owes its name to the late Peter Drummond. George Street, formed in 1876, was called after Provost George Christie (1870-79), and James Street commemorates Bailie James Ronald, who built the first (and up to this time the only) house in the street. Ed.

THE RESURRECTIONISTS IN STIRLING.

At the Spring Circuit Court in 1822, the grave-digger and some others were tried on a charge of lifting dead bodies from Stirling Churchyard. They alleged that they acted by instructions from Dr John Forrest, who made a timely flight from the town to escape prosecution. He joined the army, and ultimately rose to be Inspector-General of Hospitals. A riot took place in the streets at the time, and the 77th Regiment were brought down from the Castle to disperse the rioters. They fired on the mob in Spittal Street, but no one was injured, the soldiers intentionally firing over the people's heads. One of the bullets entered the *Journal* office, which was then in Spittal Street, in the premises at present occupied by Mrs Crocket, but did no damage. For long afterwards bodies were buried in stone or iron coffins, which were removed in six weeks or so, and a watch was kept on all new-made graves. The watch-house in the churchyard was taken down about 25 years ago. Ed.

ANCIENT TOPOGRAPHICAL DESCRIPTION OF STIRLINGSHIRE AND THE LENNOX.

The following curious notes are from the Macfarlane MSS. in the Advocates Library :—

Noats of Lennox and Sterlingshyr gotten fra Gentlemen of that country 15 May 1644.

The Springs of Kelvyn river cum from above Colyam Castle in Sterlingshyr hard by on the north hand is the Catfin burn another spring, and to the south hand another moor up then achinoyl whilk is very near the head of the water caed Beny whilk fallith down to Dunipace third yvers spring, joyned beneth the kirk of monyabrigh, beging to be caed Kelvyin and fals north, then the burn of Glaghdyr falleth in from the north about half a myl above Kirkintillo. Kirkintillo fra Kinked just south half a myl and Kelvyn betwixt, it is half a myl up on Glasdye, the tenth of Glasdye myl. The Conos fra N.W. to S.E. thereon first Kinked on the west. Woodhead 2 myl above Kinked on that same syd. Gloret a myl above Kinked on the eastsyd, Bandcloich above it on that same syd a quarter myl and a quarter from the water syd.

Kirkintillo and Partkirk at Kelvyn mouth 8 myl, Kirkintillo Glasco 6 myl Glasco Partkirk 2 myl Glasco is fra Kirkintillo SSW and Partkirk fra Glasco W.

Luggy river runs in Kelvyn at Kirkintillo on the south syd the lenth 4 myl large ther is upon it Baidlor 2 myl fra Kirkintillo upon the south syd of it. Bandheath also 3 myl fra Kirkintillo upon the northsyde it is a myl fra Monkland paroch. Monkland Kirk 3 myl fra Clyd 8 myl fra Glasco. Kinked fra Sterlin 12 myl Kinked Kilsyth 3 myl Kilsyth Sterlingshyr.

Kelvyn runs east and west inclyning somewhat to the south.

Cader-Cader-ealler is thereon 3 short myl beneth Kirkintillo. Kirkintillo—Dumbartan 12 long myl.

Bardovy a myle fra Kelvyn on the northsyd, besyd a prettie loch it is a a myle beneth Cader. Benekele is a myl and half fra Kelvyn on the northsyd just north fra Bardowye.

North west from Bardowye is Mugdock besyd a loch, 2 myl fra Bardowye 8 myl west fra Cader or thereby.

The paroch of Leinzie is on the south syd of Kirkintillo up and down Kelvynside, but most part thereof to the east.

Garguib on the northsyd of Kelvyn hard upon the river it is 3 short myl beneth Bardowy.

Northwest thesfra is Maynis 2 lang myle it beginneth Dumbartanshyr. North fra it Barie 1 quarter myl it is in the Lennox Craigtown northwest fra Barie ½ myle, and fra Craigtown just northeast ½ myle Achincloich.

Jordanhill upon the northsyd of Clyd 2 myl beneth Partkirk. Cloberhill nor'west fra Jordanhill 2 short myle a myl fra Clyd.

The river Clyd runs fra Glasco to Dumbartan north and west somewhat to the north as it were W.N.W. and fra Dumbartan to the Cloichstane it turnes a little to the south, at the Cloichstane is the entrie of it to the sea, for ther the coast turneth on the left hand to the south the breath of it at Dumbartan is a myl and half or sum less.

OLD MARKET ORDER.

Stirling, 11th March, 1794.

BY ORDER OF THE MAGISTRATES OF THE BURGH OF STIRLING.

These are to give Notice, that in order to accommodate the Public, the Magistrates propose that a Weekly Market for BLACK CATTLE should be held upon FRIDAY, within the TOWN of Stirling at the ordinary Market-Place, betwixt JOHN GRAHAM'S House and the FACTORY near the Bridge, Commencing upon the FIRST FRIDAY of APRIL, and to continue in all Time-coming.

EXTRACTS FROM THE STIRLING KIRK SESSION RECORDS.

At a sale of books in Edinburgh last year, some manuscript of local interest came into our possession. It consists of extracts from a volume of minutes of the Kirk Session of the Parish of Stirling, commencing 27th October, 1614, and ending 23rd January, 1627, which was preserved in the General Register House, Edinburgh, for some years, but has since been returned to its proper custodier, the Session Clerk of Stirling. We purpose giving from time to time such of these minutes as will bear publication.

MARRIAGES CONFINED TO PREACHING DAYS.

29 December, 1614.—The brethrein understanding that importun and untymus suitis of the compleeting of mariages suited be many personis in this congregration at times noght decent for that purpose, thairfoir the haill assemblie present inhibits the granting of all sic suites and dischairgis [forbids] the ministratione of all marriagis frathynefurth in this kirk, except on the ordinar preaching day [Thursday] immediately after sermond, and at na

uther tyme. And if any personis desyris testimoniallis to be mareit in ane uther kirk, that the samin be noght granted in respect the puiris brod is thairby hurt, except they give xxs. to the puir for helping of the said dammage without prejudice to the last act on the 10 December, 1608.

NON-ATTENDANCE AT CHURCH.

30th March, 1615.—The quhilk day compearit Janet Cowane, spous to Andro Neilsone in Castlehill, and her said husband, quha is accusit for noght frequenting the preaching of godis word in hir paroche kirk thir twa zeiris bygane. She denyes the samin albeit it appeiris to be ouer trew. Noghtheless, the brethrein passis ouer the samin with the admonitione undirwritin, viz., that she frequent the preachingis of godis word in his paroche kirk, namely on the sabboth in tymes cuming, with certificatione if she disobey the said admonitione the brethrein will hauld the former dilatione, quhairupone the said accusatione proceidit to be of veritie and injune discipline to hir thairfor and for her fault to be commited heiraftir according to the demeritis thairof.

SUPERSTITION AT CAMBUSKENNETH.

11th May, 1615.—The quhilk day compeirit Johne Keir in Cambuskynneth and confessis he tuik to Jonet Marriogh in Dunblane, ane sark of Williame Gillaspie his gude sone and askit of hir if he wald de or leive, quha ansored that he wald noght de this zeir, and that she cust ane knot on ane of the slevis of his sark and redelyverit the samin againe to him and baid him put it on him; thairfor he is warnit to compeir before the presbiterie on the xvij day of Mai instant to receave thair injunction.

A HARSH PARENT ADMONISHED.

18th May, 1615.—The quhilk day compeirit Johne Brys, flesher, quha is admonisit to detein in his awin hous all nyght, Marjorie Brys his dochter, and nowayes to suffer the samin to ly out undir any of the stairis, as it has done in tymes bygane to the great greif of the nyghtburis of this toun, utherwayes if the said las be found thairout be hir said father or his wyfis default they salbe wardit during the Magistrates' will.

WILFUL ABSENCE FROM THE COMMUNION.

1st June, 1615.—James Uttein, brother-in-law to Johne Robertsone, tailzur, is fund to have absented himself from the communion the last ministratione thairof without any just caus, and thairfor he is admonisit on his knees with certificatione if he do the lyk heiraftir that he sall mak public repentence.

GOING TO CHRIST'S WELL UNLAWFUL.

8th June, 1615.—Compeirit Agnes Young spous to Gilbert Brys and confessis she was at Christ's well and thairfor she is ordeinit to mak publict repentance in linning claythes the next sabboth.

COURTING AT NIGHT DISCOURAGED.

27th July, 1615.—The quhilk day compeirit Johne Watsone, ane baxter child and Issobell Robertson, quha being apprehendit togither in ane hous togither a litill befoir xj houris at even ar accusit of occasione of sclander togither. Thay deny the samin and thairfor thai ar admonisit to abstein fra all appeirance of evill in tymes cuming utherwayes thay wil be judgit giltie.

A SUNDAY DRINKER WARNED.

21st September, 1615.—The quhilk day compeirit Jane Richie dochter to umquhill [the late] Janet Mentayth eldar, quha is fund ane absentar fra the kirk on the sabboth, ane drinker in tyme of preaching, ane abusar of sum personis be hir drunkinness. And thairfor she is now admonesit to abstein fra the lyk in tymes cuming with certificatione if the lyk be fund in hir heiraftir that the kirk will desyr the magistrates to baneis hir the toun.

QUARRELSOME WOMEN.

5th October, 1615.—Anent the complentis producit be Chrestane Young spous to David Nicoll, and he for his interes, and Elizabeth Downy, everie ane of thame contra utheris, quhilk being tryed thair is fund mutuall wrangis done be thame ilk ane to utheris, and becaus the said Elizabeth was sumtyme servand to the said Chrestane the said Elizabeth is commanded to eschew all just occasione of craibing the said Chrestane in tymes cuming be sitting in ane uther pairt of the kirk far distant fra the said Chrestane and to eschew hir meeting on the geat. And for keeping of peace betwix thame heirafter, thay are bayth inhibit presentlie in the name of god and his kirk to nane of thame sclander backbyt or offend ane uther at any tyme heiraftir undir the paine of a merk toties quoties if the contrair sal be fund to be done be any of thame to ane uther heiraftir.

ED.

ADDITIONS TO THE "RED BOOK OF MENTEITH."—I.

Some time ago there came into the possession of Mr A. C. M'Intyre, F.S.A., Scot., Glasgow, a valuable collection of fifty-three original letters, dating from 1647 to 1668, and relating for the most part to the affairs of the first and second Earls of Airth. They are nearly all addressed to the laird of Gartmore. These documents have evidently not been seen by Sir W. Fraser, LL.D., editor of the two noble volumes entitled "The Red Book of Menteith," and we have obtained permission to transcribe and publish them in "The Stirling Antiquary." We feel sure they will be prized by Mr Drummond-Moray of Blair Drummond (at whose expense the work referred to was printed), and by others interested in the ancient and famous family of the Grahams.

William Graham, seventh Earl of Monteith, was born *circa* 1591. On 7th August, 1610, he was served heir to his father in the Earldom of Monteith. By his talents he attracted notice at Court, and rose rapidly in favour with Charles the First. In August, 1628, he was appointed Lord Justice General of Scotland, and a few months later President of the Privy Council. In 1621 he received from Adam Bishop of Dunblane, a resignation of the patronage of the church of Aberfoyle. On 25th May, 1630, he was served heir of David, Earl of Strathern, and thereafter renounced his title to the Earldom of Strathern. On 31st July, 1631, he received from King Charles First a patent ratifying to him the title of Earl of Strathern, giving to him and his heirs-male and of tailzie the style of Earls of Strathern and Monteith. He was, however, shortly after this divested of the title of Strathern, and created Earl of Airth in 1633. In 1644 he received a new investiture of the lands of Monteith to himself in life-rent, and to the heirs-male of his son John, Lord Kilpont. The Earl of Airth and Menteith died between January 1661 and 14th July, 1662. He married, in 1611, Agnes, daughter of Patrick Lord Gray, by whom he had four sons and three daughters. As appears from Dr Fraser's very interesting biography of the Earl, he fell into disfavour with the King and became insolvent. He was afterwards restored to the royal favour, but was unable to get repayment of money he had lent to Charles the First, and in 1642 his affairs were again hoplessly involved. He lost the lands of Kilbride, having previously parted with the lands of Airth. In 1645 he sat in Parliament, and was required to furnish sixty men from the parishes of Drymen. Port, and Aberfoyle for the Marquis of Argyll's regiment. In 1651 he was required by King Charles the Second, when at Stirling towards the close of July, to raise all the men he could in the defence of the kingdom. On the 15th August previous the Earl had created his cousin, William Graham, of Gartmore (to whom the first letter in this collection is addressed), his lieutenant, for calling and convening "our haill freeinds, tenents, subtenents, cottars, and hefds betuix Achyll and the foot of Lochard," recusants being ordained to pay certain fines. During the struggle then prevailing in the country, the house of Airth was made a garrison by Cromwell's troops. In 1654 the Earl was ordered by General Monck, then at Cardross, to have the woods of Milton and others in Aberfoyle cut down as they afforded great shelter to the rebels and mossers, and were a harbour for loose, idle, and desperate persons. In his latter years, the Earl seems to have been in great trouble about money matters, and the subjoined letter throws some light upon the state of his affairs.

COUSING—I receaved your letter this monday the ig at ten a clock at nicht and I coulde not delay ane houre from vretting ane ansuere too it, and I have therefor directed this berar in all haiste to Edinch—and first wheras you vrett that you have spoken with Sr James Murray and Mr Robert Bruce and that they doo contstanthe affirme that I was principall debtor in that soume wherof they have ane comprysing, I protest to God I wonder how these men can be so impudent as to affirme ane notorious falshoode. I have often vrettin to you and to Mr David Primrose to desyre ane sichte of that comprysing for give I be bot only ane cationer fer Lundie in the comprysing I shall give my lyfe and my fortune. It is trew that long efter the comprysing I gave band as debtor for the soume for reliefe of this Marquis of Argyll because the lard of Lundie gave me at that tyme ane assignation to ane band of tuelf thousand marks wch his father hade from the last Earle of Argyll, and so be that band I gave then they say I am debtor in the principall soume, bot in the comprysing they can not nor dar not say bot that I am only ane cationer, and as for ther comprysing which they doo so much boaste of becaus the legall is expyred, I protest to God I will not give ane strae for there comprysing for I shall show that wch may save me from harme and brangle there richts in ane busines wch doeth concerne them more then the doubill of that soume, for it is not there menacing and boasting that will frichte me. I know there end and drifte is that they will not setle with me in that comprysing until I setle with them in Patrick Wood his acounts. Before God they have made me alreadie pay nyne thousand mks twyse over in Patrik Woods business notwithstanding that they hade Traquair his band for it and that he tooke allowance and payment out of the soumes owing me out of the excheq[r] for it, bot they shall not deceave me so now.

You vrett to me that they desyre that we should meite for cleiring of all things amongst us. I pray you show them that I am contente and all the paines I desyre them to take is that they will come and meite me within thrie myll of Edin[ch] and I shall meite them preceislie and bring all my papers with me, with this provisione that I be advertised with this berar of the preceis day and place of there meitting and let the day be at leaste eicht or ten dayes efter you doo receave this letter and upon my faith I shall keip it. [turne ovir.]

Now I must tell you trewlie, that upon my conscience, since I did begin to vrett this letter yesternicht, I have founde this morning ane vrette that shall lett you and these men sie that there comprysing can not hurte me no more than the paying of the soume, and perhaps not all that, and for Patrik Wood his acounts they shall, at there meiting and myne, sie all that I have to say and lett them doo the lyke for upon my worde to you if they be not discreete I am weel aneuch armed against them. Show this letter to Mr David Primrose for I eschew repititiones and haist bake this berar. I wonder that nather Mr David Primrose nor you did not vrett ane ansuer bake of that I vrett to you concerning Cap: Alexr Bruce, for his money shall be ready, so vrett to me concerning that busines. My lord Gray hath vrettin me most earnestly entreating me to coome into Edin[ch] and that, if I will coome in, my effaires may setle, bot if I doo not coome thair, they will go vrong. Trewlie I beleive that he vretteth out of his love to me but I know my busines so weeli that no man knoweth them better. I confess it is trew that my coming thair will conduce much for the good of my busines and I will coome thair or neire about, bot that my not coming woulde vrong me much in good faith they ar deceived. I know that my lord Gray is informed by those who have their awin ends, and I have myne, bot I shall vrong no man, bot I will not be frechted with idill shadows. Show Mr David Primrose this letter and haiste bake the berar for efter his returne I shall not be long in coming to these pairtes. Cause this berar delyver this wther letter from my sone James to Sr James Hope and if he be not in toune cause the berar leave the letter at his house. So expecting the hastie returne of the berar I rest evir.

Yo[r] loving cheife

20 Julij AIRTHE.
1647

Address on back—For my loving cousing William Graham of Gartmore

These.

STIRLINGSHIRE MEMBERS OF THE DARIEN COMPANY.

The story of the ill-fated Darien Company fills a gloomy page of our Scottish annals. A colonising and commercial enterprise, supported enthusiastically by all classes of the community throughout the country, and inaugurated amidst the highest prospects of success, was suddenly blasted by the narrow jealousies of the English and Dutch Trading Companies and the active hostility of Spain. The capital subscribed, amounting to £400,000 sterling, constituted almost the whole available wealth of the kingdom, and therefore the ruin of the undertaking brought poverty to many families who had embarked their all in the undertaking, while the national exasperation nearly ended in open war with England. Perhaps it may prove of interest to give a list of the shareholders in Stirlingshire, so far as can be distinguished in the official roll, which was published at the time under the following title :—

"A Perfect List of the several Persons, residenters in Scotland, who have subscribed as Adventurers in the Joint-Stock of the Company of Scotland trading to Africa and the Indies; Together with the respective sums which they have severally subscribed in the Books of the said Company, amounting in the whole to the sum of £400,000 sterling.
Edinburgh: Printed and sold by the Heirs and Successors of Andrew Anderson, Printer to the King's Most Excellent Majesty. 1696."

Sir John Areskine of Alva - -	£300
Captain John Areskine, brother to the Laird of Alva - - - - -	300
Lady Alva - - - - -	300
Sir Alexander Areskine of Cambo, Lyon King at Arms - - - - -	200
Penelope Areskine, sister to Cambo -	100
William Allan, taylor in Stirling -	100
Carry forward	£1,300

Brought forward	£1,300
John Burd, merchant in Stirling -	200
John Bowie, merchant in Falkirk -	100
John Callender of Craigforth - -	600
Cowan's Hospital in Stirling - -	500
Mungo Campbell of Burnbank - -	400
Henry Chrysiston, Commissar of Stirling	100
Wm. Callender junior, merchant in Falkirk	100
Anna Cunningham, daughter to the deceased Mr James Cunningham in Alva -	100
The Guildry of Stirling - - -	200
John Knox, portioner in Falkirk - -	100
Mr Wm. Livingstoun of Kilsyth - -	1000
John Murray of Touchadam - -	500
Mr Wm. Mackgie, precenter in Stirling -	100
Mr Francis Napier, Baillie in Stirling -	100
James Russel, Deacon of the baxters in Stirling - - - - -	100
George Stirling of Herbertshire - -	300
The Town of Stirling - - - - -	200
John Stevenson, Provost of Stirling -	200
Robert Stirling, brother to Glorat -	100
Spittell's Hospital in Stirling - -	100
George Shaw of Sauchie - - -	100
David Trail, son of James Trail, Ensign in Stirling Castle - - - -	100
James and Robert Watsons, merchants in Stirling, sons to Duncan Watson, late Baillie in Stirling - - -	200
Thomas Wordie, merchant in Stirling -	200
	£7,200

Perth. R. S. F.

GENEALOGICAL MEMOIR OF THE MACFARLANES.

(From Maidment's County Collections.)

The distinguished family of Macfarlane, one of antiquity and eminence in a part of the empire where ancestry and exploit have ever been held in enthusiastic admiration, was founded by Gilchrist, fourth son of Alwyn, second Earl of Lennox, who obtained from his brother, Earl Maldwin, a grant of the lands and barony of Arrocher, in the time of Alexander I. Gilchrist's son Duncan was compelled, after a gallant defence of the national independence, to submit to Edward I of England, and died soon after, leaving a son,

Maldwin, inheritor of his broad lands and his unflinching patriotism. During the adverse fortune of Robert Bruce, the laird of Arrocher, with his kinsman the Earl of Lennox, was the faithful attendant of the heroic prince who found safe retreat in the Lennox when deserted by almost all his other subjects. To Maldwin succeeded his son,

BARTHOLOMEW, or as that name is called in Gaelic, Pharlan. He lived in the reign of David Bruce, and was father of

MALCOLM MACFARLANE, or the son of Pharlan of Arrocher, who became, on the demise of Donald, sixth Earl of Lennox in 1373, undoubted heir male of that noble family. He died not long after, and was succeeded by his son Duncan of that Ilk, who married Christian, daughter of Sir Colin Campbell of Lochaw, and died in the reign of James I., having a son and successor,

JOHN MACFARLANE of that Ilk, who died *temp.* James III., having had two sons, Walter his heir, and John, from whom descended the Macfarlanes of Kenmore, Muckroy, and Dunnamanich. The elder son,

WALTER MACFARLANE of that Ilk and Arrocher wedded a daughter of James, second Lord Livingstone, and left two sons, the younger Dugal, ancestor of the Macfarlanes of Tullichinthall, Finart, &c., while the elder,

ANDREW MACFARLANE of that Ilk, marrying one of the daughters of John Stewart, Lord Darnley, left a son,

SIR JOHN MACFARLANE of that Ilk, who received the honour of knighthood from James IV. and attended that prince to the fatal field of Flodden, where he was slain with the pride and flower of the Scottish gentry. His eldest son,

ANDREW MACFARLANE of that Ilk married Lady Margaret Cunningham, daughter of William, Earl of Glencairn, Lord High Treasurer of Scotland, and dying in the commencement of the reign of Mary, was succeeded by his son,

DUNCAN MACFARLANE of that Ilk, a gallant warrior of the troubled period in which he lived, who joined with 300 of his clan the Earls of Lennox and Glencairn, and participating in the battle of Glasgow Muir in 1544, was attainted, but shortly after obtained a reversal under the Privy Seal. He married first Isabel Stewart, daughter of Andrew Lord Ochiltree, by whom he had no issue, and secondly, Anne, daughter of Sir John Colquhoun of Luss, by whom he had a son, Andrew, his heir. The laird of Macfarlane ultimately fell at Pinkie, and was succeeded by his son,

ANDREW MACFARLANE of that Ilk, a zealous promoter of the Reformation, and a warm partisan of the Regent Murray, in opposition to the ill-fated Mary Stuart. We find him at Langside enrolled under that nobleman's banner, and to his "valiance" Holingshed ascribes the success of the Earl. He married Agnes, daughter of Sir Patrick Maxwell of Newark, and was succeeded by his son

JOHN MACFARLANE of that Ilk, a gentleman of great piety and benevolence, who founded a noble almshouse at Brintford on the mainland-opposite to his castle of Elenore for the reception of poor passengers. By the Lady Helen Stewart, his second wife, daughter of Francis Farl of Bothwell, he left a son and successor,

WALTER MACFARLANE of that Ilk, a devoted Royalist, who was fined 3000 merks for joining the standard of Montrose, and was twice besieged by the Parliamentarians, who burned to the ground his castle of Inverouglass. He married Margaret, daughter of Sir James Semple of Belltrees, and had issue—

JOHN, his heir, who died leaving daughters only. The eldest, Jean, married John Buchanan of Lenie; the second, Gilis, Alex. McMillan of Dunmore; and the third, Grizzle. Archibald Buchanan of Torie. The second son,

ANDREW MACFARLANE of Ardesss, but eventually of that Ilk, married twice and had several sons, of whom three were slain at Malplaquet. The eldest, John Macfarlane of that Ilk, colonel of a regiment of foot, left by Helen, his second wife, daughter of Robert, second Viscount of Arbuthnot, three sons—

WALTER of that Ilk, a distinguished antiquary, who married Lady Elizabeth Erskine, daughter of the sixth Earl of Kellie, but died childless; William, of whom presently; and Alexander, who settled in Jamaica, where he was one of the assistant Judges, and a member of the Assembly. He was a distinguished mathematician. He died unmarried. The second son,

WILLIAM MACFARLANE, Esq., who succeeded his elder brother Walter at Macfarlane, married Christian, daughter of James Dewar of Vogrie, and was grandfather of General Sir Robert Henry Macfarlane, K.C.B., K.G.H., &c., Colonel of the 89th Regiment of Foot, a gallant and highly distinguished officer, who married at Palermo, 10th February, 1815, Maria Gertrude, eldest daughter of G. Henry Vanhemper, Esq., Captain in the Dutch Navy, and Consul of the Netherlands at Tripoli.

Some of our correspondents may be able to bring this genealogy down to date.

MEMORIAL AND ABSTRACT OF PROCESS OF SALE OF MACFARLANE OF MACFARLANE'S ESTATES, 7th July, 1784.

at the instance of

Hugh Norman, eldest son and heir served and returned to the deceased Hugh Mossman, writer in Edinburgh

Agt.

William Macfarlane Esq. of Macfarlane, John Macfarlane Junior thereof, and their creditors.

Rental of the lands and Barony of Arrochar and others in the Shire of Dumbarton.

DOWN.—The ½ of the lands of Down—Malcolm Macfarlane and his mother lease 21 years from Whitsunday 1766, money rent £10 13s.

DOWN—The other ½ of Down, Peter and Donald Macintyre, 19 years 1768.

ARDLEISH—Ardleish, Dougal and Alexander Macdougals, now Malcolm Macfarlane, a stone of butter at the proven conversion of 10s is added to the money rent.—19 years.

Blairstaing and Stuckmud. Malcolm Macfarlane and Margaret Campbell.

Garvual, Margaret Lauder. After Whit. 1787 the rent rises to £42.

Garrachie and Ardluie, Alexander Macfarlane Shicandroin.

Upper Ardvorlich.

Upper Inverouglass and forest of Beinvourlic and Nether Ardvourlic.

Caenmore and Blaireunich.

Part of Tarbet called Inverchulin.

Hill of Tarbet.

Part of Tarbet called Claddochbeg.

Claddoch mire with the laigh park of Balhenaan.

Coinlach.

Tyunloan.

Part of Tarbet.

Another part of Ditto.

Easter Balhennan.

Pendicle of Balhennan and House and Wynd at.

Ty Vichattan.

Part of Balhennan.

Stucknacloich.

Upper and Nether Stuckintibbert.

Firken.

Mill of Cambusnaclach and mill lands.

Nether Inverouglass.

Choilchorran and Invergroin, Gartanfaired and Greitnein, expiration of present lease £88 4s8 ½d.

Tynalarach Ardinny and Muirlagan.

Stronfyne Glenluyns and the lands and mill of Portchirble and hill of Beinvein.

Tynaclach.

The Baron Officers sons pay for attune.
Tullichentaal.

The tenant pays over and above his rent the stipend to the minister of Luss, being 3 bolls meal, 8½ stone to the boll, and 40s Scots or 3s 4d of money and 3s 1d for Communion elements, and as the payment of stipend agrees with the teind duty in the feu charter to the superior, it is not here added to their rental nor is it hereafter stated as a deduction. The school salary being 4s 3d, is also paid by the tenant over and above the rent. Stuckgown comprehending Stuckdon and Stuckvolge—George Syme, vassal, John Brock in Garshuke, and Archibald Maclachan, tacksman in Bunnackrae, both bred farmers and grassers concur in deponing that they both together visited and inspected the farms of Inveresk and Balfrone and parks about the mansion house of New Tarbet, all in the natural possession of Macfarlane, and that in their opinion they are worth upon a 19 years' lease of yearly rent £47 10s.

Money Rent.			Hens.	Chickens.	Doz. of Eggs.	Wedders.	Loads of Peats.	Days of a Man and Horse.	Days of a Man.
£	S.	D.							
10	13	0	1	10	10			6	
10	13	0	2	10	10			6	
43	5	0							
24	0	0						6	
26	11	6							
30	0	0				3			
27	10	6	1	12	12			12	
14	13	0	2	10	10			6	
79	17	9							
23	3	0	2						
4	16	4	1	6	6				6
9	7	7 7-12ths	2	6	6		12	6	
6	9	9 4-12ths	2	6	6		12		8
20	19	11⅙	3	6	6			6	
6	4	2 2-12ths							
3	2	6	1	6	6		4	4	
2	0	0	1	3	3				
0	15	0	1						
10	3	10 4-12ths	2	6	6			6	
9	4	0	2	6	6				6
3	15	0	2						
3	0	0	1						
11	13	2⅙	4	12	12				12
12	13	0	4	12	12			6	
5	5	6 8-12ths						10	
4	4	8						2	
17	19	10 4-12ths						10	
47	7	7							
53	15	6							
66	19	2 9-12ths							
6	10	0							
1	10	0							
32	0	0	2						
0	10	0							
47	10	0							
677	3	7 2-12ths	36	111	111	8	28	98	32

	£677	3	7 2-12ths
36 Hens, at 8d each	1	4	0
111 Chickens, at 4d each	1	17	0
111 Doz. Eggs, at 3d per doz. .. .	1	7	9
3 Wedders, 10s each	1	10	0
28 Loads Peats, 6d per load	0	14	0
	£683	16	4 2-12ths
Tenants pay cess above Rent, total valued rent of the above lands £738 3s 4d after deduction of lands feued to George Syme.			
Total Cess of these lands	13	3	3 4-12ths
	696	17	7 6-12ths
Deduction	34	14	2 7-12ths
Free Rent	£662	5	4 11-12ths
Abstract of the different proven values.			
1st The lands and Barony of Arrochar and others in the Shire of Dumbartonshire, 25 years purchase of free rent and value of woods (£3200)	£19,756	15	2 11-12ths
2nd Lands of Burnhouses, in the Shire of Berwick, 22 years' purchase	1501	10	0
3rd The lands of Bartlaws and Huntfield in the Shire of Lanark, 22 years purchase of free proven rental, 5 years' purchase of land (£38 13s 4d)	1604	18	10 8-12ths
	£22,863	4	1 7-12ths
Debts			
Due and noted £42,918 2 4 8-12ths			
Lands in Dumbarton, deductions			
Tullichintane held of Sir James Colquhoun of Luss feu	£0	11	1 4-12ths
At entry 20 merks every successor 40 merks.			
Stipend to minister of Arrochar out of these lands £28 17 9 6-12ths			
Schoolmaster of Arrochar 5 5 3 9-12ths			
	£34	3	1 3-12ths
Tiends of Macfarlane's, Arrochar, 80 merks Scots.			
Tiends of Nether Arrochar 12 merks, or ..	£0	13	4
12 Bolls Meal, at 10s per Boll	6	0	0
	6	13	4
Considerably below Stipend			
Macfarlane's, Arrochar, 400 merks	22	4	5 4-12ths
Nether Arrochar	6	13	4
	£28	17	9 4-12ths

Glasgow. A. C.

THOMAS CHALMERS, THE STIRLING BELLMAN.

[The following sketch of the famous Stirling bellman appeared in a newspaper now 33 years old. Thanks to its preservation by Chalmers' widow, we are able to reproduce it for the information of the present generation of readers.]

The advent of a public character is always viewed with a certain degree of curious interest. We do not merely allude to the ephemeral class of functionaries, such as Town Councillors for example, or to any other mere temporary luminaries, who may be said to go out like rush-light when their brief term of official authority comes to a termination. A public character, properly so called, has a more permanent and tangible existence, and is not to be overthrown by any single blast, however strong, of capricious public opinion—and a one-sided current, that would at once extinguish half a dozen of other public luminaries, has generally no other effect on the steady light of an established public character than to fan the flame of his popularity, and make it burn the brighter. We defy any one to point out a more public, or a more popular functionary than the Public Crier, or Public Bellman. Few matters of importance occur in which he has not a *voice*. His ideas or notifications are not whispered in back shops or rooms, for the peculiar edification of private cliques, but are at once, and without hesitation, conveyed to the public in the most audible voice, in all the principal places of the town. It is this direct and uncircuitous way of conveying his sentiments and information that serves to make him so great a favourite, for, if the public hate one thing more than another, it is the concealment of anything if which they imagine they have a right to be consulted. The Public Crier does not only come up to the height of their wishes in this respect, but is a kind of notable example to all public personages to beware of anything like concealment, hole and corner meetings, cliques, out-of-the way schemings, jobbing, bagging, private buttering, cajolery, &c., which have hitherto been the bane of public officials, and that they ought to declare their honest sentiments and convictions in as open and public a manner as possible—and perfectly free from anything like sniffling, indistinctness, or concealment, and in such a way that all may understand them. In fact, if a Public Crier fails in this indispensable requisite of his profession, he is immediately cashiered by common consent. How then can it be expected that other functionaries can escape, should they be made amenable to the same salutary rule? We have been led into these remarks from the circumstance of a new Public Crier having lately made his appearance amongst us, and as he asks the suffrages of the community on public grounds alone, he is the more entitled to a fair and partial hearing. He is not, as yet, it would appear, invested by our civic rulers with the insignia of office in the shape of a salayr and uniform, but has philanthropically come forward on the Free or Voluntary principle. In short, he does not belong to the town establishment, the former crier not yet having made up his mind to give in his final resignation. The name of the new crier scarcely requires to be announced with any comment, having been, fortunately, already sufficiently celebrated. When we mention that he bears the famous name of THOMAS CHALMERS, our readers will at once perceive that, from respect to the very name he has the honour to bear, it is impossible that he could have come forward on any other than independent grounds.

About two years ago, it would appear, Thomas Chalmers was a tartan weaver at St Ninians—an occupation which he still continues to follow in Stirling, his native place. The duty of public crier in St Ninians, previous to that time, had been discharged by a person named Murray, a nail-maker, who had got into trouble through a proclamation he had made in the village regarding a game at "*Rowly Powly*" to be played on the high-way, which resulted in an accident to a boy, and led to the apprehension of Murray and the player, who were jointly and severally tried before the Sheriff, at the instance of the public prosecutor, the upshot being that Thomas Chalmers was requested to perform the duties of crier. This situation he did not hesitate to accept, as he had all along believed that he was destined to act in a prominent public capacity, and if he had any doubts about the matter at all, they were speedily dissipated by his better half, who pointedly informed him (what he had previously been sufficiently aware of) that the financial resources of his establishment were entirely exhausted. Forth then he went as Public Crier, and his first proclamation was prohibiting the theft of slates from the roof of the Temperance Hall—appropriate enough, when we consider that in ancient times all proclamations were made from the house-tops, and that before proceeding farther, he wanted to make a sure footing. A serious obstacle soon presented itself. He had frequently to officiate in the neighbouring villages, where he was saluted by the boys with—"A good Crier, but a horrid bad Bell!" The abject poverty in which Chalmers was at this time, rendered it an utter impossibility that he could of himself procure a new bell. His thoughts ran then upon getting a second-hand article, with which view he procured for himself a list of the brokers in Glasgow, with the intention of writing to them for a second-hand bell. But even the postage of the letters could not, it seems, be afforded from his limited exchequer. It was in these circumstances that he thought of appealing to the public spirit of the inhabitants of St Ninians. The appeal was responded to by a public meeting or social entertainment being held in the Temperance Hall, and the projectors of the meeting, with an eye to the object in view, wisely provided that a small sum should be charged for admission, which, we need scarcely say, was willingly paid. By this means Chalmers was enabled to obtain possession of the Bell, which had been used by the former crier, and which, as an act of charity, he purchased from the wife of the previous functionary. And this is the identical Bell which now rings so frequently among the ancient streets and buildings of our Royal Burgh. We must not omit to mention, that the history of this famous Bell has been celebrated in verse by an unknown poet, named Taylor, native of the village of St Ninians, who recited the poem on the occasion of the entertainment. With the generosity which characterises the followers of the Muse, he immediately handed over the poetical effusion about the Bell to the proper custodier of such a work—namely, to the Bellman himself—and it is said that Chalmers has some thoughts of giving it at no distant date to the public. The name of the Public Crier frequently figures in documents of no mean importance, and the services of such a functionary were highly valued by our former Town Councillors. For many years, however, we know not for what reason, a Drum has been used in preference to the euphonious sound of the Bell. It would appear, also, that not many years ago Irishmen were preferred to most public situations in Stirling. In proof of this, and also that the compliment to the present Town Drummer may be preserved—although we do not see its force—we shall briefly allude to a proclamation which was thickly posted on the walls of the town, at the time that the late Rev. Archibald Bennie was removed to Lady Yester's Church in Edinburgh. It was in nearly the following terms:—"Whereas by the resignation of the Rev. Archibald Bennie, the First Ministerial Charge of the Parish of Stirling has become vacant; and whereas the charge is in the gift of the Town Council, no candidate should apply who is not provided with proper documents to show that he is by birth and Education, as well as habit and repute an Irishman, and that for the following very cogent reasons, namely, that the burgh has been and still is, very faithfully served by a whole batch of Irish functionaries—viz, his honour the

Provost, his sub-honour the Jailor, and two Subalterns; the TOWN DRUMMER, *a most admirable crier!* and the two Leeries. Neither of which offices, in the opinion of Bailie Frosty Face, could be fairly filled by an inhabitant of Stirling. Scotsmen, therefore! whatever be your qualifications, you are sure of disappointment if a single Irishman is pitted against you, though his brogue be as broad as Ballyporeen itself, and his outward man like Paddy of Cork, with his coat buttoned behind, and his hair growing through his hat!

God Save the Queen!"

The compliment conveyed to the drummer in the above extract will not fail to be observed. Happily, however, the days of exclusive privileges have gone bye, and the humble Thomas Chalmers, by the mere force of his public eloquence, can win his way to public favour and public usefulness, without having to lean on the precarious patronage of civic dignitaries. Such has the universal approbation been of his exhibitions as public bellman in Stirling, that already we understand a number of the spirited inhabitants intend to supply him with a suitable costume—thereby giving to his public appearances the importance due to the dignity of the Royal Burgh of Stirling and its PUBLIC CRIER.

STIRLING KIRK SESSION RECORDS.

PRIVATE PEWS IN THE EAST KIRK.

11th November, 1617.—Presentes—Mr Patrik Simsone, minister, Duncan Watson, Johnne Johnsone, beallies, Walter Cowane, dean of gild, Thos. Cowper, convener, Mr Robert Murray, commissar of Stirling, eldar, James Robertsone, James Spitell, Andro Jeffrey, Johnne Adamesone, William Murhed, Johnne Andersone, tailzur, eldaris and deacunis of the said kirk. The quhilk day the haill brethrein foirsaid quhairof sum of thame are memberis of the Counsell of this brugh, and sum of thame memberis of the kirk, upon the earnest sute of James Short, provost, James Forrester, beally, Johnne Willamsone, town clerk and Johnne Cowane, nychtbur of this brugh, hes all with ane consent granted and gevin licience to ye suttaris above wreten, to big on thair awin expensis dasks and commodious seatis to thame selfis, thair wyfis and childrein in thair paroche kirk betwix the east syd of that pillar quhair the pulpit standis and the uther nixt pillar be east the samin for thair bettir aisiament and commodious heiring of god his word to thair comfort and salvatione, and for decoratione of the kirk, provyding alwayes that it sall nocht be lesum to thame nor none of thame to big thair daskis and seatis any farther out in the body of the kirk nor the utmost syd of the Reedaris letrein. Also the said suittaris ar ordeinit to big commodius saitis on the north end of the daskis above wretin of sic length as the passaige ben and but that Ill callit the Lady Ill will permit for commodius saiting to everie honest man in the toun, as many as thay may contain.

THE PROVOST'S BURIAL VAULT.

22d November 1617.—The quhilk day the haill brethrein of this assemblie being advysit with the sute of James Short provest, and Johnne Sharrar beallie, hes granted unto thame libertie and licience to burie thair famelees and thair successoris of thame selfis and sic utheris as thay pleas to adjune to thame in that plaice without the Kirk lyand betwix the porche dur and the Boweyis Ill on ther conditionis following—To wit *propter decoram* that thay big ane aistlar wall befoir the samin with ane tabill and ane sealze on the hed thairof and ane honest zet in the entrie thairof. That thay pavement the grund thairof with thrughis and uphauld on thair expenssis the glassin windois in the kirk that ar within the boundis of the said buriall plaice. Reservand also priviledge to the maisteris of the Kirk wark to set up ladderis in the samin buriall plaice to repair the Kirk quhen neid requyris.

THREAT OF THE BRANKS.

18th December 1617—The brethrein findis be sufficient probatione that Agnes Hall, servand to Robert Hog hes odiuslie sclanderit Euffame Watsone spous to Duncan Thomeson for the quhilk upon her kneis she is ordeinit in this sessionehous to ask the said Euffame forgivenes, as also in the plaice quhair the fault wes done, and certefeit if she misuse and sclandir ane manis wyf at any time heiraftir that she salbe brankit.

25th December 1617.—The brethrein findis be sufficient probatione that Euffame Henresone spous to James Robertsone fleshur, hes odiuslie sclandirit Cathrein Strathie and thairfor besyd hir present punishment she is ceritfeit if the lyk be fund in hir heirafter that the braukis sall be put on hir.

ED.

CULDEE CHAPEL AT DUNSWOOD.

Mr Mackenzie of Castlecary Castle, having mentioned to our contributor, Mr A. C. M'Intyre, F.S.A. Scot., Glasgow, the existence of a ruinous structure at Dunswood, he visited the place and pronounced the ruins to be the remains of a Culdee

Chapel. At his instance drawings were made of the relic and shown to the members of the Glasgow Arceæological Society, the result being that an excursion was made to the spot on Saturday, 17th November. In a hollow in the midst of the surrounding uplands this interesting relic of antiquity lies apart, and through the valley the Red or Rood Burn—a name suggestive of the vicinity of a chapel, flows in a zig-zag course. On its western bank, and about 30 feet above its level, the eye is arrested by a rising ground or knoll, on the top of which is a structure in ruins, lying due east and west, and known as the Chapel of Dunswood. Little is left save a portion of the walls, the doorway through which being still extant, and there are traces of windows in the southern and eastern walls. At the western end there is a square indentation something like the "ingle neuk" still visible in old dwellings, but having the sides perpendicular; and at the eastern end there is a semi-circular projection of the wall, pierced apparently by two windows, and forming a sort of apse, in the centre of which a square flag is let into the ground. Outside the western end of the building there is a group of enormous boulders, which appear to have formed part of a cromlech, near which an oak tree, affording evident signs of great age, still survives, whilst close by a huge stem of privet is entwined amidst the ruins. To the westward the ground slopes downward, and then rises gradually to a considerable height above. There is a tradition that about two centuries ago Dunswood Chapel formed a place of retirement for the inmates of Cumbernauld Castle, but another suggestion regarding it is that it is all that remains to our day of an ancient Culdee cell.

CASTLECARY CASTLE.

This interesting mansion is similar in appearance to the old Border peels or fortalices, and reminds one of the external appearance of Barncluith, in the neighbourhood of Hamilton. The lintel-stone bears the date 1679, but the western portion of the edifice is of much more ancient date. Inside the wooden door an iron gate of massive proportions still swings on its hinges. It is an interesting example of ancient Scottish hammered ironwork. At the western end of the ground floor is a spacious vaulted chamber, lighted by narrow slits in the thick walls. It has been thought that this formed the dungeon of the keep, but there are features in it strongly suggestive of its having been the kitchen or servants' hall. Access is had by a narrow winding stair to the upper stories, where there is ample living accommodation. From the top floor a private stair in the thickness of the wall led to the vaulted chamber in the basement. From the leads on the roof and over the battlemented wall a magnificent prospect of the surrounding country can be enjoyed, with the gardens sheltered under the protecting walls of the castle; and far below, the meandering course of the Red Rurn flowing on its northerly way. An interesting relic of the past in the shape of a handsome sword was found when digging out the floor of the vaulted chamber. Castlecary, besides being widely known through its association with the still prominent remains of the Roman occupation, was rendered more famous still in Scottish ballad literature by Hector Macneil in his ballad, published in 1791, entitled, "The Wee Thing, or Mary of Castlecary." This exquisite lyric was founded on the elopement of Mary Baillie of Castlecary with Duncan Graham of Gartartan. The window through which Miss Baillie leaped into her lover's arms is still pointed out.

ADDITIONS TO THE "RED BOOK OF MENTEITH."—II.

The learned editor of the "Red Book of Menteith" was unable from the materials at his command to fix the date of the death of William Graham, seventh Earl of Menteith and first Earl of Airth. He states that the Earl died between January 1661 and 14th July, 1662. The letter we give below proves that the Earl was alive in April 1661, as his grandson signs himself "Kinpount," a title he assumed after his father's death at the hands of James Stewart of Ardvoirlich, in 1644. The letter itself is peculiarly interesting, revealing, as it does, a passage in the life of the last Earl of Monteith which has not hitherto been known. At the age of 27 he seems to have fallen in love with a young lady, whose name and parentage are, unfortunately, involved in mystery, and his anxiety to have his prospects represented in the most favourable light can easily be understood when it is remembered that his grandfather's affairs were in an embarrassed state at the time. The laird of Gartmore may have been unable to conceal the truth, or the lady's father may have felt dissatisfied with the explanation made to him, or the lady's love may have cooled. At all events, no marriage took place, and it is remarkable, as proving the strength of Lord Kinpont's affection, that he did not marry for sixteen years afterwards, when he wedded

Anna Hewes, who was divorced in 1684, her husband marrying a second time before the final decision in the divorce case.

Edr 13 Apryle
1661

Much respected Cusing,

The want of of (*sic*) so reale a friend as you ar in tyme of neid proves verie disadvantagius to the partie concerned as I att present. Sir, I have a bussines now in hand, I mean of mariage, but to whom I will not reveall till meitting, bot on thing I will show you off with is this, yt matching wt yt partie is better for me—I mean for to mak a greatt esteatt—then the greattest mans daughter in Scottland wold bee. So far have I proceeded in this bussiness wtout the speciall consent of my noble friends who thinks yt altho I had sought and got my choyss of all the ladies in the kingdome I could not have pleacett my fancie better then I have doon in this. It is cumd yt lenth yt hir father desyres to know reallie ane information in wreatt from my self the true condition yt our famylie is unto and what debt the land is burdened wtall, both as to my fathers debt and grandfathers, and what comprysing is on the estaitt and the rent of the land. Now, Sir, consider this for he is a verie wyse prudent man who seeks this. This wes hir father's ansyre to the gentellman who proponed the mater from me so yt upon this information depends all the bussiness. Hir father desyred this againe munday nixt, bot yt [is] impossible, for it most be wele devysed or he gett the information of so weightie a bussines, so I humblie desyre and intreatt you cusing to spare nether night nor day till you cum to me here, for I will advyse this wt non but you allennerly. You may be here on tuesday nixt in the morning, and be assurred any thing yt I [am] able to doe to you againe shall never be wanting in me. I rest being in heast, yor. most assurred and verie loving cusing to serve you.

KINPOUNT.

On the margin of the letter are the following postscripts :—

Let no breathing know of this letter bot yorself alone and cum wt all heast possible.

If I can give satisfaction to hir father in the contract and marriage will immediately go [on]. Hir father is to go for England, and if this be instantly after I am married I intend to go wt him.

Address—For my much respected cusing the laird of Gartmore, heast thease.

LETTER FROM THE PRINCESS CHARLOTTE TO HER MOTHER.

The following letter is transcribed from an old document so worn in many places that we have been unable to supply the missing words. The letter was found among the papers of a person descended from one of the household of the unfortunate Princess. It is not the original, but has every appearance of being an authentic copy, the watermark on the paper giving the date 1814. We shall be glad to learn whether the letter, which is an exceedingly interesting one, has been published before, and if so, where it appears. We are indebted to Mr James Rae, Glasgow, for the document.

My Dearest Mother,—A very few days will elapse before I may claim to be addressed by the endearing appellation with which I have commenced this letter: when Providence may develop to me new duties, which may in some measure temper, but can never supersede those moral and pious obligations which have been hitherto imposed on me. Were I to disguise my true sentiment or to affect feelings other than which occupy my bosom, in the prospect of becoming a mother, I would feel myself unworthy of that paternal affection which constitutes at least the second bliss of life. United to a man whose whole attentions are directed to the promotion of my happiness, I cannot but feel a pleasure in the anticipation of that hour of perilous hope, which shall enable me to present a new tie of connubial love, and to the nation an abundant source of future promise and consolation. Political considerations, in this instance, stand in competition with the more near and natural feelings of the breast. While as a wife I am alive to all these anxious susceptibilities which accompany my peculiar situation: I am compelled by circumstances to extend my views to contemplations widely different in their kind as in their latitude—contemplations involving the nearest and most durable interests of a people to whom I owe a debt scarcely to be liquidated—gratitude for unbounded affection to relieve in some degree this weight of obligation, and to justify this universal confidence in the strength and consistency of my character. I have determined, should it please Providence to bless me with offspring, so to regulate its early reason and so direct its infant energies, that the lessons I have received from you, and the wisdom which time and observation have confirmed may be handed down to my child, with a view to the perpetuation of the great principle — the legitimate end of all governments is the welfare of society, and that political and private virtue is the surest foundation and the best bulwark of a throne. But O my mother, when my timid imagination revolves upon the uncertainty which veils futurity; when I look to the dark possibilities which may put a period to the dreams of hope, even [ ] shake my courage, and I feel myself the [prey of] terrors which reason would almost denominate [. At] such a trying moment, why am I debarred from [the cheering] voice of maternal affection? Why is not my [dear mother] allowed to pour cheerfulness into the sinking soul [of her] inexperienced and trembling child? I have no friend, no relation near me whose advice may guide or whose admonitions may check my conduct. Surrounded by strangers with a single exception, my heart feels itself alone, and should the protection of heaven for a moment leave me and I fall, the presence of a mother would assuredly impart a serenity and resignation to my mind which would smooth the pillow for my dying head, and prevent my distracted soul from erring in the hour of her severest trial.

Secluded from the giddy world, I have learned to set a true value on that retirement which has taught me a more perfect knowledge, not only of myself, but of the society over which I may one day be called to rule. Folly and pride no longer wear to me the imposing blazoning which they exhibited to my early years. I have read, reflected, and conversed; and I trust the evidence of a future day will rescue me from having read, reflected, and conversed in vain. The sufferings of my early years, acute as they were in their opinion, have not been unproductive of instruction; their effect has been to correct that sanguineness of disposition [which] was too commonly a source of severe disappointment, and which uniformly led me to view things through a prejudicial medium. A sort of premature experience has given me that insight into human life and human character which in ordinary cases and circumstances is the result of the study and observation of years. Your virtues, my dearest mother, and your afflictions, add a strength to the affections which nature had entwined about my heart, and [lead] me to cling to you in all changes and under all [phases] of persecution with a constancy which those who [hated] you termed obstinacy; but which those who loved you termed by the name of honourable perseverance. I felt that I was not merely acquiescing in [ ] of my moral you, do I now feel the bitterness of your absence. You have no substitute in this [heart; there] is none to occupy your place to my seeking. Even the affectionate attentions of an [ ] person are insufficient to supply the chasm in my bosom, but leave me unsatisfied. I have illustrious relatives it is true, but they offer me no kindness; and if they did, there are certain slumbering recollections would awake in my brain and check my ardour to receive them. I have but one mother, and no variations of place or circumstances can remove her from my sight. Heaven impressed her image on my soul, and time has established it there as its native and legitimate sphere. By a refinement of cruelty indeed we may be separated on earth, and I, as well as yourself, may be doomed the victim of an unjust and malignant spirit of persecution. But in a better world our congenial [souls] will rush to meet each other, where no envious or hating fiends can interfere or impede the pleasures which flow from the pure fountain of filial and maternal love. Such sentiments as these naturally arise out of contemplation of my situation at this moment. Should it be the pleasure of Providence that I survive the hour of approaching danger, I may at some future period be endued with power to restore you to that situation which you were formed to embellish but in which the jealousies of inferior minds would not suffer you to remain. But if an all-wise decree should summon me from this sphere of anxious apprehension, not for myself but for my mother, a pang of horror shoots across my wildered brain. Even then, however, my last prayer would be to Heaven to gift you with that sublime feeling of pious resignation which would teach you to bow submissive to the chastening stroke of our common Father, and to console your afflicted heart with the anticipation of our reunion in a world felicity is unimpaired and to which malice is inadmissible.

Believe me my dearest mother, I fear less to die than to live. The prospect of protracted existence is so blended with dangers and difficulties, so shadowed with clouds and uncertainties, so replete with anxieties and apprehensions, that I must shrink from the contemplation of it, and fly for refuge even to the probability of my removal from so joyless an inheritance. The page of history has determined that happiness is not the possession of those who move in the [ ] circles to which my birth entitles me to look. I cannot hope for an exception in my favour—all the joys of life are centred in my present retirement, and they are even poor, because you are not a participator in them; duties. In proportion have [ ] I have loved but even this qualified enjoyment of them must be brief, and I must emerge into a situation uncongenial to my soul and destructive to all my hopes of felicity on earth. What cause, then, have I to shun that issue which others may behold with horror? What have I to court that existence which others so highly prize? Death would obliterate no image of delight from my heart, save that which in the portrait of a beloved mother nature has still left to the hoping, doubting, yet fearing

CHARLOTTE.

Claremont, October 10, 1817.

Original letter addressed by the late Princess Charlotte to her mother, the Princess of Wales, in October, 1817.

A STIRLING HOTEL IN 1762.

[The following advertisement appeared in the *Caledonian Mercury* for 27th December, 1762.]

A LARGE INN AT STIRLING TO SELL.

That upon Thursday the 4th of January next, at twelve o'clock mid-day, there is to be exposed to sale, by free and publick roup, within the Coffee-house of Stirling, that LARGE NEW TENEMENT OF HOUSES, below the mealmarket of that borough, pretaining to Baillie William, merchant, and which a few years ago was possessed and occupied by Ambrose Hickson, Vinter, as a publick inn. This tenement consists of a large kitchen, and five fire rooms, besides two large cellars on the ground story; a large dining room, and five bed rooms in the second, and seven more bed rooms in the third story; there are likewise two more bed rooms above the kitchen, and four garret rooms, all which have fire places; and there is good stabling, and a large hay loft for between thirty and forty horses. This tenement is still proper and convenient for a publick inn, and the purchasers entry will be from Whitsunday next. The articles and conditions of roup, with the title deeds of the subjects (which make a clear and complete progress) will be seen in the hands of Baillie William Allan, or of James Tower, Writer in Stirling, any time betwixt and the foresaid day of sale; and in case any person shall incline to make a private purchase, he may transact in that manner, on reasonable terms, betwixt and the day of roup.

LOCAL RECORDS.

Letter from the Earl of Linlithgow to James VI., as to the falling in of part of Linlithgow Palace, 6th September, 1607 :—

Pleas zour most sacred Maiestie

This sext of September, betwixt thre and four in the morning the north quarter of your Maiesties palice of linlythgw is fallin rufe and all within the wallis to the ground, bot the wallis are standing yit, bot lukis everie moment when the inner wall sall fall and brek your Maiesties fontan. I had bene to blame if I had nocht maid your Maiestie forsein tua zeiris sence with the estait of it, bot saw na furtherance in thes your Maiesties offisers quhomto your Maiestie gave directionne at that tyme for repairatioun of zour Maiesties said palice. Heirfore it will pleas your Maiestie tak sik ordour thairanent as your hiness thinks gude, and seing the taxationne is grantit for repairing your Maiesties housis according to your hiness directionne, I sall endeuor my selfe to sie zour Maiesties wille performit thairanent. So praying god to grant many happy and prosperous day and long to ring over ws, Zour Maiesties humble subiect

and Servant

LINLYTHGOW.

From your M. palice of linlythgw
the 6th of Septembr 1607

Addressed—To his most sacred Maiestie.

Prices of a number of articles in Kilsyth, in 1676 and 1795.

	1676.			1795.		
A pound of Tobacco - - -	£0	1	6			
Do. Powder - - -	0	0	8	£0	2	2
Do. Shot - - -	0	0	3	0	0	4
A Pint of Wine - - -	0	1	6	0	6	0
A Barrel of Herrings - -	0	16	8	1	7	0
A Stone of Salt Butter - -	0	5	8	0	13	0
A Pair of Worsted Stockings .	0	2	2	0	6	6
A Pair of Gloves - - -	0	1	4	0	3	0
A Yard of Linen for Shirts -	0	0	10	0	3	6
Making 6 Shirts - - -	0	1	0	0	6	6
A Stone of Lint - - -	0	10	0	0	14	0

Rate of Wages and Annual Fees.

	1676.			1795.		
Groom to Lord Kilsyth - -	£5	8	0	£18	0	0
A thicker per day, with meat	0	0	5	0	1	8
A dyke builder do.	0	0	6	0	1	8
A coallier do.	0	0	10	0	3	9

	1676.			1795.		
A labourer, with meat -	£0	0	6	£0	1	6
A tradesman do.	0	0	8	0	2	0
A leg of Beef - - - -	0	5	0	1	0	0
A cow's tongue - - - -	0	0	4	0	1	0
A horse's hay and corn in Glasgow - - -	0	0	9	0	1	8
One horse shoe and 3 removes - - - - -	0	0	7	0	1	3
A stone of skimmed milk cheese	0	4	6			
do. cheese not skimmed -	0	8	0			
A threave of straw for thatch	0	3	0			
A stone of do. do.	0	0	2			
A stone of tarry wool -	0	7	0			
do. of white do. -	0	9	6			
A mutchkin of sweet milk -	0	0	0½			
A Scottish pint of churned milk	0	0	0½			
Weaving a yard of linnen -	0	0	8			
A man, a horse and cart per day	0	5	0			
A spindle of linnen yarn spun	0	1	6			
A peck of potatoes dug for -	0	0	0½			
A woodcutter a day - -	0	1	3			
A pealer - - - - -	0	0	8			
A stone of bark - - -	0	1	6			
100 slabs, 3½ feet long - -	0	3	6			
do. 4½ do. - -	0	4	6			

Excerpts from the Expenditure of Lord Kilsyth in 1676.

	£	S.	D.
Ane Advocate's retaining fee for my Lord,	20	0	0
The Chamberlayn's allowance,	44	0	0
A year's board for my Lord at Glasgow College,	82	0	0
A Physician from Glasgow for a visit,	1	4	0
Do. do. Edinburgh do.	4	10	0
A Surgeon's visit from Glasgow,	0	7	3
To the Physician man,	0	4	3
A furnished velvet Hunting Cap to my Lord,	1	5	0
A hat to my Lord,	0	12	0
A gun to my Lord,	0	16	8
A pair pocket pistols,	1	13	0
do. hulsters furnished	0	18	0
A Suit of Cloths for his Lordship's page,	0	15	0
A saddle and bridle furnished to my Lord,	1	0	3
Matriculating his Lordship's Arms,	1	8	0
Small seeds for his Lordships garden yearly,	0	4	10

A. C.

Glasgow.

LIST OF THE OFFICERS OF THE STIRLINGSHIRE YEOMANRY.

Rank.	Christian and Surname.	Date of Commission.
Lieut.-Colonel	William Murray,	13 July, 1820.
Major	Thos. Graham Stirling,	28 June, 1821.
Captain	David Monro Binning,	15 Feby., 1804.
Do.	M. Stewart Nicolson,	16 Aug., 1819.
Do.	H. Fletcher Campbell,	15 July, 1820.
Do.	Sir Archd. Edmonstone,	11 Sept., 1819.
Do.	Sir Samuel Stirling,	24 March, 1820.
Lieutenant	John MacVicar,	7 June, 1817.
Do.	Campbell Riddell,	16 Aug., 1819.
Do.	John T. Davidson,	11 Sept., 1819.
Do.	C. C. Graham Bontine,	28 June, 1821.
Do.	James Smith,	24 March, 1820.
Cornet	James Smith,	16 Aug., 1819.
Do.	William Galbraith,	16 Nov., 1817.
Do.	John Corbit,	11 Sept., 1819.
Do.	Michael Bruce,	22 April, 1820.
Do.	Alexander Dunlop,	24 April, 1820.
Surgeon	George Anderson,	23 July, 1825.
Adjutant	John Murray,	1 June, 1804.

I do hereby certify that commissions have been granted to the several officers herein named according to the rank and date specified.

(Signed) WILLIAM MURRAY, Lt.-Col.,
Officer Commanding.

Dated at Stirling this 3d day of August, 1825.

LOCAL DOCUMENTS RELATING TO THE REBELLION OF 1745.

[The following original letter, recently obtained by us from an Edinburgh bookseller, would seem to indicate the existence of documents in connection with the Rebellion of 1745, which have not yet seen the light. Mr James Lucas, who writes the letter, was a solicitor in Stirling, and a zealous antiquarian, while his correspondent was the late Mr James Maidment, advocate, Edinburgh, whose learned labours are well known.]

Stirling, 5th Feby., 1841.

My dear Sir,

I received your note accompanying le Roman de Fregus. Mr Morison has now had his final answer from Mrs Murray of Livilands; and I am sorry to say that it is quite unfavorable. She either has not the Autobiography of Lochiel, or is unwilling to lend it; Mr Morison thinks the former. Her statement is, that at the death of her mother, the late Mrs M'Gregor, a few years ago, there was a considerable mass of family papers, not bound up or arranged, as you seem to consider the Autobiography to have been, but in a very loose and confused state, and that they were all destroyed at that period, with the exception of a number of detached letters relating to the Rebellion of 1745. These she acknowledges to be still in her possession; but she says that she will neither part with them, nor allow access to them for the purpose of publication. In short, our friend may give up all idea of obtaining a single document from her. If any body could have moved her Mr Morison was the person; for he is intimate in the family, and I believe a favourite of her ladyship.

Can you tell me whether any letter from Claverhouse to any of the nobility detailing the particulars of the affair of Drumclog, has ever been published? If not, I think that I have fallen in lately with a very valuable document. I can see nothing from him in the shape of an official report of the battle, in Woodrow. I presume that the words "sic subscribitur" prefixed to a signature uniformly infer that a document is merely a copy, and not the original letter itself. May I now ask you whether you have ever seen any letter from Lord Ross, giving an account of the subsequent engagément with the insurgents in the streets of Glasgow.

Mr J. W. M'Kenzie lately gave me a commission to send him half a dozen of the casts of the Stirling Heads. Being anxious to save him the expence of making a box to pack them in, I suggested to him to apply to you for the box in which yours had gone, and send it to me by the carrier; and stated to him that if it had not been already broken up by your servants, I had no doubt that you would willingly give it to him. I have not since heard from him. With my best respects to Mr Turnbull, I remain, yours truly, JAS. LUCAS.

FIFTY YEARS' PROGRESS IN STIRLING.

The following population and trade statistics of Stirling in 1820 and 1870 respectively, show the progress made by the burgh during half a century.

1820.

Population, 6000. Auctioneers, 2; bakers, 17; bankers, 2—Stirling Bank, St. Mary's Wynd, and Bank of Scotland, Broad Street; booksellers, 7; boot and shoemakers, 9; brewers, 3; cabinetmakers, 9; carpet manufacturers, 7; coachmakers, 2; confectioners, 3; coopers, 4; copper and tinsmiths, 3; corn merchants, 2; cotton manufacturers, 2; dyers, 4; earthenware manufacturers, 2; flax dressers, 2; gardeners and seedsmen, 2; glass, china, and stoneware dealers, 3; grocers, &c., 21; haberdashers, 3; inns, 2; ironmongers, 5; land surveyors, 3; linen and woollen drapers, 14; merchants, 2; painters, 2; perfumers, 2; physicians, 5; printers, 1; saddlers, 3; spirit dealers, 7; soap manufacturers, 1; surgeons, 6; tailors, 5; tanners and curriers, 2; tallow chandlers, 3; tartan manufacturers, 2; timber merchants, 3; umbrella makers, 2; vintners, 35; watch and clockmakers, 3; wine and spirit merchants, 4; writers, 13; miscellaneous, 14—including 1 hat manufacturer; 1 stocking maker; 1 trunk maker; 1 upholsterer; 1 plumber; 1 straw hat maker; 1 wright; 1 musician; 1 flour dealer; 1 rope maker; 1 cork cutter; 1 bookbinder; 1 oil and colour man; and 1 lime merchant. Carriers by land, 32; "Lady of the Lake" steam packet; coaches, 4—Edinburgh, Glasgow, Perth, and Castle Cary. Of the 222 persons in business, 76 were in Baker's Wynd (Baker Street), 34 in Broad Street, 12 in Bow (Bow Street), 21 in St. Mary's Wynd; 4 in Spittal Street; 1 in St. John Street; 46 in Quality Street (King Street); 17 in Port (Port Street); 3 in Cowane Street; and 5 in Craigs (4 carpet manufacturers, and 1 coachmaker, Jno. Thomson). Amongst the names were Archd. Watt, baker; Robt. Smith, carpet yarn manufacturer, Cowane Street; John Christie, brick and tile manufacturer; W. Drummond & Sons, seedsmen; Dan. M'Ewen, grocer; Forrest & Dunsmore, physicians; John Shearer, bookbinder; G. & D. Dalgleish, tallow chandlers; Alex. Baird, umbrella maker; Archibald Mouat, vintner; George Harvey, watchmaker; Robt. Campbell, writer; Jas. Chrystal, writer (Allan Park); Robt. Hill, writer; Robt. Sconce, writer; Peter Burden, vintner.

1870.

Population of Royal Burgh, 10,873.—Ærated water manufacturers, 2; agricultural implement makers, 3; architects, 3; artists, 2; auctioneers, 7; bakers, 10; bankers, 7; basket makers, 2; Berlin woolsellers, 3; bill posters, 3; blacksmiths, 11; booksellers, 7; boot and shoemakers, 23; brewers, 3; brick and tile makers, 3; brokers, 9; builders, 7; cabinetmakers, 14; carters, 14; carvers and gilders, 2; chemical manufacturers, 3; chemists, 6; china merchants, 7; coachbuilders, 2; coal agents, 16; commission agents, 6; confectioners, 6; contractors, 4; coopers, 3; dairykeepers, 34; dentists, 3; drapers, 13; dressmakers, 40; dyers, 2; engineers, 6; fishers, 3; fishing-tackle makers, 3; fishmongers, 5; fleshers,

11; green grocers, 15; gardeners, 11; glaziers, 2; grain dealers, 8 ; grocers and spirit dealers, 22 ; grocers and provision dealers, 50; hairdressers, 3; hamcurers, 2; hatters, 3; hotel keepers, 7; iron merchants, 2 ; ironmongers, 4 ; joiners, 12; lath splitters, 2; laundresses, 3; leather cutters, 4; maltsters, 5; manglers, 10; manufacturers, 6; medical practitioners, 10; outfitters, 9; painters, 6; pawnbrokers, 4; photographers, 2; plasterers, 2; plumbers, 6; potato dealers, 4; printers, 4; publicans, 50; refreshment rooms, 8; ropespinners, 4; saddlers, 4 ; seedsmen, 5; shipowners, 6; skinners, 3; slaters, 3 ; surveyors, 7; tailors, 6; tailors and clothiers, 11 ; teachers of music, 10; tea dealers, 5; tinsmiths, 3 ; temperance hotel keepers, 2; tobacconists, 6; toy shops, 6; umbrella makers, 2; upholsterers, 2; veterinary surgeons, 2 ; watchmakers, 11 ; wood merchants, 5; wool merchants, 5; writers, 17; procurators, 8; miscellaneous, 34—total, 726.

LOCAL EXTRACTS FROM "EDINBURGH ADVERTISER," 1793.

[ADVERTISEMENT.]

Feb. 5.—Wanted at Whitsunday first for the Incorporation of Bakers of Stirling a flour miller who is well experienced in making flour and keeping the machinery in good order. None need to apply but who have an undoubted character. Good encouragement will be given.—At the same time there is an apprentice wanted for their mills, who will bind himself as a servant for the space of three years, and who will be allowed a certain sum per year.

N.B.—Letters addressed to Robert Watt, deacon, will be pointedly answered.

[ADVERTISEMENT.]

Feb. 8.—Bounty to Seamen. For speedy manning His Majesty's ship the Robuste, under the command of the Hon. Keith Elphinston, by the Provost and Magistrates of the Town of Stirling. These are offering a bounty of two guineas to every able seaman, and one guinea to every ordinary seaman or able-bodied landman residing within this Town and Parish *(over and above all other Bounties)* who shall within two months from this date turn out volunteers to serve on board of the above man-of-war to be paid upon being approved of by Sir George Home the regulating Captain at Leith.

Given at Stirling the 7th day of February 1793.

(Signed) HENRY JAFFRAY, Provost.

An address to the King from the Provost, Magistrates, and Town Council appeared in the *London Gazette* on March 5, 1793. In this address is offered to His Majesty "our unanimous and firm support in the prosecution of a war in which we are now involved by the unjustifyable conduct of the present rulers of France." His Majesty is also congratulated on the "failure of those sinister attempts which were lately made to disturb our internal quiet by the dissemination of seditious and inflammatory writings which have been completely frustrated by a universal display of patriotism from all corners of the kingdom."

Signed at the Town-House of Stirling the 23rd day of February, 1793.

HENRY JAFFRAY, Provost.

[ADVERTISEMENT.]

Mar. 5.—At a meeting of manufacturers in the Burgh of Stirling held within the house of Mr Wingate, of the Golden Lion Inn, the 26th day of Feby., 1793. The meeting unanimously made choice of Mr Robert Young, carpet manufacturer to his Royal Highness the Prince of Wales, to be their preses, and Robert Banks, writer, to be their clerk, and having thereafter taken into consideration an advertisement inserted in the *Caledonian Mercury* of the 18th Feby. curt., purporting to be the sentiment of persons styling themselves manufactuıers in this place and some neighbouring villages, they find themselves called upon to declare in opposition thereto their firm attachment to the constitution of this country as established in King, Lords and Commons, at the glorious era of the Revolution, and that they will with heart and hand, lives and goods, defend His Majesty's person, crown, and dignity, against all traitorous conspiracies and attempts whatsoever.

[Several declarations of a general kind follow, and a copy of the Resolutions is appointed to be left at the shop of Mr John Sutherland, for signatures by absent Brethren, and the whole names to be afterwards advertised. The advertisement is signed "Ro. Young, Preses," and "Ro. Banks, Clerk."] Immediately below is the following:—

To the Public.

John Dick, manufacturer in Stirling, was sorry to observe in the *Caledonian Mercury* of the 18th Feby. curt., Resolutions of the Manufacturers of Stirling and neighbourhood, signed by him as Presis. He takes this public method of mentioning that he was called off the street a market day, hurried into the said meeting, and immediately elected Preses without knowing anything of their intentions. No sooner was he chosen Preses than one of the members read a copy of resolutions, and he as Preses was appointed to sign them, which he did without considering their contents and scarce knowing what they contained. Since they have appeared in the newspaper he has had an opportunity of considering them attentively, and finds they are perfectly different from his known and avowed sentiments. He hereby disclaims all connection with them. He has never attended any of the meetings for Reform. Loyal to his King and faithful to the constitution of his country, he wished to live in peace and oppose instead of support these views which seem to be entertained by the members of the meeting he was carried to attend.

JOHN DICK.

Stirling, 25th Feb., 1793.

PASS FROM THE EARL OF PERTH TO BALHALDIES, 1684.

James, Earl of Perth, Lord Drumond and Stobhall, Lord High Chancelour of Scotland.

Whereas the bearer Alexander Drumond of Balhaldies is about to travel into the kingdom of England, and particularly to the City of London, about his lawful affairs. These are to desire you to permit him to pass and repass without any let or molestation, he behaving himself as becometh a good subject. Given at His Majties Palace of Holyrood Hous, this 3d of March, 1684.

To all Gouernars, Commanders of His——Perth. Majties forces. To all Magistrates, Justices of the peace, Constables, and all els whom it may concern."

Note.—MacGregor of Balhaldies took the name of Drummond, his own name being proscribed.

POMP OF THE RUSTIC GODS

Bearing gifts to James the Sixth and Mary, King and Queen of Scotland, at the Supper that followed the Baptism of the King at Stirling, December 1566.

SATYRS, to the King.

Woodland Satyrs we, we bring
Rustic gifts to grace the King;
Thee the country's nurslings greet
With the glad country's nurslings fleet;
Stags that can the winds outrun,
Though trusting to their feet, undone.
With years when thy strength shall increase,
With keen Molossian hounds in chase,
Thou wilt pursue and catch the roes,
And the wild boars in nets enclose;
And learn how greatly rural joys
Surpass the city's din and noise.

2. NEREIDS, to the Queen, his mother.

Struck with the Magnesian Marble's
Quick contagion, streaming forth,
Th' iron's hard force turns the needle
To the cold star of the North.

So whose heart the love of virtue
With its mighty force imbues,
'Neath whatever quarter dwelling
Of the sky, thee only views.

This the secret force has drawn us
Hither from the Indian shore,
Nor the flint Heraclian ever
Could have drawn the iron more,

That the clear light of thy virtue
Nearer still we may enjoy;
And with gifts our country readers,
Our observance testify.

3. NAIADS, to the King.

Nor lone wayfarer when the sun arises,
Nor seaman in the calm so much rejoices,
As, babe, the happy tidings of thy birth
Refresh'd our sadden'd hearts with joy and mirth.

Therefore we Naiads gifts bring, small and slight,
Yet they're not small if they are judg'd aright
If gifts be by the heart with which they're made;
And not the heart by gift be judg'd and weigh'd.

4. FAUNS, to the Queen.

O Queen, on whom their lavish gifts
Virtue and form and genius pour,
More happily endow'd with them
Than happy forefathers of yore;

Who now are happiest of all
In fruit of royal wedlock's bands,
Whose cradle, to honour and to grace,
Come embassies from foreign lands:

Whom honour, love, and duty yield
The rural gods of field and floods,
The Naiads from their fountains drawn,
And Satyrs that have quit their woods.

The King of the celestials bids
   The Fauns this oracle declare,
In pledge and promise of an age
   That speeds to better drawing near :

All the machine of nature joins
   To make this Prince a King and great ;
Not chosen he by lot or law,
   But sent by the decrees of Fate.

Not otherwise than hive of bees,
   Though there is none the chief to show,
Led by the instinct nature gives,
   Their leader and their chieftain know.

5. OREADS, to the King.

The Oreads are we, whose dwellings lie
'Mong the recesses of the mountains high,
And from the mountains fetch'd 'mong which we live,
To thee as gifts the whelps of wild beasts give.
And when thy body firmer grows apace
With years, with hounds Molossian in the chase,
Thou wilt thyself pursue the fleeing roes,
And the wild boars in toils of nets enclose ;
Unless, perchance, to catch thou rather love
Napaen Nymphs in glade of sylvan grove,
Who, like the roses, are apt to flee away,
But fear not to be caught so much as they ;
Thou shalt perchance the shaggy wood's retreat
Prefer to towns, though they be rich and great.

A. G.

—*From the Latin of George Buchanan.*

AN OLD TUTOR OF ROYALTY IN STIRLING.

While searching some of the Maitland Club books, I came upon a most interesting letter from Sir Peter Young, which I thought worthy of transcription, and the letter set me wondering if anything was known of the writer. My limited researches have brought me a few facts, a very few.

But who was Sir Peter Young may very fairly be asked, and what had he to do with Stirling? Now the very necessity for asking these questions is at once the best reason for disturbing the perhaps well-earned obscurity of the now nearly forgotten knight, and for offering the unfortunately meagre account of him which the materials at command enable me to furnish. Sir Peter was born in 1544, and died in 1628. When King James the Sixth was but four years old, his education was entrusted to George Buchanan, Peter Young, David Erskine of Cambuskenneth, and Adam Erskine of Dryburgh, the two latter being related to the Earl of Mar. By a decree of the Scottish Council, dated February 1573, the custody of the king was assigned to the Earl of Mar, and the care of his education was continued in the charge of Buchanan and Young, "his present pedagogues." It is matter of history that Buchanan was chief among the tutors of the king, but Young's share appears to have been not inconsiderable. The high favour in which the king held him at once attests a genuine respect for his abilities as a teacher and his amiability as a man.

Sir Walter Scott, in an amusing paragraph anent Sir Mungo Malagrowther in the "Fortunes of Nigel," makes reference to Sir Peter:—

"Having little or no property save his bare designations, Sir Mungo had been early attached to court in the capacity of whipping-boy, as the office was then called, to King James the sixth, and, with his Majesty, trained to all polite learning by his celebrated preceptor, George Buchanan. The office of whipping-boy doomed its unfortunate occupant to undergo all the corporeal punishment which the Lord's annointed, whose proper person was of course sacred, might chance to incur, in the course of travelling through his grammar and prosody. Under the stern rule, indeed, of George Buchanan, who did not approve of the vicarious mode of punishment, James bore the penance of his own faults, and Mungo Malagrowther enjoyed a sinecure; but James' other pedagogue, Master Young, went more cermoniously to work, and appalled the very soul of the youthful king by the floggings which he bestowed on the whipping-boy when the royal task was not suitably performed. And be it told to Sir Mungo's praise, that there were points about him in the highest respect suited to his official situation. He had even in youth a naturally irregular and grotesque set of features, which, when distorted by fear, pain, and anger, looked like one of the whimsical faces which present themselves in a Gothic cornice. His voice also was high-pitched and querulous, so that when smarting under Master Peter Young's unsparing inflictions, the expression of his grotesque physiognomy, and the superhuman yells which he uttered, were well suited to produce all the effects on the monarch who deserved the lash that could possibly be produced, by seeing another, and an innocent individual, suffering for his delict."

Whatever the method James's instructors had, they had much credit by their pupil. When Henry Kyllgrew visited Stirling in 1574, Buchanan and Young put the King through his facings to the great astonishment of the Englishman. In a letter to Walsingham, he speaks most highly of the King's attainments, and mentions that he translated *extempore* a chapter of the Bible from Latin into French, and from French into English, and also danced well. That Young was a scholar and a lover of books is borne out by the letter already referred to, which is addressed to the Lord-Justice Clerk, and is printed in the first volume of the Maitland Club Miscellany:—"My Lord,—Eftir maist hartly commendation of seruice, I haue causit the Librare Hercules lay a syde a nomber of Buikis for the Kingis Majestie, and sum for my Lady Mar, and some for Mr George and for myself seuerally. The catalogue of the Buikis for the Kingis hienes, I send to your Lordship heirwith, to the end it vald pleis your Lordship gett the samyn subscryuit be my Lord Regentis grace, or ellis a precept of the lyik sowme to the thesaurare, with a command that the samyn be ansuerit with expeditioun, seeing it is our soueranes erand. The causis quhairfoir I haue tain the baldnes to trouble your L. heirwith ar sindry, bot cheifly the great affectioun I am assurit ye beare unto our Maisteris furtherance in lerning: and alsua in caise any persoun suld say as the fascioun of the maist part is, quhat neidis his Majestie sa mony Buikis, hes he not anew alredey? that in that caise your L. vald schaw thame thair errour, and persuade my Lordis grace alwayes to graunt. Seeing I mycht not cum thither at this present, I knew nane culd or vald do this mater sa fauorably as your L. In respect quhairof, I hoip your L. sall appardone my baldnes. As I vryt the last tyme, I vald wish to haue the Cæsar of Uenise for a saison to conferr him with utheris. I pray your L. for the panegyriques gif they may be had. As for the Cæsar correctit be Hotomans, I haue reseruit ane in Kingis catalogue. The Librare will think lang for payment, and I for a sicht of the Buikis. Your L. may put us baith out of payne. Sua after my seruice again recommendit to your L. and my Lady, I committ you baith with all your family to Goddis protectioun. From Stiruiling Castell this fryday late.—Your L. seruitour at command, P. YOWNG. To the rycht honorabill and very guid Lork, my Lord Justice-Clerk."

Young was appointed Elemosinare in 1577, received a piece of land from the Crown in 1580, was sent as ambassador to Denmark to negotiate for possession of the Orkney Islands in 1586, was knighted in England in 1614, and wrote a vindication of Mary, Queen of Scots. He is in several places styled as Sir Peter Young of Seaton, afterwards of Auldbar, so that he probably possessed these estates. Now, is there anything more known about this fine old gentleman whom we can fancy must have loved old Stirling well?

THE WALLACE SWORD.

Councillor J. W. Small, F.S.A., Scot., has sketched for us the sword which was transferred from Dumbarton Castle to the Wallace Monument in November, 1888. According to Dr Rogers, when Wallace was captured, as he slept at Robroyston on the night of the 5th August, 1305, he had this great blade resting by his pillow: and when he was conveyed to London to meet his death, it was borne to Dumbarton as the prize of its governor, the recreant Scotsman who had betrayed its possessor. At Dumbarton the sword had for six long centuries remained as a protest against treachery and injustice, and now it has become a trophy in our patriot's monument. As governor of Dumbarton, Sir John Menteith received the sword in August 1305, and two hundred years thereafter, namely, on the 7th December 1505, the accounts of the Lord High Treasurer inform us that, at the command of James IV., the sum of twenty-six shillings, equal to about thirty pounds of our present British money, was paid to an armourer for binding a riding sword and a rapier; also for the "binding of Wallas sword with cords of silk," and providing it with "ane new hilt and plomet," also a "new scabbard and a new belt." And it will be remarked that while the rapier and the riding sword are named as being simply repaired, the Wallace sword is described as adorned with trappings of silk; also as having been provided with the specified additions of a new hilt and pommel, a new scabbard, and a new belt. Concerning the weapon we learn nothing further for 320 years; but a letter which, in October 1872, Dr Rogers received from the War Office, informed him that in the year 1825 the sword was sent for repair to the Tower, when the Duke of Wellington, as Master-General of the Ordnance, submitted it for examination to Dr Meyrick. This gentleman, afterwards Sir Samuel Meyrick, was an authority as to ancient swords, but in estimating the age of the Dumbarton weapon he was guided by its mountings only. Judging from these, he concluded that the sword was not older than a sword in the British Museum connected with the Earldom of Chester, and belonging to the reign of Edward IV. Sir Samuel in his work on "Ancient Armour," at vol. II., page 177, when referring to the reign of Edward IV., wrote:—"The two-handed sword, shown at Dumbarton Castle as that of Wallace, is of this period, as will be evident to any one who compares it with that of the Earldom of Chester in the British Museum."

WALLACE'S SWORD.

The Chester sword was afterwards examined by Mr George Ormerod, of the Society of Antiquaries, who, in the fifth volume of *Vetusta Monumenta*, showed that the weapon was the Sword of State which Edward V. had borne before him when, as Prince of Wales, he, in 1475, made a triumphal entry into Chester Castle. If then, the Chester sword belonged to the year 1475, Sir Samuel Meyrick approximated nearly to the date of the mounting of the Wallace sword, which occurred just thirty years later. But the Wallace sword was in 1505 an old blade, which required a new hilt and pommel, a new scabbard, and a new belt. And as the weapon was then so materially shattered, it seemed reasonable to conclude that it was decidedly ancient; moreover, that before it was allowed to rest in the Dumbarton Armoury it had been subjected to much hard usage. And its being adorned with silk tassels, by the King's command, says Dr Rogers, leaves us in no doubt as to its being held in special veneration; while in the register the weapon is described as "Wallas sword," no qualifying word of doubt being expressed as to its genuineness. And apart from the circumstance that by two separate weldings the blade has been shortened, it is otherwise a duplicate of the two-handed blade of Sir Richard Lundin, used at the battle of Stirling, now preserved at Drummond Castle. Dr Rogers compared the two swords in 1861, when they were together under his charge. One blunder led to another. Consequent upon Sir Samuel Meyrick's judgment, pronounced in 1825, the mountings of 1505 were removed and a common handle of the 15th century substituted. This information he obtained in the letter which, in 1872, he received from the War Office. He has thus no doubt of the genuineness of the relic. The blade, which is double-edged, is 4ft. 4in. long, and 2¼in. broad at the top, narrowing to 1in. at the point. The hilt, which is mounted with leather, is a foot long, and the size of the pommel is 2in.

ARDOCH CAMP IN 1672.

The following interesting letter is from the Blair Drummond M.S., and is printed in Vol. 7 of Historical Manuscript Commission Reports, the writer being James, Lord Drummond, afterwards fourth Earl of Perth, who communicates the discovery of a Roman gold ring and a number of coins :—

"Stobhall, 15th January, 1672.

"My dearest friend,—Your Almanacks arrived last week with the Book directed to me. My father was mightily pleased with his part. I assure you mine was no less satisfactorie to me. I have not read it quite through, for I was engadged in Doctor Broun's Vulgar Errors. On Saturday I read his Discourse of Vrn Buriall, with which I was so taken, that in a very short time I read it. No doubt he is an extraordinarie person both for learning and piety; His Religio Medici I never saw nor is it in Scotland to be had. My reading the first lines of the discourse I mentioned puts me in min to show you that latly near Drummond (that is to say within 5 myles) amongst the hills which lie at its back, towards the Forest which belongs to my Father, two countrymen intenning to build a new kiln for corn in the seat of an old oregroun one, and searching deep to lay its foundation, found a great ring of gold, and a considerable deal of money, which they disposed of to pedlars, for its weight in the common coyne of this countrie; they carried it to goldsmiths in Perthe; and for a very inconsiderable gain sold them. Only one accidentally came to Drummond, where my father was about his affairs in that place, who bought about 24 of the pieces. They are about the bredth of a very large 3 pence, and thryce as thick or more. I have not yet taken particular notice to them, bot these I saw had upon them Domitian, Commodus Antoninus Pius, Trajan and Diva Faustina. I belive there be more heads amongst them. The figurs are excellently uell stampt and by their dresse appear to haue bein as old as those they represent. If you intend to speak of them to any, send me word and I will aske some of them from my father; for most of them he has tuice or thrice The thing I am most concerned at is the goldsmith's put them in work (lyke fools) for they might haue had much gain by them, bot the siluer was so good, it would not mix with thers until a third part of alloy was joyned to them. They say ther was more than a bushel of them; bot all the inquiry I made I could not get me any of them. The Leaguer of the Romans for one whole winter lay at Ardoch, some 4 miles or more towards the south from that place, and ther is to be sein their intrenchments and fortifications in circular lines deeper in some places then a man on horsback can be seen: and northeast from that there are more trenches, alyke in form and largeness; bot the ground being much better has made the people against my grandfather's orders till them doune in some places. Ther was near these a round open lyke the mouth of a narrow well of a great depth, into which my grandfather ordered a malefactor to go, who (glad of the opportunity to escape hanging) went and brought up a spur and a buckler of brass; which were lost the time that a garrison of Oliver's dispossessed us of Drummond. Ther was found a stone ther vpon which was cut an in scription to show that a Captain of the Spanish Legion died ther. If you please I shall coppie it for yow. It is rudely cutt," &c.

LOCAL EXTRACTS FROM "THE EDINBURGH ADVERTISER," 1793.

Mar. 5. [Advertisement]. Villa very near Stirling To be Let and entered to at Whitsunday 1793. The Premises are a house consisting of dining-room, drawing-room, seven fire-rooms, kitchen, laundry, cellar, closets. &c. A stable, byre, coach-house, hay-loft, garden, and about four acres of rich grass ground surrounding the whole. The buildings are modern. The picturesque situation of Stirling and the rich country about it are well-known and the Villa lies upon the great road leading to Edinr. Glasgow &c.; and within about two English miles of perhaps the cheapest and best coal on the south of the Forth. The grass-ground will be retained if the tenant does not want it. Peter Littlejohn, writer in Stirling, will inform as to other particulars.

Mar. 19.—Intimation of raising Seven Regiments of Fencibles. Stirling to be head quarters of Marquis of Lorn's corps.

[N.B. This corps was the first filled up.]

Mar. 19. [Advertisement]. Houses in Stirling for Sale. To be sold by public roup within the house of Malcolm Monro, vintner in Stirling, upon Friday the 5th day of April, 1793. The following subjects either in whole or separately as purchasers may incline: viz. Lot 1st. That new-built house at the junction of the roads leading from Stirling to Dumbarton, Glasgow and Edinr. near the Port of Stirling, consisting of a kitchen, parlour, dining-room, drawing-room, eight bedrooms, including the garrets; also a back-court sufficiently enclosed, containing coach-house, poultry-house, &c., and a pump-well of fine soft water which is conveyed into the kitchen. The number of conveniences makes this lot a desirable purchase for a genteel family, and which can either be occupied by one or two families, as it has two separate doors or entrys, and from the prospect it commands of the country round Stirling, makes it by far the most pleasant in that part. The building is done in a most substantial manner, and finished with taste, the proprietor having built it for his own residence:—it has been rented to two families at £50 per annum. 2d. A back house adjoining lot 1st with garden ground before the door neatly enclosed presently possessed by Michael Potter Esq. at the rent of £10: 10s per annum. 3d. A court with stables for eight horses and a coach-house above with an extensive loft or granary mostly enclosed, fit either for a garden or buildings, and as the whole of this lot has great command of soft water within 6 ft. of the surface it would answer very well for manufactures of different kinds. The whole premises will be shown on any lawful day between the hours of 12 and 2 o'clock in the afternoon ; and for further particulars application may be made to Mr Buchanan the proprietor at the house ; Mr James Wright, writer in Stirling ; Mr Alex. Stewart, mercht. St. Andrew's Square, Glasgow, or to Mr John Campbell, junior writer to the signet, Edinr.

April 19—Advt. of House and Lands of Broom near Stirling to be Let for any number of years. Also a farm of 47 acres rich kerse ground inclosed and subdivided on the banks of the Forth.

April 23—Notice to the Public—That the business formerly carried on at Stirling by John Glas junior and William Glas & Son, was dissolved by mutual consent in May last, which notice though directed to be inserted in different newspapers, appeared only in one.

William Glas.

Stirling 18th April, 1793.

April 26.—Died on Monday last (22nd) the Rev. Mr John Muschet minister of Stirling—[33d yr of ministry]

May 3. [Advertisement] Money Wanted—Five Hundred Pounds Sterling immediately or at Whitsunday, on heritable security at 4½ per cent. Apply to Mr James Chrystal, writer, Stirling. Not to be repeated.

May 14. [Advertisement]—Country House, Stirlingshire—To be let and entered upon at Whitsunday, The House of Tarbrex, consisting of a kitchen and two convenient cellars on the ground floor, a good dining-room and drawing-room on the first flat two good bedrooms on the second and two excellent garret-rooms above with fire-places; together with a stable and byre and a large garden mostly laboured, and sown with kitchen stuffs. The house stands on a dry and healthy soil in a pleasant situation a good neighbourhood and within 20 minutes walk of the Cross of Stirling. For particulars apply to Mr William Wright, Stirling, or to Mr Jas. Aikman mason, St. Patrick's Square Edinr.

May 27—We hear from Stirling that on Thursday se'ennight the Magistrates and Council, waving their right of patronage, met with the Kirk Session and heritors and unanimously elected the Rev. Mr Sommerville to be first minister; and that on Tuesday thereafter Mr William Innes, preacher of the Gospel was also unanimously elected second minister of that town by the Magistrates, Kirk Session and Delegates from the Guildry, Trades, and different communities.

Aug. 16—Inn at Stirling Port advertised to be let with the whole stables malt barn and garden for seven years. Miss Margt. Willison, daughter of Widow Willison, to show the premises.

Oct. 1—Easter Livelands advertised to be let furnished or unfurnished. "The house sheltered with wood and in the midst of a rieh beautiful ond fertile country is situated about half-a-mile from the town of Stirling, where there is an easy communication with Edinburgh and Glasgow by stage-coaches every day and by carriers once a week." Application may be made to Mr Forman, writer to the signet, Edinburgh, or to Thomas Wingate, writer, Stirling.

Oct. 15—The first division of the Argyly Fencibles arrived at Stirling on Thursday under the command of Sir Alex. Campbell and the second division under the command of Major Maclaine. Their appearance and good order are remarkable for so young a corpse.

Oct. 22.—Advertisement of Houses to be Let at Stirling suitable for a dyer or an inn. The dwelling-house, shop and offices nigh the old toll-bar of Stirling, as possessed by the deceased John Connal. The premises most complete for a dyer, or a public or stabling house. If an active person was inclining an inn this is an excellent situation.—Apply to Alexr. Peebles, merchant.

Dec. 10.—Advertisement of House and Orchard to Let. The Middle House at the Houffe of Stirling, with or without garden ground and offices. It is capable of accommodating a genteel family, and in point of situation is almost a country residence. The town of Stirling is well known for cheapness of living and genteel society, and the conveniency of almost all branches of education. Large orchard well stocked with fruit trees of a proper age to be let along with house or separately. Apply to John Burn, writer in Stirling.

LETTER FROM KING JAMES THE EIGHTH TO WILLIAM MACGREGOR OF BALHALDIE.

"Rome, Decmre 3d, 1748.

"I received last week yours of the 4th Novemer. I had already heard of Lochyel's death, it is a loss to the cause, and I am truely concernd for it: If my recommendation to the Court of France comes in time, and has its effect, young Lochyel will have his Father's Regiment, and on this and all other other occasions I shall be always glad to show him the great sense I retain of the merits of that Family. Poor Lochyel did not long outlive his friend Lord Semple, in whom I have also lost a very zealous subject, and who had given many proofs of his being so. I wish I had been able to have been more kind to his Family, But the truth is my straits were never so great as they are now, and Therefore I cannot neither authorize your keeping up a correspondence, the expences of which I am not able to defray. The Prince in his present situation can best judge of what use it may do in that respect by his directions. I desire Lochyels Lady, his Brothers, and son may find here my compliments on their late loss, which I sincerely share with them, and have nothing else to add at present but to assure you of my constant kindness and regard for yourself.

JAMES R."

THE OLD BRIDGE OF STIRLING.

The following Writ for the Repair of the Bridge of Stirling appears in "Historical Documents Relating to Scotland," vol. II., p. 491 :—

DE PONTE DE STRIVELYN REPARANDO.

Rex delecto suo Johanni de Sandale camerario suo Scotiæ salutem.

Volentes quod exitus provenientes de custuma cujusdam passagii apud Strivelyn convertantur in reparationem et emendationem pontis ibidem, qui dirutus est et confractus vobis mandamus quod omnes exitus præditos ad reparationemet emendationem pontis prædicti, per visum et testimonium dilecti nobis Willelmi constabulari nostri de Strývelyn, assignari facias. Exitus enim prædictos in compoto vestro allocari faciemus.

Teste rege, apud Westm. xx die Octobris.

CHARLES II. AND THE MAGISTRATES OF STIRLING.

The following letters which are preserved in the Town Clerk's Office, Stirling, are of considerable value as showing the severe straits to which Charles II. was reduced whilst Scotland was under the control of Cromwell and the Parliamentarians. These documents enable the reader to trace the course of the King's adventures during a portion of the fatal year 1651. A short time before the date of the first letter he was in Dundee ; thence he had gone to Dunfermline in May, and he was at Stirling in the following month. The siege of Dundee by General Monk had begun before the date of the last document, and the cause of the Royalists was temporarily overthrown by "the crowning mercy" of Worcester on September 3d. The date of Colonel Leighton's receipt is especially interesting, as it was written on the very day when Charles set out from Stirling at the head of 14,000 men to endure defeat at Worcester.

"CHARLES R.

"Trustie and weill beloved, wee greite you weell. The necessitie of our affaires forceth us at this tyme (our awne propper rentes lying where the enemie hes power, our customs made ineffectuall, and that which the Parliament did give us, being for our necessarie intertainment, and uther neidfull affaires, alreadie super expended) to crave your assistance for the present advance of some money for our necessarie provisione against our going to the fields. These are therefoir earnestlie to desire you presentlie to advance to us twa hundreth pund sterling, for which soume you shall have securitie aither upon our proper rentes, customes, imposts, or casuallities, within this our Kingdome, or other wayes what private securitie you can in reasone demand from the commissioners of our treasurie for the same, and interest thereof. And for that effect that you appoynt one of your number whom you trust to speack with the commissioners of our treasurie (on Wednesday next the 7th of this instant), whom we shall authorise to give you securitie, aither private or publik, and the publik securitie shall be authorised and confirmed by the next ensueing parliament for your further securitie. So expecting your care to provyde the said soume with all diligence, as you tender the good of our service, and honour of this Kingdome, we bid you fare weill. From our Court at Dunfermlyne, this third day of May, 1651.

"To our trustie and weill beloved The Magistratts, Councell, and Comunitie of our burgh of Stirling."

---

(2) "CHARLES R.

"Our will and pleasure is that upon sight hereof you pay or cause to bee payd, out of such moneys as shall come into your hands from the town of Sterlin, for our use, the sume of two hundred pounds sterlin, unto our trusty and well beloved Arthur Areskin of Scotscraig; and for your so doing this shall be your sufficient warrant. Given at our Court at Sterlin this 28th day of June 1651, and the third year of our reign."

"To our trusty and well beloved the Provost of Sterlin, and to our right trusty and well beloved the Treasurer-Deputy."

"Whatsoever of the above written sum shall be delayvered to my Lord Duck of Buckingham, his servant Mr Way, or Col. Lugton, upon their reseitt, it shall be by me allowed, as if I had reseaved it myself."

ARTHUR ARSKEN.

(3)

"Receyved the 31st of July 1651, the sume of one hundred pounds Sterlin, in part payment of his Majesty's precept to me.

"E. LEIGHTON."

"You shall be pleased to deliver lykwaise to John Short, Provist, the uther hundred punds sterling, which, with his reseit, shall be acknowledged be mee."

Sir Arthur Erskine of Scotscraig referred to in these letters was the sixth son of John, Earl of Mar, and represented Fifeshire in the Convention of Estates in 1643-4, 1645, and 1648-9. When the troubles began after the death of Charles I., he seems to have taken refuge in Dundee, as did many of the Royalists of the time, since his name appears in the Register of Baptisms in Dundee under date March 4th, 1651, in these terms :—

"Arthur Erskyne of Scots craige, a man-child Charles ; Sponsors, Lord Balcleugh, Lord Yeaster, Lord Balcaras, and Sir Robert Murray."

He died before October in the following year, as according to Lamont his creditors were summoned to Edinburgh to give sworn statements as to the sums due to them, at which time they "did each subscribe that, for their pairt, they sould not troubell the aire, young Scotscraige, his person, for the speace of five years to come ; and if in that time he and his mother were abell to redeime the lands, it was good and well ; and if not, the aire was to reseigne his right of the lands to his creditors, to dispose upon them at their pleasure. All this time the creditors were to receave no annual rents, for the Lady Scotscraigie was infeft in the haile lands during hir life-time. The burden was thought to be above 300 thousand merks of debt." Lady Scotscraig died at Edinburgh in October 1657, and was buried there. The estate of Scotscraig was then acquired by the unfortunate Archbishop Sharpe.

A DEFUNCT LOCAL INSTITUTION.

The following advertisement refers to an Institution which did much good in its time, but has long been extinct :—

STIRLING AND BANNOCKBURN CALEDONIAN SOCIETY.

THE FIFTH ANNIVERSARY GENERAL MEETING of the SOCIETY will be held in the GUILD-HALL, of Stirling, on Monday the 25th of June next, at 10 o'clock of the morning, in order to elect Office-Bearers for the ensuing year, Ballot for new Members, and arrange other matters connected with the Society ; *and also to have a public examination of the Boys admitted to the benefits of the Institution.* After which, the members of the Society, with such deputations from other Societies as may honour the meeting with their attendance, will march in procession to the Bored Stone, in commemoration of the ever-to-be-remembered Battle of Bannockburn ; and from thence return to the Guild-Hall and Bowling Green, for the purpose of adjudging the following premiums :—

Two Sovereigns to the best Performer of Pibrochs, on the Great Highland Bagpipe.

One Sovereign and a Half to the best Performer of Reels and Strathspeys on the Great Highland Bagpipe.

The Society's Honorary Silver Medals, to the best Dancers of Reels and Strathspeys, of members belonging to the Society.

Half a Sovereign each, to the two best Dancers of Reels and Strathspeys, of members not belonging to the Society.

A handsome Sporan Molloch, to the best, and a pair of Stocking Hose to the next best Dancer of the Sword Dance.

All those intending to compete, must be equipped in the Highland Garb, and have their names enrolled with the Secretaries, betwixt and 10 o'clock of the morning of the 25th ; at same time mentioning what they are to compete for.

RULES OF COMPETITION.

1st, Those intending to compete for the two first Prizes, must lodge with the Secretaries, the names of three Pibrochs, and Reels and Strathspeys, any of which the Committee shall have it in their power to call for.

2d, Should only one competitor appear, for any of the Prizes, the Committee are to have it in their power either to award the whole, or such part of the Prize, to that Competitor as they judge proper.

3d, Tickets of admission, one shilling each, to be issued by the Sub-Committee.

N.B.—The Society dine in the Saracen's Head Inn.—Tickets of admission to be had at the bar; and such gentlemen as are friendly to the institution, although not members, will be at liberty to join.

Stirling, 31st May, 1827.

THE ORIGIN OF PARISHES.

The present division of parishes is purely of ecclesiastical origin, and seems to have been more the result of gradual development than fixed and determinate plan. In fact, it would appear that boundaries were not clearly defined till the teinds of each pastorate were by law confined to the limits of said pastorate or parish. In England, an Act in Queen Elizabeth's time directed "That the church wardens of every parish, and four, three, or two substantial householders therein" should be nominated as overseers of the poor, to provide a rate for the maintenance of the poor. This poor-rate of our southern neighbours, doubtless, had the effect of producing fixity in the parish boundaries, so that assessments should not overlap. In Scotland, their origin is more obscure. Forbes, in his *Treatise on Tithes*, published in 1705, says all perhaps that can be said on the subject:—

"It is owned that Bishops at first lived with the clergy about them in their proper seats, or the Cathedral Churches, where the stated services and publick offices of religion were alone performed, and to which all the people of the Diocese considered as one parish resorted, especially at the more solemn seasons of devotion; and that some Presbyters used to be sent forth into the remoter parts as itinerant preachers, for dispensing of the Word and Sacraments to such as could not conveniently come to reap the benefit thereof in the Episcopal College. Nor is it controverted that the institution of rural Parishes was got up to the end Pastors might notice more particularly the people committed to their immediate care. But it is not so clear when or by whom this was done. . . . Sometimes the missionary preacher found encouragement to settle in a populous place, and by the liberal assistance of the zealous inhabitants to raise up an Oratory or Chappell with a little adjoyning manse. Sometimes princes erected conveniences for devotion at their country houses, called Royal Free Chappells, with sufficient revenues to priests to officiate there. But more frequently Lords and great men founded churches on their own lands, for the use of their families and tenant; whereby the Parishes were of no larger extent than the founder's possessions. As these came to be divided among more proprietors, the new masters obtained new churches, with a parochial circuit commensurate to their proper estate, pretending frequently that all their design in the matter was to supply the inconveniences of distance from, and different access to the *Ecclesia matrix*, or Original Parish Church. These new churches were therefore called auxiliary churches, but must not be confounded with Chappells of Ease. . . . . . . The ministers of the Reformation were distributed among the Burghs of Scotland. . . . . But the first Act of Parliament that I find for bounding the ministerial duty by distinct parishes is the Act 100, parl. 7, James VI. King Charles I. gave order for dividing the town of Edinburgh into four distinct parishes . .

. . . but these parishes are now increased to the number of eight."

After the Reformation, Commissioners of Parliament for the "plantation of kirks" were from time to time appointed, who confirmed old boundaries and established new as the exigencies of each particular case suggested, dividing or uniting parishes as their wisdom saw fit. The same powers continued till the union, and are now under its provisions exercised by the Court of Teinds, which is in reality a permanent Commission of the Parliament of Scotland. Parishes are now subdivided or united under the provisions of Sir James Graham's Act of 1845 (properly known as the *Quoad Sacra Churches Act*), but these latter exactly correspond to the "Chappels of Ease" of pre-Reformation times.

D. D.

AN ELECTION PETITION.

Upon Tuesday, 28th November, 1826, a petition was presented to the House of Commons by the Honourable John Maitland, lieutenant colonel of his Majesty's 32nd regiment of foot, setting forth that, at the last election of a member to serve in Parliament for the class district of burghs, consisting of the 5 burghs, Stirling, Dunfermline, Inverkeithing, Culross, and Queensferry, on 3rd day of July last, Robert Downie of Appin, Esq., and the petitioner, were candidates. That, at the said election, James Gibson Craig of Riccarton, Esq. commissioner or delegate legally chosen for the burgh of Culross, the presiding burgh (and producing a commission duly executed and authenticated as the law requires) voted for the petitioner, and also declared that, in case of an equality of votes, he gave his casting vote for the petitioner. That James Stuart of Dunearn, Esq., commissioner and delegate for the burgh of Inverkeithing (and producing a commission duly executed and authenticated as the law requires) voted for the petitioner, and also declared that, in case he should be found to have the right of a casting vote, he gave it for the petitioner. That John Thomson, pretending to be duly elected delegate from the burgh of Stirling, James Blackwood, pretending to be duly elected delegate from the burgh of Dunfermline, and Campbell Innes, pretending to be duly elected delegate for the burgh of Queensferry, voted for the said Robert Downie. That the said burgh of Queensferry had, previous to the said election, by violation of its set in the election of its magistrates, councillors, and other members of the incorporation, and by the common clerks of burghs at election of delegates for choosing members of Parliament, were not taken and subscribed, or not duly taken and subscribed by the magistrates, councillors, and other members of the incorporation, and by the common clerks of the said burghs of Stirling, Dumfermline, and Queensferry, or either of them, on the occasion of the election of the said delegates of the said burghs, or either of them; and other essential irregularities were then committed, whereby they were respectively disqualified from voting or acting at the election of such delegates: That the elections of the said delegates for the burghs of Stirling, Dumfermline, and Queenferry, were made by persons not duly qualified, and not having right to elect, and were otherwise conducted in a manner informal, illegal, and contrary to the statutes in that behalf made and provided: That the elections of the said delegates were null and void, and the votes of the delegates, so illegally constituted, ought not to have been received or admitted at the said election: That the petitioner had the majority of legal votes, and was entitled to be, and ought to have been, returned the Burgess to serve in Parliament for the said district of burghs, but that nevertheless, the Common Clerk Depute of Culross, the presiding burgh, who acted as returning officer at the said election, did return the said Robert Downie as Burgess or Commissioner to represent the said district of burghs in Parliament.

The petitioner therefore humbly prays the house to take this petition into consideration, to declare the election and return of the said Robert Downie to be null and void, and that the petitioner was duly elected and ought to have been returned, and to grant him such other relief as to the house shall seem meet.

The House (28th November, 1826) ordered this petition "to be taken into consideration upon Tuesday the 9th day of January next, at half an hour after three o'clock afternoon; and Mr Speaker to issue his warrants for persons papers, and records:" But, upon 13th December, 1826, this order was discharged, and the petition ordered "to taken into consideration upon Thursday the 1st day of March next, at half an hour after three o'clock in the afternoon."

On Saturday, 17th March, 1827, Provost Thomson received a letter from Mr Downie, intimating his success in the contest into which he had been dragged before a Committee of the House of

Commons, relative to the merits of his election. Owing to the fall of snow, it was late in the afternoon before the letter arrived announcing the triumph, but the Magistrates lost no time in communicating the news, by causing all the bells in the town to ring a merry peal.

The evening of Saturday being too late to admit of farther demonstrations of public joy, the Magistrates resolved to defer these until Monday evening, when the Council, along with Mr Downie's voters at the election, assembled in the Town House at 7 o'clock, to celebrate the happy event, by drinking Mr Downie's health, the bells again ringing a merry peal. The company vied with each other in manifesting their joy on the happy occasion. Many loyal and appropriate toasts were given.

NORRIESTON COMMUNION CUPS.

The two silver Communion cups belonging to the Norrieston Church are graceful, but of quite a common make. As the inscription tells us, they were presented by Robert Downie, Esq., late of Bengal, in 1815.

Early in last century, George Downie married, 1st, Margaret M'Culloch, co-heiress of Ashentree, and their son John, born 1727, inherited his mother. Thinking he could thrive better as tenant than as laird, John sold Ashentree, which he and his son continued to farm till within the memory of some that are still alive.

George Downie, above mentioned, married 2nd, Mary Murdoch in Arnieve, in 1734. Their son, Robert, was born in 1735. He established a distillery at Spittalton; and there is preserved at Knock o' Ronald a bottle bearing his name, and dated 1771, which was used in the business. His son, Robert, born 1771, opened a spirit shop in Broad Street, Stirling, but he did not prosper. His relatives at Ashentree advanced him a considerable sum of money, with which he went to Bengal, where he amassed a large fortune. Having returned, he took up his residence in Newton, near Doune. He represented the Stirling Burghs in Parliament from 1820 to 1830, having been re-elected in 1826. He was suspected of having bribed the limited constituency of the Burghs, which was too common in these days. When the estate of the old Stuarts of Appin came to the market, Robert Downie secured them, and on his death on 10th Sept., 1841, the Appin property passed to his daughter. It is now vested in trustees in behoof of her nephew, the son of MacAlpin Lennie of Dalswinton.

The gift of the two cups was made by Downie soon after the erection of the Church, and must have been much appreciated by a congregation that had usually to bear its own burdens.

W.

THE GUISERS IN STIRLING.

(From the MS. of the late James Lucas.)

GALATIONS.

As the schoolmaster is so busy in effacing any vestiges of ancient customs and habits, the preservation of this relic of the olden time will afford gratification to those who take pleasure in their early recollections of what happy Britain once was. Some account of this fragment of the Old Mystery or Interlude will be found in Hone, and a Cornish version has been given in the recent valuable publication of "Ancient Christmas Carols."

DRAMATIS PERSONÆ:

Sir Alexander.
Galations.
Admiral
Farmer's Son.
Doctor.

Sir Alexander.

Keep silence, merry gentlemen, unto your courts, said I:
My name's Sir Alexander, I'll show you sport, said I.
Five of us all, fine merry boys are we,
And we are come a-rambling your houses for to see:
Your houses for to see, Sir, and pleasure for to have,
And what you freely give to us we freely will receive.
The first young man that I call in, he is the farmer's son;
And he's afraid he lose his love, because he is too young.

Farmer's Son.

Altho' I am too yonng, Sir, I've money for to rove,
And I will freely spend it before I lose my love.

Sir Alexander.

The next young man that I call in, he is a hero fine;
He's Admiral of the Hairy Caps, and all his men are mine.

The Admiral.

Here am I the Admiral—the Admiral stout and bold,
Who won the battle of Quinbeck, and wear a crown of gold.

Sir Alexander.

The next young man that I call in, is Galations of renown,
And he will slay our Admiral, and take his golden crown.

Galations.

Here comes in Galations, Galations is my name;
With sword and pistol by my side, I hope to win the game.

The Admiral.

The game, Sir; the game, it is not in your power:
I'll draw my bloody dagger, and slay you on the floor.

Galations.

My head is made of iron, my body's made of steel;
I'll draw my bloody weapon, and slay you on the field.

Sir Alexander.

Fight on, fight on, brave warriors! fight on with noble speed!
I'll give any man ten hundred pounds to slay Galations dead.

[*Here Galations and the Admiral fight, and Galations falls, being stabbed.*]

Sir Alexander.

Galations ye have killed, and on the floor have slain:
Ye will suffer sore for him, as sure's your on the plain.

The Admiral.

Oh no; it was not I, Sir; I'm innocent of the crime;
'Twas that young man behind me that drew his sword so fine.

Farmer's Son.

Oh, you awful villain! to lay the weight on me;
For my two eyes were shut, Sir, when this young man did die.

Sir Alexander.

How could your eyes be shut, sir, when you stood looking on?
When their two swords were drawn, you might have sindered them.
Since Galations ye have killed, Galations ye must cure;
Galations ye must raise to life in less than half an hour.

Spoken—Round the kitchen, and round the hall,
For an old greasy doctor I do call.

Doctor.

Here comes I, the best old greasy doctor in the kingdom.

Sir Alexander.

What can you cure?

Doctor.

I can cure the rout, the gout, the ringworm, cholic, and the scurvy; and can gar an old woman of seventy look as gay as a young woman of sixteen.

Sir Alexander.

What will you take to cure this dead man?

Doctor.

Ten pounds and a bottle of wine.

Sir Alexander.

Will five not do? nor six?

Doctor.

Six won't take down a Highlandman's breeks to let the devil fart out fire.

Sir Alexander.

Seven? Eight? Nine?

Doctor.

No.

Sir Alexander.

Ten?

Doctor.

Yes, ten! and a bottle of wine.

Sir Alexander.

What will you give him?

Doctor.

I'll give him ——; and I have a small bottle in my breek pouch full of Inky Pinky*—*(sings)* a little to his nose, and a little to his toes *(applying it accordingly)*. Start up, Jack, and sing.

Galations.

Once I was dead, and now I'm come alive;
Blessed be the doctor that made me to revive.

Omnes.

We will all join hands, and never fight more,
But we will all 'gree as brethren, as we have done before:
We thank the master of this house, likewise the mistress, too,
And all the little babies that round the table grow.
Your pockets full of money, and your bottles full of beer,
We wish you a good Hogmanay, and a happy New Year. [*Exeunt.*

EPILOGUE.

Here comes in little diddie dots,
With his pockets full of groats,
If you have anything to spare,
Put it in there.

---

* Inky Pinky, about seventy or eighty years since, was used by the brewers in Stirlingshire to designate the smallest kind of beer; the medium was termed Middle-moy, and the best, or strongest, Ram-tambling.

Stories of Old Stirling.

A KING'S BIRTHDAY RIOT IN THE DAYS OF GEORGE II.

The new volume of Stirling Records contains several references to a disturbance which took place in the burgh on the occasion of celebrating the King's Birthday in October, 1734, but there is no entry explanatory of the affair. It was, in fact, one of the most extraordinary occurrences in local history, although no hint of it is to be found in any local history. There have been long in our possession the materials for telling the whole story, and this we purpose doing now. Perhaps the best way of narrating the circumstances which led to the riot, and the incidents of the disturbance itself, is to allow a contemporary writer to give his version, which appeared in a very rare anti-Government print of the period, viz., *The Thistle*, Edinburgh newspaper conducted by "Sir John de Graham, Knight," and professedly patriotic. The copy we quote from belonged to the late David Laing. Once our readers get accustomed to the old style of printing, and the writer's way of expressing himself, they will appreciate the graphic touches in his account of a remarkable *émeute*.

TO SIR JOHN DE GRAHAM, KNIGHT.

Stirling, December 21, 1734.

Sir,—As the Squabble that happened at *Starling*, on the 30th of *October*, (being the Anniversary of our most gracious Sovereign King *George*) has, in many Places, made some Noise; and, by the Artifice of some, who had no small Share in it, been most unjustly represented; Knowing that you are a Lover of Truth and your Country, setting every Thing in a true Light, I beg the Favour that you will oblige the Publick with the following Account of it, and the Spring from whence the design'd Mischief, which that Day happened, proceeded.

Some few Days before the Election of the Member of Parliament for this District of Towns, our Town-Council, (which consists of 21) met to chuse a Delegate, to go to *Innerkeithing* to vote for their Member of Parliament, when *Robert Wingate*, then Provost, with 13 more, declared themselves for the *Honourable Mr. James Erskine of Grange*, to represent them in Parliament: And *James Littlejohn*, late Provost, with 6 more, declared themselves for Captain *Charles Campbel* of Colouel *Harrison's* Regiment, or, at least, resolved to oppose Mr. *Erskine:* (For, indeed, the Truth on't is, they did not, at that Time, know who was to be their Member, till they had their Instructions from *L——d I——a*) And how it far'd with Mr. *Erskine*, is pretty well known, nor is it my Business to mention; only, that the Treatment he met with in his Election, gave *James Littlejohn* and his Adherents, (who call themselves the *Court-Party*, and call Provost *Wingate* and his Adherents, who voted for Mr. *Erskine*, the *COUNTRY-PARTY*, by which Names I shall distinguish the two Parties for the future) I say, gave the *Court-Party* Encouragement to play a Part unprecedented, except in Mr. *Erskine* of *Grange's* Case: For, as there was a great Majority in the Council, and yet a much more general Dissatisfaction, thro' the Town, against them, and, as the Election of our Magistrates drew near, the *Court-Party* left no Stone unturned, to have *Littlejohn* and his Accomplices continued in the Council, by Means of Offers, &c. and then by Menaces, &c. which, however, had not the expected Effect; for, like true honest Men, they dispised all Offers or Threatnings, when in Balance with their Country's Welfare: So that they only carried off one Merchant-Counsellor, (who, by the By, was the first among the 14, who proposed to turn out the 7) and one disobliged Trades-Counsellor, which made the *Court-Party* 9, in Opposition to 12 who stood for their *COUNTRY* in the Council.

On the 26th of *September*, being the Election-Day of our Magistrates and Town-Council, Provost *Wingate* with his Adherents, on Account of the Measures the 9 had taken to have themselves made Magistrates, and to have thrown out the 12 from being anywise concerned in the Council, unanimously resolved to turn the 9 out, and bring in others more capable of Offices in the Council, and better liked in the Place; which the 9 justly fearing, the Day before the Election, they sent to *Edinburgh* for an Adviser, (the common *Court-Hack* on these occasions) who advised them to make a separate Election (tho' in the same Room) in this manner. While the Council was incloseed, in order to their Election, he sent his Instructions to the 9, to oppose the 12 in every Vote, both in purging and filling the Council, and to vote for others to be Counsellors and Magistrates than what the 12 did; which the 9 accordingly did, and insisted, that those they had voted for, were the duly elected Counsellors and Magistrates, though our present Magistrates and Council were elected by 12: So that here was a Majority of four, (the Dean of Gild, who is Preses, being one of the 9, and having no Vote, unless in case of Equality) To manage this, and make 9 more than 12, as 2 more than 8, in the Towns, their Adviser drew up Protests against 4 of the 12, whether on Information, or if he made them himself, is not known, but, in either of these Cases, they would have been equally true. These protests were indeed taken before the Election begun, but how ridiculous they are, will appear by the Minutes, and, in due Time, will likewise be shewn to be equally false. The cutting off these 4, gave the 9 a seeming Majority of one: So that we have a Magistracy duly and legally elected, and likewise a *Mock-Magistracy* encouraged to oppose them.

As we were thus stated at our Election, so the *Mock-Magistrates* have, ever since, endeavoured to keep up a Magisterial Appearance: For, on the 30th of *October*, being his Majesty's Birth-Day, as it is usual for the Magistrates to go to the Bonefire, and to invite such Gentlemen and others of the Place, as they think proper, to solemnize the Day, the Day before being the Quarter-Sessions, and a great many of the Justices and other Gentlemen, from the Country, being in Town, the Magistrates invited all of them to assist at the Solemnity: Some of them came, and some not. Why I mention this, is, because it is said, the Magistrates had, or invited, none but *Jacobites* to be with them; when it is most certain, that all the Gentlemen then in Town, (both of the *Court* and *COUNTRY* Side) were invited, yea, by the Magistrates themselves: And there were few, if any of them, that waited on the Magistrates, but were acting Justices of the Peace: But, the Truth on't is, That all who oppose the M——r are term'd *Jacobites*. I beg Pardon for this Digression. I say, among the rest were invited all the *Mock-Magistrates*, to accompany the present Magistrates, at the usual Hour, at the Bonefire: But, about Half an Hour before the Solemnity begun, they, with some Justices who join'd them, and with all the *Court Posse*, between 30 and 40 in Number, consisting of *Custom-House* and *Excise Officers*, *Messengers*, &c. marched up the Street, (as it were in Defiance of the Magistrates) to another Bonefire, where they drank and did what they had a Mind, undisturbed by any of the other Party; and no Exceptions were taken at their Healths: But, because the Magistrates, (assisted by some Noblemen and Gentlemen) when they went to the Bonefire, among many other loyal Healths, drank, *Liberty, Property, and No Excise*, they are represented as Sowers of Sedition and Discontent among his Majesty's Subjects: And because they had Cockades with *Liberty, Property, and No Excise*, which our Courtiers represent the Magistrates wore *all that Day*, but it is an arrant Falshood, for none of them put on their Cockades till just before they came to the Bonefire, betwixt 4 and 5 a Clock, where they drank all the Royal Family's Healths, eccho'd back by a Volley of small Arms, by a Company of Townsmen, at each Health; and from thence, went to the Town-House, where all the Royal Healths were again repeated, and there they entertain'd those Noblemen and Gentlemen who did them the Honour of solemnizing the Day with them, till betwixt 8 and 9 a Clock, when they all went to their several Homes.

Betwixt 9 and 10 a Clock, two of the *Court-Party* were overheard to say, *Let us go down and pick a Quarrel with the Guard at the Bonefire;* which the Magistrates being apprised of, (whether it was told them that Night, or not, does not signify much, but, that it was said, and by whom, will be proven, in due Time, by Witnesses) ordered the Captain of the Guard to put so many of his Men around the Bonefire, as were judged proper, either to prevent any Mischief being done by, or at the Fire, or to keep Peace in the Streets. I must here give an Account who the Guard were, because the *Court-Party* give it out, that the Magistrates pickt 'em out, as Men disaffected to his Majesty, and as the most desperate wicked Ruffians in the Town; and as if the Magistrates designed what afterwards happen'd. The Truth of the Story is this. There being no Soldiers in the Town, the Magistrates ordered a certain Number of the Townsmen to parade, in order to come and fire at the Bonefire: However, there were found among the whole that paraded, 15 or 16, who either could not fire, or had not Guns that would fire; for which Reason they were ordered to mount Guard, and 5 or 6 more added to them at Night: And this, to my certain Knowledge, is Truth.

Betwixt Twelve at Night, and One in the Morning, the whole *Court-Party* and their *Servants*, (between 30 and 40) came down the Street, and, about 30 Yards from the Fire, opposite to Clerk *Nicol's* (a Tavern) they stopt, when some were for going to the Tavern, and actually did go; but others, less disposed for Peace, said, *They would go to the Bonefire, and let them see who would hinder them to do what they had a Mind at it*: And accordingly came there, where were only eight Men, and one that commanded them, placed around it, when one (noted to be always ready to begin and stir up Mischief) broke through those that guarded the Fire, and was followed by several others, who were all turn'd out, but insisted, *They were come to drink the King's Health, and, by G——D, would not be hindered*; and were answered by the Guard, providing they would keep without the Circle, they should be very welcome, and they themselves would join them in so doing; but, as they were placed to take Care that no Mischief should happen, by the Fire's being thrown about the Streets, or otherwise, they would keep betwixt them and it. Whereupon they forced their Way to the Fire, notwithstanding that they were desired by the Guard, frequently, to keep off; and, no Doubt, the Guard made what Resistance they could, tho', at this Time, much inferior in Number. But as yet little Mischief was done, till the Alarm went to the Tavern where the rest of the Party were, who came running down to the Fire, with drawn Swords in their Hands, and had certainly massacred the Guard, but, by this Time, a good many of the Townsmen came to their Assistance, so that, after some Blows on both Sides, the *Court-Party* were obliged to retire, both having got and given Wounds.

Now, whether the *COUNTRY-PARTY*, (as they are call'd) are our real and duly elected Magistrates, or the *Court Mock-Magistrates* those who should be such, and, whether the Guard, or those who attack'd them, are most to blame, is referr'd to the Determination of those who, I am perswaded, will do the Country Justice; the one being the Subject of a Process before the Lords of Session, and the other of one before the Lords of Justiciary. You'll remember, Sir, I said, our *Mock-Magistrates* are encouraged by *the Court*. My Reason for it is this. Some Days after the Election, one of the *Mock-Bailies* being asked, Why they did oppose the present Magistrates, seeing they were elected by a Majority? replied, *'Twas not they, but the Court, that oppos'd them*: which can be proved by Witnesses. Where would be our Freedom or Liberty of Elections, if those of all Kinds, how legally or unanimously soever gone about, should be threatned to be subverted, if they should not, at all Times, and all Occasions, give up their Country a Sacrifice perhaps to some *rapacious* or *arbitrary Minister*, or to some *greedy* or *ambitious Agent?* I likewise said, the Mischief which happen'd on his Majestys' Birth-day, was, for some Time before, designed; and my Reason for that is, (besides what was overheard about coming down to pick a Quarrel with the Guard) one of the *Mock-Council*, that very Night, said, *That he had, for some Time, long'd for the Consequences of that Night;* which can likewise be proven by Witnesses. I shall conclude, with assuring you, that all above narrated is assuredly Fact. And I shall only venture to say, on the whole, That the Election of the present Magistrates will be supported by a vast Majority, in Opposition to the *Court-Party*. And, for the Riot, there is one Thing certain, that, as the Guard did not molest them, they were so far to blame to attack the Guard when on Duty. From

A BURGESS OF STIRLING.

Having given the letter of "A Burgess of Stirling," which tells the story of the riot in 1734 from the town's folks' point of view, we now present the other side of the story as set forth in a Justiciary Court indictment against the Provost and Magistrates of the burgh, at the instance of the "The Court Party." Notwithstanding the involved style of the legal document, the alleged circumstances of the riot can easily enough be understood upon a careful perusal. We are indebted for the copy of the indictment which we reproduce to Mr George Gray, Clerk of the Peace for Lanarkshire, a well-known collector of books, &c., relating to the Stirling district.

GEORGE, by the Grace of GOD, King of Great Britain, France, and Ireland, Defender of the Faith; To our Lovits. [Blank.] Macers, Messengers at Arms, our Sheriffs in that Part, conjunctly and severally, specially constitute, Greeting. FORASMUCHAS it is humbly meaned and complained to Us by Our Lovits Sir James Campbel of Ardkinglass Baronet, and Member of Parliament for the Shire of Stirling, John Napier of Culcreuch, James Graham of Kilmannan, Thomas Forrester of Denovan, Justices of the Peace in the said Shire, Captain Charles Campbel of the Honourable Colonel Harrison's Regiment of Foot, Lieutenant David Cunninghame of Stirling-Castle, John Campbel Comptroller of the Customs at Alloa, James Littlejohn late Provost of Stirling, John Don younger Merchant-Burgess there, George Monro Gunner in Stirling-Castle, William Cumming Servant to the said Captain Charles Campbel, with Concourse of our right trusty Duncan Forbe , Esq ; our Advocate, for our Interest, UPON Robert Wingate present Provost of Stirling, John Gib Merchant, George Henderson Merchant, John Gillespie Chirurgeon, and Henry Allan Writer, all Bailies there, James Alexander Merchant Dean of Guild of the said Burgh, William Paterson Writer Procurator-Fiscal to the Bailie-Court of Stirling, James Dundas of Castlecary, James Graham of Buchlivie younger, James Walker younger Merchant in Stirling, and Captain of the Town-Guard of Stirling on the Thirtieth of October, One thousand Seven hundred and Thirty four, Charles Bauchop Mason there, Lieutenant of the said Guard said Day, William Bowie Flesher there, William Sorley Smith there, Alexander Smith Smith there, Alexander Graham Hatter there, John Morison Chapman-Traveller and Residenter in Stirling, Archibald Paterson younger Cordiner there, William Lyon elder Cordiner there, who were all of the Guard said Day under Command of the said Officers, James Baird Merchant in Stirling, George Nairn Merchant there, Thomas Jack Sclater there, David Duncan Sclater there, James Stark Writer there, John Anderson Baxter there, Thomas Dollar Mason there, Hugh Paterson younger Taylor there, William Chrystie Chapman-Traveller and Residenter in Sterling, John Miller Mason there, and William Anderson Horse-hirer in Stirling; which Eleven last mentioned Persons, tho not on the Guard said Day, yet came out with Swords, Guns, and other Weapons, on the Beating of the Drum, in Manner after mention'd; That by the Common Law, the Laws of all well govern'd Realms, and the Municipal Law and Practice of this Kingdom, Riot and Violence, the inciting, raising, or fomenting of Mobs, Tumults, and Commotions of the People, especially upon forethought Felony, and within Burgh, or by Magistrates to whom Power for the Preservation of the Peace is committed, the Negligence of Officers, such as Provosts, Bailies, or other Office-bearers in Burgh, culpable in not preventing or staying Mobs and Tumults; the threatning, invading, or attacking of our Subjects passing along the Streets of any Royal Burgh, in peaceable Manner to their Lodgings, or about their other lawful Occasions; the beating, bruising, mutilating, or wounding such Persons, to the Effusion of their Blood, and imminent Danger of their Lives; and the imprisoning them, or any of them, without just Cause, or lawful Warrand; or in a hostile and outragious Manner pursuing them to their Houses, or Lodgings; or the surrounding, or planting the Passages to and from the same with a furious arm'd Mob, to the great Terror and Danger of those within; and the threatning and attempting to kill them with Guns, the throwing of Stones, or other mortal weapons, and menacing to burn the House, and endeavouring to break open the Doors, and breaking and destroying the Windows; and attacking, without any just Cause or Provocation, our Troops, beating, bruising, and wounding them, are most attrocious Crimes, and severely punishable; especially, when done and committed on a Day of Publick Joy, in seditious and disloyal Manner, and by arm'd Persons brought together, under Colour, and false Pretence of preserving the Peace; and when the Persons so attacked, beat, bruised, and wounded, or otherways maletreated, are Persons of Distinction, and Justices of our Peace: NEVERTHELESS, it is of Verity, That the Persons above complain'd upon, all, and each, or one and other of them, have presum'd to commit, and are guilty and accessory, or Art and Part of all, or one or other of the foresaid Crimes, aggravated as aforesaid, IN SO FAR AS the Justices of the Peace for our County of Stirling, being conveen'd upon the Twenty ninth of October last, at a Quarter-Session within the said Burgh, and having divided upon a Proposition then made, touching Matters of Government, the Magistrates, or other Office-bearers within the Burgh, above complain'd upon, did that Night invite such of the Justices only as had appeared in Support of the said Proposition, viz, Charles Lord Elphingstoun, Francis Lord Napier, Sir George Dunbar of Mochrum, John Graham of Killearn, John Glass of Sauchie, Alexander Monro of Auchinbowie, James Graham of Airth, John Erskine of Balgownie, James Graham of Bucklyvie, James Graham of Bucklyvie yonnger, John M'Lauchlane of Auchintroig, John M'Leod of Muirevenside, Alexander Mitchel of Mitchel, John Master of Elphingstoun, and Alexander Crawford of Manwellmiln, and several others Gentlemen, not of the Commission of the Peace, and even some who were in the Rebellion in Anno 1715, and 1716, and who were forfeited for the same Crime, to celebrate with them Our Birthday, being the Day immediately following, viz, the thirtieth of October last; and no Notice having been timeously taken by the said Magistrates of the other Justices, who had opposed the Motion aforesaid, viz. Sir James Campbel of Ardkinglass Baronet, Sir James Stirling of Glorat, Sir James Livingston of Glentirran, John Napier of Culcreuch, William Stirling of Herbertshire, William Cunninnghame of Ballindalloch, Mr. Patrick Halden of Bearcrofts Advocate, Thomas Forrester of Denovan, James Graham of Kilmannan, Walter Graham of Kilmardinnie, Robert Cunninghame of Banton, John Lennox of Woodhead, William Buchannan of Drummakill younger, Gabriel Napier of Craigannet Sheriff of the Shire, and James Bruce of Powfowls, they, or such of them as remained in Town, being invited, first by Colonel Cockurn's Lady to come to the Castle, and next by the said Complainer Captain Charles Campbell, resolved and agreed to express their Joy at a Bonfire in the Garden belonging to John Duke of Argyle within the said Town: And upon the said thirtieth Day of October, a Bonfire being accordingly erected there, upon Information given at least when it was publickly known that the Complainers had so agreed, the ordinary Guard of Burgesses warned in the Morning out of that Quarter of the Town, on which it happened of Course to fall, was by the said Magistrates above complained upon, or one or other of them, discharged; and against all former Rules, Persons industriously called out from all the different Quarters of the Town were ordered to be in Arms and serve as a Guard; some whereof were of desperate Fortunes, and in other Respects proper for executing the wicked Riot that afterwards happened. In the mean Time false and groundless Reports were whispered round, and the Persons above complained upon, particularly the said Magistrates, thought fit to adorn themselves with Cockades, having Inscriptions upon them, that appeared calculated to fill and fire the Minds of the Mob with disrespectful Sentiments of our Government, and to distribute the same to the Officers of the said pick't Guard: and others their Accomplices, who having Guns, Swords, Pole-Axes, and other mortal and offensive Weapons put into their Hands, after the usual Solemnity was over, were planted, contrary to all Custom, and without Precedent, in the Market-Place, near to the House of David Nicol common Clerk of the Burgh, with whom some of the Complainers had taken up their Lodgings, and in the Way through which others of the Complainers were to pass to their Houses and Places of Abode, from the foresaid Bonfire within the said Garden, where, and in the House of the said Duke of Argyle, they continued expressing, in a decent Manner, their Loyalty to us, by the usual Demonstrations of Joy, till the Hours of Ten or Eleven at Night, when separating, and repairing to their respective Lodgings, as some of them happened to pass by a Bonfire in the said Market-Place, the said John Don stepping towards the Fire, addressed himself to one or other of the Persons above complained upon, and innocently enquiring in a civil Manner, If he and his Friends might have leave to drink a Glass of their own Wine there in Honour of the Day? The Persons complained on, particularly the said Charles Bauchope, George Nairn, James Baird : William Bowie, William Lyon, John Anderson, Thomas Jack, William Chrystie Chapman, Archibald Paterson Younger, John Morison Chapman, David Duncan, and their said Accomplices, or one or other of them, or one or other of the Persons above complained upon, all in Arms, did then beat upon the Head, and push upon the Breast, with Muskets and other offensive Weapons, the said John Don to the Effusion of his Blood, whereupon the said Thomas Forrester Complainer, one of our Justices of our Peace, having in a soft and easie Manner, moved towards the Persons above complained upon, or some, or one or other of them; and as by the Duty of his Office he was bound, after asking what the Matter was, exhorted them to keep the Peace, they, the said James Walker, Charles Bauchop, George Nairn, James Baird, William Bowie and William Lyon, or one or other of them, and their said Accomplices in Arms, without any just Cause or Provocation, invaded him, having neither Sword. Staff, nor any Weapon about him, and aimed a full Stroke at his Head with a broad Sword, which, in his own Defence he received upon his Left-Hand, whereby he was wounded on the Ball of his Thumb, and immediately thereafter was by them, or some of them, or their Accomplices, furiously attacked with Swords, Pole-Axes, and Muskets, and beat and bruised on his Head and Shoulders, and wounded in two several Places of his Left-Arm, to the great Effusion of his Blood; and not contented with treating him in this causeless and barbarous Manner, upbraided him with opprobrious Names, such as Villain and Rascal, or Words to that Purpose, and seized and dragged him to the Guard as an Offender and Criminal, and detained him there a Prisoner.

About this Time, and while the Riot herein after described was carrying on, John Gillespie and George Henderson, Two of the present Magistrates above complained upon, instead of interposing to put a Stop to the foresaid illegal Sedition and Violence, they, or one or other of them, or one or other of the Persons above complained upon, ordered an Alarm, and to Arms, to be beat through the Town, whereby the Streets were crowded with a Multitude, armed with Guns, Swords, Pole-Axes, and other mortal and offensive Weapons, beating, bruising, and committing Outrages wherever they came, the Tumult being thereby increased and fomented; nor was any Attempt made to quiet or stay the same by them or the other Magistrates above complained upon who were near at Hand, and in Duty bound, at any Hazard, to put a Stop to it: But on the contrary, Musquet-Ball and Lead-Shot were in Presence of the said Bailie Henderson, or some one or other of the said Magistrates, distributed to the Guard, and other Persons standing armed with Firelocks by the said James Graham younger of Buchlyvie, or some one or other of the said Persons complained upon, and Orders were therewith given to the said Guard, and other Persons, to load their Guns with the said Ball and Leadshot; when the said Sir James Campbel of Ardkinglass, John Napier of Culcreuch, James Graham of Kilmannan, Justices of Our Peace, Captain Charles Campbel, and Mr. John Campbel, Comptroller of the Customs at Alloa, upon hearing the sudden Noise and Tumult, altogether unexpected by them, coming from the House of the said David Nicol, and their other respective Lodgings, to the Market-place, only to enquire what the Matter was, were immediately insulted, attacked and invaded by the said James Dundas, James Walker, Charles Bauchop, William Bowie, William Sorly, Alexander Smith, Alexander Graham, John Morison, Archibald Paterson, William Lyon, James Baird, George Nairn, Thomas Jack, David Duncan, James Stark, John Anderson, Thomas Dollar, Hugh Paterson and William Christie, or one or other of them, and their Accomplices, with Poll-axes, broad Swords, Muskets, and other mortal and offensive Weapons, and beat, bruised and wounded, to the great Effusion of their Blood; particularly the said Captain Charles Campbel was then, and there knock d down to the Ground, bruised upon the Head, Shoulders, Arms and Hands, and received severe Wounds; and when he called out, that he had no Arms, and was in no Condition to defend himself, and desired them to spare his Life; their barbarous Return was, No Mercy: And they continued to beat and wound him; so that in all human Probability, he had been murdered outright, if some Persons present had not interposed themselves, who were grieviously wounded, particularly, the said John Campbel received a Wound upon his Head, above his right Eye, and another below it, and a deep Wound on his right Arm near the Shoulder, from the said James Stark, or one or other of the Persons above-complained upon, or their Accomplices, where through, he will for ever remain maimed, and disabled of his said Arm. And the said Sir James Campbel, and James Grahame of Kilmannan, as well as the other Complainers, did likewise then and there receive several Bruises and Contusions, and Wounds, over their Heads and Arms, with broad Swords, and other offensive Weapons, from the said Persons above complained upon, with their Accomplices; AS ALSO the said George Monro, Gunner, received five dangerous Wounds on his Head and Body, and the said William Cumming received a Wound on his Face, and several dangerous Contusions on his Breast and Body: and Lieutenant David Cunninghame was beat upon his Head, and bruised by Strokes of a Cane or Staff, given behind his Back by the said James Dundas, or one or other of the Persons above complained upon, and narrowly escaped with their Lives from their cruel Hands; and such was their Rage, and so relentless their Malice, that after the said Captain Charles Campbel and John Campbel had got out of the Crowd, and were retiring, they, the Persons above complained upon, or one or other of them hotly pursued them, striking upon their Heads, and other Parts of their Body, with Swords and Cutlaces, even behind their Backs, whereby the said Complainers were so butchered, and barbarously used, that for sometime they remained in a hopeless, at least in a very dangerous Condition. And their Malice, Violence and Sedition not resting there, leading on the riotious and furious Multitude their Accomplices, they, particularly the said Bailie John Gillespie, one of the said Magistrates, or some one or other of the Persons complained upon, went next to the House of the said David Nicol, where some of the Complainers so beat, bruised and wounded, had retired, and shut the Doors for their Safety, and beset the same, and planted arm'd Persons upon the Passages to and from the said House, and back Windows thereof. And when the Complainers, who were within the said House, upon hearing that Captain Charles Campbel, and the said John

Campbel were lying in the Streets, blooding in their Wounds, intreated that the Captain of the Guard, or a Party thereof would conduct in safety Provost James Littlejohn, who is a Surgeon by his Employment, to go and dress their Wounds; the said Persons complained upon, or one or other of them, in a most barbarous Manner refused the said Desire, and continued their Riot, demanding the Justices of the Peace, and other Complainers, or one or other of them, more particularly the said Lieuten- and David Cunninghame Complainer, should be delivered up to them, that they might tear out their Soul, or Words to that Purpose. And when the said James Littlejohn, from the Window of the said House, beg'd and pray'd the Persons above complained upon, and their Accomplices to abstain from further Violence, they, or some, or one or other of them threw a large Stone, aim'd at his Head; and the said James Walker Captain of the Guard, or some one or other of the Persons complained upon, presented a Gun, threatning to shoot him dead, which, in all Appearance, had been put in Execution, if the said Gun had not been beat off, and the said Provost Littlejohn retired from the Window. LIKEAS, the said Persons above complained upon, did break the Windows of the said House with Stones and other Instruments, and attempted to beat open the Doors; no doubt, with an Intention to put in Execution their wicked Malice and terrible Threats, which they continued to utter; and Information having been carried to our Garrison in the Castle, that the said arm'd Mob was demanding the said Lieutenant Cunninghame, one of their Officers, to be delivered up, and threatening to kill and destroy him; a Party of twelve Men and a Corporal, under the Command of a Sergeant, being ordered to attend him from the House of the said David Nicol to the Garrison, when they approach'd to the said House, without offering the least Provocation to any Person whatsoever by Word or Deed, the said Persons above complained upon, or one or other of them, with their Accomplices, did attack, beat, bruise, and wound them, and particularly Elisha Johnston, Sergeant, who commanded the Party, John Ross, Soldier, and others, to the great Effusion of their Blood, and Danger of their Lives. And during the said Riot and Violence, outragious Threatnings were breathed out, of burning and destroying the said House, to the great Terror of those within: And during these riotous, seditious, tumultuous and disloyal Proceedings, which continued for several Hours, none of the Persons above complained upon, Magistrates of the Burgh, so much as faintly attempted to suppress or quell the same. LIKEAS, the said William Paterson, during the Heat of this Tumult and Riot, wherein he had a chief and active Hand, did send George Stalker, Taylor in Sterling, or some other Person, to the House of Thomas Blackader, Conveener of the Trades, desiring him forthwith to give Orders to conveen all the Seven Trades in Arms: And, while the said Thomas Forrester remained, as aforesaid a Prisoner in the Guard, and blooding in his Wounds, he, the said William Paterson caused serve him with a Summons at his Instance, as Procurator-fiscal of the Town-court of Stirling, early on the Morning of the Thirty first Day of October last, to appear before the Magistrates by Ten of the Clock, or some other Hour of that Day; and, on the First Day of November immediately following, did likewise, at his Instance, cause summon the said Captain Charles Campbel, Lieutenant David Cunninghame, James and William Burgesses, John Christie, John Don, younger.—[Here our copy of the indictment ends, but enough has been given to indicate the charges it contains.]

(To be continued.)

DUNBLANE CATHEDRAL IN HISTORY.

By Rev. Mr. Ritchie.

Saint Blane, said to have been buried here at the end of the sixth century, and who has given our Cathedral its name, and the Culdees, who for centuries lived and taught at Dunblane, and of whom a trace remains as late as the year 1237, I only name. Nor must we linger over the century which elapsed between the time when, in 1140, King David I. founded or established, the Bishopric, and the year 1233, when there comes upon the scene one Clement, consecrated Bishop of Dunblane by William of St Andrews in the Church of Stow in Midlothian. At the character and work of Clement we call our first halt. It is to the determination and unwearied efforts of Bishop Clement we owe the restoration, or rebuilding of our Cathedral, which converted its nave into what it continues to be to-day, one of the gems of Gothic architecture in its prime. It is he who recovered for his Bishopric the lands which greed and rapine had seized and turned to secular uses. It is he who procured and put in operation a new and better Constitution than that under which the affairs of the See had hitherto been conducted. It is he who thus made it possible for Dunblane Cathedral to figure in Scottish history. All honour to the man who, as we learn from a letter of Pope Gregory IX., accepted, as Bishop of Dunblane, an office which "no one for ten years last past, would undertake, seeing the revenues available would not maintain a bishop for two years," and connected himself with a church which stood "bare and roofless," and who by a determination, energy, tact, and patience, which Gregory IX. was quick to note, left Dunblane Cathedral a glorious sanctuary, and raised the See to state of prosperity, and gave it an importance it had never known.

If there is one thing which Scotchmen love more than another, and for which they have contended to the utmost, it is independence. Two Bishops of Dunblane in their day were distinguished supporters of civil and religious liberty. In the year 1268, one Ottobuoni, legate of the Pope for England, summoned all the Scottish Bishops to compear before him. The bishops, says an old chronicler, "in general council, deputed Richard, Bishop of Dunkeld, and Robert, Bishop of Dunblane, on their behalf, so that nothing which could damage or aggrieve them might be enacted in their absence. So the legate enacted some new statutes, which the Bishops of Scotland utterly refused to abide by." Robert de Praededda of Dunblane was evidently one on whom his brethren relied as willing and able to maintain the independence of the Scottish Church against unjust demands and unwarranted encroachments on the part of the Pope and his haughty legate. Peaceful and beautiful though the situation of our Cathedral be, it stands too near the Carse of Stirling, that natural battle ground of Scotland, not to have had its quiet frequently broken by the din of war, even though it be not the case, as is affirmed, that the edifice suffered grievous damage at the hands of Edward I., who stripped the roof of its lead to make bullets for his engines employed in the siege of Stirling Castle. Once at least there reigned in the Episcopal Palace, of which but a few vaults and a remnant of a wall now remain, one who owed his Bishopric to his patriotism and personal bravery as much as to his piety and learning. Maurice, Abbot of Inchaffray, said mass in the presence of the Scottish army on the morning of the eventful battle of Bannockburn, and inspired the soldiers by the words of cheer he spoke. So pleased was King Robert the Bruce with the patriotic and martial abbot, that he appointed him his private chaplain, and some years after, when the See of Dunblane fell vacant, had him installed in the Bishop's chair. If it be the case, as surely it is, that religion is not the foe but the friend of true and wise patriotism, we have reason to be proud of the connection which Bishop Maurice establishes between Dunblane Cathedral and so important an event in our national history as the battle of Bannockburn. The next Bishop I shall mention is Finlaw Dermoch, whom I select not because he figured in any great national event or crisis, but because he built in 1409 the bridge over the Allan which, widened in 1849, we still use every day. The recumbent stone figure beside the present pulpit in the choir is said to represent this practical prelate.

If Scotland has always loved freedom, she has, all through her history, loved learning too. We must not forget when we associate zeal for learning with Knox, that we owe St Andrews University to the old, unreformed Church of Scotland. When St Andrews University was founded in 1412, one William Stephen was appointed first lecturer in Divinity; and some years after his learning was acknowledged and rewarded by presentation to the bishopric of Dunblane. Nor was William Stephen merely a learned man. He was a man of capacity and judgment, so much so that he was selected as one of three ambassadors sent to England to treat of the ransom of King James I., held so long prisoner there. When James I. was assassinated at Perth, another Bishop of Dunblane, Michael Ochiltree, a man of high standing and dignity, though labouring under some physical defect, crowned his infant successor, James II., at Holyrood, in 1437; and on more than one occasion the name of this Bishop occurs in connection with matters of State. His effigy in stone lies in the south-east corner of the nave of the Cathedral. In the centre of the parapet of the tower, and of the choir, as well as on the oak stalls in the church, you will see cut a boar's head surmounted by a mitre. This device is the crest of a powerful, family of Chisholm of Cromlix, which gave to our Cathedral its three last Roman Catholic Bishops, each of whom was noted in his way. James Chisholm was a man of weight and authority, but seems to have chiefly confined his energies to ruling well, and conserving and extending the property of his diocese, as well as adorning his Cathedral within and without. It was in his reign that the unfortunate Margaret Drummond and her two sisters died mysteriously at Drummond Castle, and were interred in Dunblane Cathedral. We all know the slabs of blue stone on the floor of the choir that mark their supposed resting-place, but the masses appointed by James IV. to be perpetually sung for the rest of her soul have long ceased to be chanted. The second bishop of the name of Chisholm, half brother of the first, was a resolute adversary of the Reformation which was accomplished in his day, and he was one of the few prelates who ventured to protest, in the Parliament of 1560, against the adoption of the reformed faith, and the overthrow of the Romish Church. The third bishop, Wm. Chisholm, nephew to the two former, was appointed by the Pope coadjutor to his uncle in the year 1561, at the request of Queen Mary, whom he served as ambassador to France and Rome on several occasions, in connection with her marriage to Darnley and afterwards to Bothwell. On the accusation of harbouring papists he was forced to fly the country, found his way to Rome, where he was well received, and was ultimately in the year 1670 appointed by the Pope Bishop of Vaison in the south of France, which Bishopric he was to hold till such time as a change in ecclesiastical affairs in Scotland should permit him to return to his diocese of Dunblane—a turn which never came. Of Protestant Bishops I shall mention but two. James Wedderburn was greatly esteemed by Archbishop Laud, and gave material help in framing the new liturgy, which the stool of Jenny Geddes silenced once for all. He was ejected from Dunblane in 1628, and went to England, where he died in the following year. The curious pilgrim to Canterbury Cathedral will find a stone erected to his memory, on which his learning and goodness are eloquently described. I may fitly close this hurried glimpse at Dunblane Cathedral in history by reminding you of Bishop Leighton, whose association with Dunblane from 1661 to 1670, under the second Protestant Episcopate, would by itself give our Cathedral an honourable place in the annals of our country. Of Leighton I cannot now say more than that he is an illustrious example of humility, learning, goodness, and the spirit of wise tolerance, and desire to obliterate little distinctions and unite Christians in catholic unity.

MISS ELIZA HAMILTON.

The destruction by fire of the cottages at the Crook a week or two ago has revived the association of Miss Hamilton with the locality, and we are indebted to an esteemed townsman for the following correspondence on this subject :—

Miss Eliza Hamilton, authoress of "The Cottagers of Glenburnie," lived for some years at "Ingram's Crook," and was a great friend of the Polmaise family and of Mrs Alexander Murray, widow of Alexander Murray, 22nd Regiment [the parents of the late John Murray, Esq. of Livilands.] An extract from Miss Hamilton's letters to Mrs Murray may be interesting, written from London, preparing for her return to the Crook :—

"68 Charlotte Street,

Rathbone Place, London, March 11th, 1791.

Thank you, my dear madam, for your kind wishes for my return. There is one favour in which I must particularly request your assistance; it is as to a servant. When Mrs John Murray [mother of the late Polmaise] took Peggy, she told me it was with that provision that she should come back to me when I again took up house at the Crook; but in the present situation of my friend, I cannot think of applying to her by letter upon the subject, but must beg you to have the goodness to settle the matter for me. If Mrs Murray would at this time find it inconvenient or disagreeable to make a change, she may be assured I would rather put up with any inconvenience myself than subject her to it at present, and in that case, my dear Mrs Murray, who can I apply to but yourself for engaging another for me? I am conscious of the trouble that this must give you, and do not know what apology to make for offering it, but when you consider the necessity of my case, I hope you will excuse it. You know what qualifications will be necessary for an *only* maid servant, so will only mention that, as my brother, I hope, will be with me in summer, something more of cookery will be requisite than a *maiden* family. As to the terms, I leave you *carte blanche*. If Mrs Murray has no objection to parting with Peggy, you will be so good as let her know that, as far as I can judge at present, I think I shall be at the Crook about Whitsunday, sooner or later, as fellow-travellers may determine. If later, I shall give her directions of all that I would have her to do to prepare for our reception. I likewise purpose to keep a boy, and if any of your acquaintances hear of a smart lad of from 12 to 15 years of age, that would be willing to *do bidding* (as poor old Donald used to say), and would look a little smartish, I would be happy to have him. That I shall hear of my dear friend at Johnstone's [where Col. and Mrs John Murray lived] happy recovery, yet until I know that she has regained her usual health, I could not run the risk of giving her any disturbance about these matters, but if she is now as well as I could wish, I must just leave it to you to communicate to her what I have said."

"London, May 9th, 1791.

You forbid me to make any apology for the trouble you have been so good as to take in the settlement of my household, and I will not disobey you so far as even *to say* that *I am very much obliged to you*, but I assure you at the same time that that will not prevent me from *thinking it*. The maiden will, I hope, turn out as we could wish, and if she is a good girl, I think the wages will be moderate enough, with the little additions you mention. But I am afraid the young man's ideas are too extravagant for the economical plan to which I must limit myself, as, if he is to be furnished in all necessaries, I must think £4 a year a great deal too much for pocket money; but as boys are so scarce a commodity in Stirlingshire (for I well remember the difficulty we used always to have in getting one), I should like to take one so well recommended, at least for the first half-year, if he will agree to such terms as I can possibly afford to give. The utmost that will be is *the wages he mentions* (£2 in the half-year), without any other clothes than a suit to wear occasionally in dress, and which, if not worn out at the time of his quitting my service, leaves to his successor: but for keeping him in shoes, stockings, linens, &c., is more than I think I ought to do. If you can make a bargain with him on such terms, I will be much obliged to you for doing so; but if he insists upon *his own*, I must take my chance of finding some one that will be more moderate. At the time I last wrote I had some thoughts of embracing an opportunity of going down to Scotland by sea, but my brother was so averse to the proposal that I have given it up. He insists that I shall not go until we break up house altogether, which will probably delay my arrival in Stirlingshire two or three weeks beyond the time I at first intended, as I daresay it will be *at least* the end of this month before my brother can quit London. He will then accompany us as far as Lancashire, and from thence take a trip to Bath, which is recommended to him as very necessary for his health, which has received some injury from the intense application he has given to his laborious work all the winter, but I hope that before harvest I shall have the pleasure of his company at the Crook. I intended writing Mr Campbell along with this, to desire him to tell the Robinsons that they must return to their own habitation at the term. I would wish the girl to get into the house as soon as she quits her place, till my arrival (which I suppose will be about a fortnight or so from that time.) She will, I dare-say, find enough of employment in putting things in order. I intend taking up my abode in my own old garret, which, by Tibbie's directions, she will put in order for me. I do not intend moving my bed in the room under it. Peggy wrote me that the lady who had the house last summer had made some alterations, which makes me mention it. As I hear that the house will require to have its face washed, will you, my dear madam, be so good as send down the painter who you formerly recommended to me, but whose name I forget, to do just what he did before, to give the drawing-room a new *coat of blue*, and to whiten the roof, as likewise the roofs of the other room of passage and kitchen. The girl will have the same board wages that Peggy had till I come; if she wants money for coals and soap, &c., she will get it from Mr Campbell. Mr brother joins me in affectionate compliments to Miss Wordie and our young friends. My friend John [the late John Murray of Livilands] will be quite the Buck of the town, and his sister grown out of all knowledge, before I see them. Adieu, my dear madam, and believe me that no *time* can lessen the regard of your gratefully affectionate friend and obedient servant,

ELIZA HAMILTON."

Note.—It is said that while living at Ingram's Crook, Miss Hamilton wrote her celebrated work, "The Cottagers of Glenburnie." The Crook was used by the late William Murray of Polmaise (who married Miss Maxwell of Monreith) as his factor's house, and the late Mr M'Micking, while acting as such, lived there for many years.

THE LANDS OF BRAENDAM.

Braendam, or as it some times spelt, Breandam, is a small property in the parish of Kincardine, situated midway between the bridge of Frew over the Forth, and the bridge of Callander over the

Teith. It was anciently designated the twenty-five shilling land of the Brae of Bowhapple. Boquhapple may have suggested the name Balmawhapple to the author of "Waverley." This singular-looking word probably means Chapelton (Bal Chapel). The existence of a chapel here is indicated in the name of a holding in the vicinity aed in the now ruinous steading Rottenraw (the Raw to the Rude, the road to the cross). The Twenty-five Shilling Land has been explained by Cosmo Qunes to mean ⅝ of the old unit of land which being holden of the Crown constituted the old county electoral qualification. The unit of land was a three-mark land, 104 acres of extent, and Braendam would measure about 65 acres on this calculation. One of the dams of the Little Mill would give the farm its more specific designation.

This property has had a long list of lairds since the beginning of last century. In 1701 it was owned by Lieut. Colin Fairfoul. We came across a James Fairfoul of Braendam as a Justice of the Peace in the proceedings against Rob Roy's sons for the abduction of Jean Key *alias* Wright from Edenbelly in 1750. In the same year James Fairfoul entered into an engagement with "the Sucken of the Little Millyn of Bowchappell," wherebyhe is to uphold the farmers for six years at a specified sum from eight ploughs of the "thirlage," and the two ploughs of Braendam. In case of non-payment the miller is authorised to "detain in his own hand the peopell's meall who does not pay, ay, and whill payment be made notwithstanding of any law to the contrair." In the event of the farmers breaking at work "the owner of the vittwall has liberty to send for ane sufficient wright upon Mr Fairfoul's charges." It may be worth mentioning that "as their is not sufficient roum to sighn upon the first page we unanimously agree that sighning this page which is upon the back of the first shall be as sufficient as we had sighned both papers as witness our hand day and date forsaid."

Braendam passes to Andrew Buchanan in 1760. The following is a copy of a lease granted by him:—

It is contracted, agreed, and finally ended betwixt the parties aftermentioned, viz., Andrew Buchanan of Breandam, heritable proprietor of the lands, and others aftermentioned on the one part, and David Ferguson, tenant in Spittletown, conjointly and severally with John Ferguson, his son, on the other part, in manner and to the effect following:—

That is to say, The said Andrew Buchanan setts, and hereby in tack and assidation for the yearly duties and others underwritten, letts to the said David and John Fergusons, and their heirs conjunctly and severally, secluding assigneys, all and haill that part of the Mains of Breandam at present possest by William Gilespie, tenant there, together with the houses, biggings, yards, grass, mosses, muirs, pertinents, and privileges thereof, all lying within the parish of Kincardine and shire of Perth, as the same is presently possest by the said William Gilespie, together also with the liberty of carrying of ffulzie from the marle bog at Breandam, viz., such places thereof as the master shall allow and direct them, the said Andrew Buchanan also hereby reserving to himself the liberty of quarrying and carrying off stones from any part of the said lands so set, and that for the hail space of nineteen years from and after the term of Martinmas first to come, which is hereby declared to be the term of their entry thereto, and from thenceforth to be peaceably possest, laboured, and occupied by the saids David and John Fergusons and their foresaids during the said space. Which Tack the said Andrew Buchanan binds and obliges him, his heirs, exers., or assigneys, to uphold good and sufficient to the said David and John Fergusons and their foresaids at all hands and against all deadly as law will. For the which causes and on the other part, the said David and John Fergusons jointly and severally bind and oblige them, their heirs, exers., intromittors, with their goods and gear and successors whatsoever, thankfully to content, satisfy, and pay to the said Andrew Buchanan, his heirs, and assigneys, yearly, and ilk year during the currency of this tack, the sum of fourteen pounds ten shillings sterling money, and that too by two payments, the one just and equal half at the term of Candlemass first after separation of the crop from the ground, and the other half at the term of Whitsunday next following thereafter, and so on, yearly and termly, during the space foresaid.

As also the said David and John Ferguson bind and oblige them and their foresaids to pay to the said Andrew Buchanan and his foresaids, yearly, during the said space, the quantity of seven bolls good and sufficient oat meal and one boll good and sufficient bear betwixt Yule and Candlemass, after the crop is separate from the ground, and to carry the said victual, if desired, on their own horses and in their own sacks to the distance of three miles from the house of Breandam, and further they bind and oblige them and their foresaids to cast win and lead to the house of Breandam yearly twenty cartloads of Peats, which Peats are to be cast in the moss belonging to the said Master, as also to carry four loads of coals yearly to the said house, and to pay two plough Dargues and two Kane hens yearly, all at the ordinary seasons for the like, and to carry their hail grindable victual yearly to the Little Mill of Buchapple, and pay the accustomed multores therefor, and keep up of the ordinary service belonging to the said mill, according to use and wont, and to free and relieve the said Andrew Buchanan and his foresaids of cess and all other publick burdens imposed or to be imposed conform to the usual valuation laid on the said lands hereby set. And likewise the said David and John Fergusons further oblige them and their foresaids to lay on the said lands, during the currency of this tack, the quantity of twenty chalders of lime stones, to be brought by men from Lenny or Ballochinduy, of which twenty chalders the said Andrew Buchanan obliges him and his foresaids to pay one half at the quarry: And it is hereby expressly agreed by both parties that whenever the said quantity of twenty chalders of lime compleat shall be laid on the said lands, the said tennents shall thenceforth pay only fourteen pounds sterling of money rent, with the victual and casualties above named, yearly, instead of the fourteen pounds ten shillings mentioned above, which said money rent shall continue accordingly to the end of this tack. And the said tennents moreover oblige themselves and foresaids at the expiry of this tack to leave the houses and dykes on the said possession in a sufficient habitable condition at men's sight, and to give up one of the barns at the term of Martimass and the other at Candlemass thereafter, when they remove from the same, and to leave the summer fulzie at their removal on the ground, as they received the same at their entry thereto. And lastly, both parties bind themselves and their foresaids to the performance of the premisses to each other under the penalty of pounds sterling, to be paid by the party failzier to the party observer, or willing to observe by and attour performance, consenting to the registration hereof in the books of council & session or others competent to have the strength of ane decreet interponed hereto that letters of horning on six days and others necessary may pass thereon as effeirs and thereto constitute.

In witness whereof these presents, consisting of this and the preceding page wrote on stampt paper by Alexr. M'Gruther, schoolmaster in Norriestown, are subscribed by the said parties att Thornhill the seventeenth day of May seventeen hundred and sixty-three years, before these witnesses, Walter Mackison, farmer in Spittletown, and John Spittle, feuar in Thornhill, witness also the marginal note on the first page.

Signed WALTER MCKISON, Witness. ANDREW BUCHANAN.
(torn) itness. D. F. I. F.

Andrew Buchanan is succeeded in 1768 by Richard Miller, whom tradition speaks of as "Dick Miller." He is said to have married a sister of the MacNab of that period. We meet his name in a document of date 1789 in connection with another farmer for the new mill of Little Mill, bought from James Dick, wright, Bridge of Allan, for £4 4s sterling. His brother John succeeded to the property at his death. A saying of John's is handed down—"Eh, sirs, it's an unco sairious thing being a laird." After disposing of the property he took up his residence at Torrie.

The next proprietor of Braendam was Ebenezer Brown, M.D., who purchased it in 1818. He was probably a son of Ebenezer Brown, weaver, Stirling, who subscribes for a copy of Erskine's works in 1755. Dr Brown had been in the army, and he brought home with him a Spaniard, one of the prisoners, as well as a bear, which for its tricks on breaking loose one night had to destroyed. The young Spaniard married and settled in Leith.

Braendam house was built by Dr Brown. He has the reputation of being a very skilful surgeon and although he never practised in the district he was always ready to help any one that called upon him. He was succeeded in 1829 by a person of the same name, whether a son or a nephew tradition does not say.

James Kinross, who had been land steward at Abercairly, bought the property in 1834. Several of his descendants hold a high position in legal circles in Stirlingshire.

In 1844 Braendam became the property of the Rev. Peter Robertson of Callander. This family sold it in 1862 to Henry Wm. Landers, Esq., who, on account of an unsuccessful plea at law regarding a right of way, disposed it to Andrew Jardine, Esq. of Lanrick. It is now an integral portion of the Lanrick estate, and has been increased by the purchase of adjacent kirklands when Norrieston was erected ino a parish several years ago.

THE SIBYLS AT LIVILANDS.

We are indebted for the following interesting paper to Miss Wright, granddaughter of the late John Murray, Esq., a former proprietor of Livilands:—

Paper on the Sibyls in the Dressing-room at Livilands, by Keith Milnes, Esq., and sent by him to Mrs Murray of Livilands, April 11th, 1833.

"Accounts vary as to the number of the Sibyls, from one to ten. They were of different nations. Those at Livilands are the Persian, the Libyan, the Delphic, and probably the Cumæan. One of the Sibyls came to Tarquin, King of Rome, and offered him nine volumes at a very high price. He refused, and she returned, after burning three, with the remaining six, and asked the same price for these. He refused again. She then burnt three more, and returned with the three left, still asking the same price. Struck with her extraordinary behaviour, he purchased the books. They were preserved under the care of priests appointed for that purpose, and were called the Sybelline verses, and consulted when the State was in danger. When the capitol was burnt in the time of Sylla, these verses, which had been deposited there, perished in the flames. Commissioners were afterwards sent to Greece to collect whatever could be recovered of the inspired verses of the Sibyls. The fate of what were thus collected is not known. There are said to be eight books of Sybelline verses extant, but considered as spurious. They speak so plainly of our Saviour, His sufferings and death, as to make it evident that they were composed by some of the followers of Christianity, who made use of this pious artifice to assist the cause of truth. The paintings, I have no doubt, were done at the date affixed, 1629, as the ornamental scrolls, in imitation of framework, round them, as well as the rude pilasters and sort of Corinthian capitals, is much like what was commonly made use of about that period. They are well worthy of careful preservation, not only as being not without some degree of good design and correct drawing, but as a specimen of the style of decorating private houses in those days. They could have no relation to any religious house formerly at Livilands, having been done after the Reformation."

Writings below the Sibyl paintings at Livilands. Copied by Keith Milnes, Esq., 1833.

A King of Jewes shall the Redeemer be,
Just, gentle, guiltlisse, for the guiltie He
Shall suffer much: the Scribes with scornefull brow
Shall him forbid his Father to avow
Within their Synagogue, yet shall He preach
The way of Life, and it the people teach.

The Mother of th' eternall Father's Sonne,
A mayde shall be: His Birth, Salvation
Shall bring the world, and life; yet farre from pride
Though King of all, He on an asse shall ride
[Into Hiersoalem], where with wrongfull wrath,
[Condemned by] wicked, He shall suffer Death.

After some years' dive Revolution past,
God, of a virgin borne, to man dis-grac't,
Shall make the Hope of Sinne's Remission shine,
And, though Almighty (and his throne divine
Have bin for ay in Heaven), yet, His to save
From Death, will He both suffer Death and Grave."

[The late Mr James Maidment contributed an article on this subject in 1866 to *Notes and Queries*, which will be found reprinted in *Stirling Notes and Queries*, vol. I., p. 326. From this article we have got the words bracketed in one of the above inscriptions. Mr Maidment's opinion was that the date 1629 had reference to a renewal, and not to the original erection of the house, and that the place where the Sibyls are painted may have been an oratory. The mention of "Chapel Croft" in the title deeds of Livilands, he looked upon as indicating that part of the estate which was originally church land, and his suggestion was that it might have been a pendicle of the Blackfriars Monastery. The Chapel Croft, however, was connected with St Ninian's Chapel, and had nothing to do with the Blackfriars. Mr Maidment also notices that at a very short distance to the north-east of the house of Livilands is a row of fine lime trees, placed at regular distances, presenting very much the appearance of an avenue, which goes by the name of the "Bishop's Walk." Livilands, we may mention, was the residence of General Monk when the Cromwellian troops besieged Stirling Castle, and among the title deeds of the property is a precept of Lord Protector Cromwell in favour of John Murray.—ED.]

KIRK SESSION DISCIPLINE IN KINCARDINE.

The kirk session was in former generations a very real terror to evildoers. The discipline exercised thereby was for the most part public. There is, or lately was, a board in the Church of Kincardine inscribed, "The Place of Repentance." The transgressor, dressed in sackcloth, sat during worship on a black stool, the observed of all observers. Here is a specimen of discipline from the Records of Kincardine:—

A. B. had already been before the session, and it would appear that his case had been transmitted to the Presbytery, and sent back to Kincardine, to take end according to the laws of the Church.

"Octr. 26, 1777. This day the session being met and constituted, A. B.'s request was laid before them anent not appearing in sackcloth. The session were of opinion that if the sackcloth should be laid aside, his appearing before the congregation would not give the satisfaction intended. The minister therefore represented to A., that he, the said A., could appear upon no other terms, as the design of it would not answer the end, and begged of him to consider the matter more sincerely. In the interval between sermons A. met with the minister and some of the elders, and condescended upon taking the sackcloth and making his appearance in the afternoon, which accordingly he did, and was rebuked and ordered to continue his appearance. Closed with prayer."

But the case does not end here, for—

"Novr. 2nd, 1777. This day A. B. appeared the second time.

Novr. 9th. This day A. B. appeared the third time.

Novr. 16th. This day A. appeared not, being not in health.

Novr. 23rd. No sermon.

Novr. 30th. This day A. B. appeared with the sackcloth on, was suitably exhorted by the minister, and absolved by authority of the Presbytery."

The following was an attempt to get the discipline over comfortably. In 1728 a woman took her place on the stool of repentance, and sat out the service. But, on the following Sabbath, the kirk session observed "her carriage befor the congregatione was not soe becoming, in regaird she appeared not soe penitent as could have been expected, but slumbered and slept away ye day." She was rebuked very sharply and required to compeir on the following Sabbath and ordered to pay "her mulct."

Sometimes, in the exercise of discipline, the kirk session met opposition. In 1789, "I. M. did not think the session had any business with that affair, seeing he had not been accused before them, and since he had never applied for church privileges."

Sept. 15th, 1811, Mr Watt, Wester Boquhapple, compeared for breach of the Sabbath, he having cut Little Mill Dam on that day. He came furnished with a certificate from Robert Stewart, Siock, and Duncan Macfarlane, Whirriston, the Birlaymen, which mentioned damages done formerly to Mrs Graham's lands by the breaking of the dam. The case was accordingly dismissed.

When a transgressor felt reluctant to sit on the black stool in "the place of repentance," he might offer a sum of money to purge the scandal. The potent guinea found its way to the box and the wrong was put right. "Jeanie, woman;" said the laird of Dumbiedykes, "Jeanie, woman; dinna greet, its sad wark, but siller will help it." Even so; the money was usually effectual, and was always laid out in the support of the poor—a source of constant trouble to the kirk sessions of last century.

OLD SCOTTISH MARKET CROSSES.

By J. W. Small, F.S.A., Scot.

The origin of the Market Cross was no doubt ecclesiastical, and the transition from its original character to its ordinary use is simple, if, as the late James Drummond, R.S.A., says:—"Let us suppose, in the rude and lawless times, a paction of any sort being made, and considered binding, if contracted at a Cross with all its sacred significance, the place where it was situate thus becoming a place of bargain-making and the Cross gradually losing its religious significance," till it became the usual market place of the town in which it was situate, and in the transition of time the Cross proper at the top of the shaft being lost altogether and its place supplied by carved shields of arms or other emblems as seen in those examples from Airth, Kincardine, Clackmannan, &c.

Market Crosses are generally placed in some open square or broad street in the towns where they are situate, to mark the spot where the markets are held. They are also used to publish edicts of a royal or burghal nature. They were also used as a place of punishment for offenders against the burghal laws, for a place of meeting for the inhabitants to celebrate any naval or military victory, and to burn any proclaimed books and papers.

In our own Burgh Records, published last year by the Glasgow Stirlingshire and Sons of the Rock Society, we find that our old Cross was used for all these purposes.

On 23rd October, 1682, it was used as the place from which to issue a proclamation for securing the peace of the kingdom. Folio 37.

On April 16, 1689, it was used to proclaim their Majesties, King William and Queen Marie, with all solemnitie. Folio 54.

In 1714, it was used for the more commercial use of regulating the time of sale of fish, butter, cheese, and fowls. Folio 137.

In May, 1691, £11 4s was spent in wine by the Magistrates and Council, and several gentlemen with them at the Cross, upon the news of their Majestie's victory at sea. 8 pynts wine.

On 7th July, 1708, £5 5s worth of glasses was thrown at the Cross at the solemnitie upon account of the Confederates victorie over the French. Folio 116.

On October 14, 1688, in commemorating the King's Birth Day, a sum of 28s was paid to them that served at the Cross. Folio 332.

Other items of money were paid for proclamation, and a few days ago we find the Magistrates have had to advertise the new Cross to be the Market Cross of Stirling.

It is also a common occurrence to read in the newspapers of such and such a proclamation being read at the Cross of Edinburgh by Heralds dressed up in all the gorgeous livery of a by-gone age.

Market Crosses, as I said before, were also used as a place of punishment. In many of the examples an iron collar and staple inserted in the shaft of the Cross is all that remain of the jougs, a form of punishment which consisted of an iron collar being put round prisoner's neck and locked and attached by a chain to the shaft of the Cross, to be there exposed in the market place to the gaze of and endure the taunts of the multitude. The jougs, in the example of Kinross, are now hung over the top. This mode of punishment was only abolished by Act of Parliament in 1837.

There was another form of punishment in use by an instrument called the Branks, an open iron-work cage which enclosed the head, a flat piece which went into the mouth and lay over the tongue for the purpose of preventing the offender speaking. This may also have been attached to some of our old Market Crosses, as, in two examples, these from Crieff and Ormiston, which have remains of staples on either side of cross and at different heights suggesting the jougs on one side and the branks on the other. The branks were generally used on female scolds, a punishment which put an effectual stop to their talent in that direction, when shut up in what we might call an iron cap.

Referring again to Stirling Burgh Records, we give a reference to the punishment of the branks.

In 1654 there is an item of 12s given to officers for going through the town with the branket woman. On October 21, 1702, there is another entry of 12s for conveying a woman with the branks through the town. In our case, therefore, it is evident that the branks were kept separate from the Cross, although the woman and officers may have commenced their peregrinations from the Cross.

In March, 1746, a sum of money was paid for attending James Baird, when on the Cross, with a paper on his breast for treason.

You will readily classify these twenty examples on the walls into two parts.

The first, these which have the shaft of the Cross resting on a series of steps and sometimes on a built pedestal, resting on the street.

The second, these which have the shaft of the Cross resting on the roof of an octagonal building of one storey in height.

The first lot having the greatest number in it, and being the earlier in point of date.

Several of the examples have dates on them, which is of great importance in fixing the dates for those which are without.

In the second lot of examples, the late James Drummond, Esq., says as far as I have been able to ascertain there were only 5 crosses in the style of the Edinburgh one, viz. :—

1. Edinburgh, built in 1617, taken down in 1756.
2. Preston, erected 1617. This example is still standing.
3. Perth, pulled down in 1651, rebuilt 1669; removed as an obstruction in 1765.
4. Dundee, pulled down in 1777.
5. Aberdeen, erected in 1686. This example is still standing.

In the Edinburgh example, which was taken down in 1756, the shaft only remained, crowned with its Gothic capital of curly cabbage foliation and grotesque animals, and it was re-erected a few years ago on its old site under the shadow of St Giles' Church, as near to its 1617 original as was possible.

The Prestonpans example is still extant. The privilege of holding weekly markets was granted in 1617, and no doubt the Cross was erected at this time. It now stands in the middle of a market garden, the town having removed in course of time nearer the shores of the Forth, the Cross and the foundations of houses only remaining to mark its former site.

The Dundee Cross, the shaft of which, with the arms of the burgh—a pot of lilies—carved on it, is all that remains, and this was re-erected a few years ago near the old churches there, but in a style which cannot be commended as a restoration.

The Perth one underwent two erections and two castings down. The shaft only remains, and is in a gentleman's possession in the neighbourhood, and we hope that the Fair City will yet follow suit with the other burghs and cities of Scotland, and restore its ancient Cross on its old site to adorn and embellish her streets. We find that when the Magistrates of Perth in 1669 re-erected the Cross, so much importance was attached to the gilding of the thistles with which the shaft was spangled, that an agreement was entered into between them and the Lyon King in Epinburgh to send one from the Herald's Office to "gilde the croce."

The Aberdeen example is still in existence although it has been removed from one site to another. We have on record that it was executed by a John Montgomery, mason, in old Rayne, for the sum of £100 Scots, and was paid for out of the Guild wine funds.

Of the first lot of Crosses, an exception has to be made with the examples from Inverary and Campbeltown, which have been purloined from the churchyards of their respective neighbourhoods and set up and appropriated as town's crosses. All the other examples of various dates and forms, have an average height of pillar and capital of from 9 to thirteen feet.

I will now describe these in our immediate neighbourhood in detail, beginning with Inverkeithing, which is perhaps the most beautiful. I think it may rank amongst the oldest examples, at any rate, we can almost get at the date of its erection from the shield armorial with which the capital of its shaft is embellished. There are 4 shields carrying—1st and 2nd, the Arms of Scotland; 3rd, Queen Annabella Drummond; 4th, Douglas. The 3rd shield is impaled with the Royal Arms and the Drummond, thus fixing it as the shield of Annabella, Queen of Robert III. The king's eldest son, the Duke of Rothesay, was married to the daughter of the Earl of Douglas in 1398, and it has been suggested that this cross may have been a marriage present, or remembrancer of that occasion and erected by the Queen—a very feasible and not at all improbable suggestion, and well butressed by the heraldic reading of these 4 shields. I have the idea that the sun-dial and unicorn are not of the same age as the shaft. The iron band with the staple for the jougs and branks still remain in the shaft of the cross. The steps at the bottom of this fine old Cross are modern.

The example from Airth is of much later date, viz., 1697, but it is a very fine example also. The shaft is octagonal in plan, with five octagonal steps at bottom, and crowned with an ornamental sun-dial and coats-of-arms of the Elphinstoun family.

The one from Kincardine is very graceful with its long octagonal shaft, with base and five octagonal steps surmounted with a capital and square abacus, on which is set an achievement of arms.

The Clackmannan Cross has its shaft square, with large chamfers off the corners, which make it virtually an octagon in plan the greater part of its length, set on the top of seven octagonal steps, and having as a capital a trefoil-shaped head with carving.

The example from Doune has its shaft like the Clackmannan one, but five steps at bottom are square.

The Culross Cross has its shaft oblong in section, with a cross arm at top like a cross proper, the whole resting on an octagonal base and five octagonal steps.

The example from Kinross stands in a recess off the principal street, and is in one stone, and seems to be of a very old date, probably as old as Inverkeithing. The plinth and steps are modern.

Dunfermline also possesses a Town Cross, the shaft and elaborately carved capital of which only are old, the base and steps being modern.

These examples from the lot No. 1 are all in our immediate neighbourhood, and it is to be noted that the whole of them have their shafts octagonal in plan, or where square at base have chamfered edges, which virtually make them octagonal. The steps at the base of all those that have octagonal shafts also take the same form. And in one example of square shaft with chamfered edges the steps take the octagonal plan, and the remainder of the examples have the steps square.

The other examples, which I may call without our own immediate neighbourhood, also bear out the same rule, and taking my stand on these old examples, I have no hesitation in saying that it is a pity that whoever designed the erection of our new Market Cross should have made the steps at the base of it circular in plan, and so few in number.

The shaft of Stirling Market Cross must have been octagonal in plan. The only reliable piece of it that we know of at present as being in existence is the unicorn which crowned the top. It is in the usual position of the unicorn of other old examples, with the exception that the shield is surrounded by the collar of St Andrew, and rests on an octagonal moulded base, the plain part being enriched with notches or square incisions; the octagonal form of the base thus indicating the shape of the shaft of the column to be also octagonal in plan. Any other information regarding the Cross I have not been able to procure, with this exception, that in 1792 the Town Council petitioned the Court of Session to allow it to be taken down, as it was in a ruinous condition. It will be noted here, that about the same date, or a little before it, Edinburgh, Perth, and Dundee also did the same thing with their old Market Crosses, showing the contagious nature of the destroyer's hand. In the case of Stirling, one of the Lords of Session, before whom the petition for its demolition was brought, said he would visit the spot when here on circuit. This he accordingly did, and to his visit we owe the short stone pillar at the side of the pavement in Broad Street, erected exactly opposite the site of the old Cross in the centre of the street.

In this same petition the following occurs:—"The Cross being composed of a pillar with several circular steps, occupies a large space, and is a great incumbrance to the street." This, I presume, is all the designer of our new cross has to go upon to make the steps at bottom circular, which we have seen is against all precedent. I do not think that the old steps of the Stirling Market Cross were circular. I have no doubt in my own mind that they were octagonal, like the rest of our old examples, and I can easily imagine the writer of this report looking at the old Cross and its surrounding steps in its dilapidated and ruinous condition, much the same as the example from Airth is at present, with the corners of all the steps rounded off by the constant use of centuries, and the sharp corners of the octagon also rounded off until, to the casual observer, or to those who had no love for the subject, might in truth write of them, as he does in this written report, as *circular* steps. He also says it occupied a large space. The present new Cross certainly does not occupy a large space; but if there had been six or seven steps to it, the correct number from our old Crosses, it would have occupied a "large space."

It is in my recollection of reading a report of Arnot, the historian, anent the old Edinburgh Cross when it was taken down, in which he described the capital of it as *Corinthian*, while in reality it has nothing classic about it, but dates from the late Gothic period with the characteristics of that time carved upon it. I therefore do not place much dependence upon a destroyer's written description of our old historical landmarks, but prefer to base my restoration ideas on contemporaneous existing examples. It is stated there is mention of the Stirling Cross in 1473. I do not doubt this, but the present unicorn is not of this date. From the detail and enrichment of the moulding of its base, and from itself, I would not date it later than James the Sixth's time.

I have a list of 37 Market Crosses in Scotland, viz.:—Auchtermuchty, Airth, Ancrum, Aberdeen, Aberlady, Anstruther, Biggar, Bowden, Clackmannan, Culross, Crieff, Coldingham, Canongate, Cupar, Cockburnspath, Cellardyke, Campbeltown, Dundee, Doune, Dunfermline, Elgin, Forfar, Gifford, Inverkeithing, Inverary, Kinross, Kincardine, Lochmaben, Melrose, Mussleburgh, Newbigging, Ormiston, Pencaithland, Prestonpans, Perth, Scone, Thornhill. Twenty of these are shown to-night, of which 13 are from my own sketches, 4 from photographs, and 3 from Mr James Drummond's illustrations. Of the total 37 examples, there are 9 of them I have not seen, nor any photo or drawing of them, but 3 of these are not now in existence, namely, Auchtermuchty, Forfar, and Perth, leaving 6 to be sketched, namely, Ancrum, Aberlady, Biggar, Gifford, Lochmaben, and Coldingham.

The following are additions to the list:—Kettings, near Coupar Angus; Bervie; Dumfries, removed 40 or 50 years ago, solid octagonal table; Leven, old sundials.

STIRLING CARPET WEAVERS' BROTHERLY SOCIETY.

Long before the Friendly Societies with which we are now familiar were instituted, Stirling had a Society under the above title, for the purpose of giving aid to sick members and paying funeral money to surviving relatives. It began on the 10th May, 1805, the entry money being 2s 6d, and the periodical payments 6d every six weeks. The rate of aliment allowed was 1s a day or 7s a week. From a statement of the income and expenditure of this Society from its institution till 1823, we find that no aliment was paid until 1807-8, when the sum of £1 11s appears in the accounts. In 1822-3 it had risen to £28 15s, showing that the carpet weavers were a numerous body in Stirling at that time. The following is a minute of the Society, dated March, 1824:—

"At a Meeting of the Stirling Carpet Weavers' Brotherly Society, held in the Trades-Hall, on the 19th instant, Bailie Jaffray having previously seen the Society's Regulations, and having highly approved of the same, attended the above Meeting, and addressed the members to the following purpose:—He remarked that Stirling, in which our lot is cast, is on an elevated spot of ground, so as to be seen at a distance—it is more, it is built upon a rock; it is also blessed with faithful gospel ministers; its inhabitants are greatly increased; its merchants numerous; its manufacturers respectable; its manufactories increased and improving, among which, her carpet manufactories are none of the least, having of late years been greatly extended both at home and abroad. He then expressed his high approbation of the Society which the journeymen Carpet Weavers had so successfully instituted, and remarked that the stock of the Society now amounted to upwards of £200, by which means the wants of their sick are amply provided for, they receiving 7s per week, which keeps them from becoming a burden on the public, and their families from penury and want, and all this is effected by a small item from the working members. The whole, he said, did great honour to the Society, and added, that he wished other towns and villages would adopt the same plan, and follow the manly example of the Stirling Journeymen Carpet Weavers, who had reared so creditable an institution. He then highly approved of the manner in which the Society was conducted, and wished that the principles on which it is founded were more generally known, as they could not fail to prove an inducement to others to enter into similar associations. After which, the preses rose, and in name of the Society, thanked Bailie Jaffray for his kindness in paying the Society a visit, and stated that if magistrates, ministers, and others in the higher ranks of life, would give their countenance to similar meetings, he thought such attention could not fail to benefit not only this, but all friendly institutions of the like nature."

STIRLING SOLDIERS AT WATERLOO.

UNPUBLISHED INCIDENTS OF THE BATTLE.

By the kindness of Mr David Chrystal, solicitor, Stirling, we have had the use of a peculiarly interesting copy of Siborne's "Waterloo," in which Mr Chrystal's grandfather, who was one of the subscribers to the work, inserted at the end of each volume a munber of notes by himself descriptive of incidents which he had from the parties concerned, and which, so far as we know, have not hitherto been published. We give below the notes referring to soldiers belonging to Stirling and Bannockburn, who were present at the battle of Waterloo. The date of the MS. is 1848.

George Macnie.

George Macnie, pensioner and plasterer, Stirling, who was in the 79th Highlanders, was through the whole of the Peninsular War, and at Waterloo. At Quatre Bras the regiment suffered most when returning through a hedge after having charged the French. The regiment was a good deal broken when going back to their own line. The enemy were too numerous for them to face, and kept firing when the 79th were getting through the fence. Their adjutant, Mr Kynock, was killed there while waving his bonnet encouraging the men.

Corporal Macnie and a party were sent out at night to collect the wounded. One of them whom they picked up was John Geary, of their own regiment. His leg was broken by a cannon ball, and when they tried to lift him, he begged to be let alone, as he would rather lie and die, so pained was he when lifted. They then spread a blanket, and the wounded man trailed himself upon it. They carried him to a house for the wounded, but as they could not wait to get him with them, they left him with a canteen of water at his head. Macnie some years afterwards met Geary on the North Bridge of Edinburgh, terribly lame. He was like to devour Macnie with kindness, and said he saved his life.

Macnie says that the closest fighting they had with the French was at Fuentes d Oneres. Walls only separated the combatants; the raising of a head was almost death. Upon making a rush to put the enemy out of the village, they came upon a number of killed and wounded men, both 79th and Imperial Guards, from a struggle with the bayonet. This had arisen from the parties meeting without being aware of their nearness, at the corner of a street, and none had time to turn about when they were upon each other. Colonel Cameron, of the 79th, was killed at Fuentes d'Oneres, by a shot through the neck. He was riding too conspicuously into a street at the head of his men.

Peter Rankine.

Peter Rankine, pensioner, Stirling, was in the Royal Horse Artillery, and was attached to the howitzer battery at Waterloo. The position was overlooking Hougomont. The French were coming down upon the place in a dense mass. The Duke of Wellington happened to be beside the howitzers at the time, and asked the officer if he had a new kind of shell of a larger diameter than they used in the Peninsula, and desired him to try it upon the columns. They fired two shells, one close after the other, and they both dropped into the column. They saw distinctly the effect by a scattering and opening among the French. The Duke remarked that it was very good practice, and desired them to go on as they had begun.

David Eadie.

David Eadie, pensioner, Bannockburn, was an artillery driver like Rankine, whom he did not know, and was through the whole of the Peninsular War. He was thereafter sent to America and was present (dismounted) at New Orleans. Upon nearing Plymouth, they were ordered to Ostend and not allowed to land in England. The gun Eadie was attached to was in a park near the farm house of Mont St Jean on the night before Waterloo, and the weather was very bad. Pretty early in the morning of the 18th, they were sent to the right along the Nivelles road, and were stationed a little forward or in front of a bit sandy brae. In the course of the battle the death of Major Ramsay damped the spirits of the men sadly, as it arose from the following accident:—Major Ramsay did not belong to the battery Eadie was in, but he rode to it to see if they could spare any ammunition, as his was getting done. At that instant two of the guns were slewed a little to a new range, and in the confusion and agitation of the moment, the men who were working the guns fired. Major Ramsay and his horse were most unfortunately in the line of fire, and both were killed on the spot. To conceal and get over the accident as speedily as possible, the men dug a slight grave in the sandy brae in rear of the guns, where they laid the body wrapt up in a cloak. After the army advanced to France, David Eadie was sent back with the Major's servant to point out the place, and the body was sent home. (I observe an elaborately-carved covering over a grave in the churchyard of Inveresk, to the memory of Major Norman Ramsay.)

At Fuentes d'Oneres, David Eadie was one of the drivers of a gun under Major Ramsay. Once, when retiring, they were hotly pursued by the French. A dragoon tried to cut down Eadie, who had nothing in his hand but a short whip. They galloped as fast as whip and spur could make their horses go, and the Frenchman still kept alongside cutting at him. Eadie could not get his sword drawn, and saw no escape, when, unseen by both, an English dragoon dashed up and with one blow at the neck struck off the Frenchman's head. The Englishman called out to David, "You owe me a bottle for that," and galloped on. Eadie never saw his deliverer again.

Such hand-to-hand encounters occasionally happened in the Peninsula. William Kilpatrick, gunner, pensioner in Stirling Castle, belonged to the Foot Artillery, and was at Albuera. The weather was bad and thick, and so unaware were the artillerymen of a sudden attack by the enemy's lancers, that the gunners had not time to fly from their guns. Kilpatrick was defending himself with his rammer from a lancer, when in the midst of the struggle the latter fell off his horse from a cut on the head dealt by an English dragoon. The lancer was killed by the blow.

James Leonard.

James Leonard, pensioner, was in the 40th. A sergeant of the regiment at one time of the battle gave an alarm. The arms were piled at the time, and "Stand to your arms!" was called out. Just as the men were falling into their companies, Ensign Clarke asked Leonard for a drink from his canteen. The latter could not get it unstrung, and Mr Clarke went behind Leonard and put his mouth to the canteen. The company had just formed when a round shot took it in flank, nine men being killed or wounded. Mr Clarke was the last struck by it. He lost an arm, and several ribs in the same side were broken. He survived, but his side was always padded till he died, about 1828.

James Baad.

James Baad, guildbrother of Stirling, and pensioner, was in the 27th regiment, which lost more officers and men than any other in the British army. They had a long march on the 17th June. The Duke of Wellington met them accidentally early on the morning of the 18th, and asked what regiment it was. Bead heard him answer, on being told their number, "Very well, lads, you are in good time." Bead was hit by a musket ball on the top of the hip joint, the ball forcing a bit of his flannel jacket into his flesh. The irritation of the wound towards the close of the day became most painful, and his officer told him to fall out. He got into the hospital at Bruxelles. Before he left, the regiment were in square, but the killed and wounded inside the square were more numerous than the men who were standing and firing.

John Macfarlan.

John Macfarlan, pensioner and porter to the Edinburgh and Glasgow Bank, Stirling, was a private in the distinguished 52nd through the whole of the Peninsula and at Waterloo. When the regiment had bivouacked on the night of the 18th, where the rear of the French army had stood, it was observed that the regimental colours were lost. This annoyed the men very much, but it was then too dark to search for them. As soon as light would admit on the morning of the 19th, a party retraced the ground gone over by the regiment in following up the Imperial Guards, and to their joy they found the standard where its bearer had fallen in the advance. It was a good deal soiled from being trampled upon. Macfarlan says that such was the mixed crowd of fugitives of all arms the 52nd got amongst in following up the French, that they were like to be carried away, and some bayonetting and blows with the butt of the firelock were dealt out in the crowd.

Paymaster Hugh Mackenzie.

Hugh MacKenzie, Esq., Melville Place, Stirling, h.p. 71st Highland Light Infantry, was with his regiment at Waterloo. The regiment formed one of Adam's brigade, but was not moved forward till the afternoon. It suffered several casualties in the earlier part of the day from heavy shot dropping amongst the men. While waiting, a great noise of shouting and firing occurred, but from the rising ground intervening, the cause, which proceeded from one of the vigorous assaults of the French, could not be seen. Several officers of the 23rd Welsh Fusileers, which lay nearer the front line than the 71st, ran to the rising ground, in the excitement, to see better, when three of them were struck down by a shot.

Mr MacKenzie, as will be seen from the enumeration of the actions (hereafter stated) at which he was present, served in the four quarters of the globe. Few veterans can show such a length of service, not even the great Duke himself. Mr MacKenzie is shy in detailing what he saw, but occasionally tells an anecdote. At Vimiera, he heard Sir Brent Spencer exclaim, "My God, Sir Arthur, look at the poor 50th, what will become of them?" The 50th was a weak battalion, and was advancing with colours displayed towards the French, who were greatly superior in numbers. Sir Arthur, upon turning his spyglass in their direction, answered, "No fear of them, they will show the bayonet immediately." This proved to be the case, and the French were soon running away in great confusion.

Mrs MacKenzie (sister of John Murray, Esq., of Livilands) was with her husband at Corunna. She and other officers' wives were in one of the transports in the bay when the French opened fire upon the shipping. Amidst great noise and confusion, the ladies were sent down to the cabin, and instantly a heavy shot passed through it. Mrs MacKenzie, not aware of the danger, called out, "Will nobody shut that hole and keep the wind out?"

The following is the inscription on a gold box presented to Mr MacKenzie:—

"From the Officers of the 71st Highland Light Infantry to their esteemed friend, Paymaster Hugh MacKenzie, who served in the corps from 5th October, 1780, to 19th May, 1824, during which period he was present at the sieges and actions here detailed, and commanded the forlorn-hope at Nundydroog, October 18, 1791.

Siege of Gibraltar.
Siege of Policatcherry.
Siege and Storm of Bangalore.
General Action at Carrigate Hills.
Storm of Nundydroog.
Storm of Tippoo's Camp at Seringapatam.
Surprise of Tippoo's Horse Camp.

Capture of the Cape of Good Hope.

Capture of Buenos Ayres.

Rollia.
Vimiera.
Retreat to Corunna.
Walcheren.
Massena's Retreat from Portugal.
Arroyo de Molenos.
Almarez.

Storm of Savendroog.

Retreat from Madrid.
Vittoria.
Pyrenees.
Nive.
Nivelle.
Bayonne.
Orthes.
Tarbes.
Toulouse.
Waterloo."

At a review of the Austrians, who reached Paris after the British and Prussians were in possession, the Austrians appeared very splendid, their clothes and equipments being new. A Prussian officer, to the annoyance of a Parisian gentleman, was enlarging upon the size and imposing appearance of the Austrians, and Mr MacKenzie, who was beside the Prussian and the Parisian in the crowd, heard the latter say to the former, "Do you see that fellow there? (pointing to a little 71st soldier in dirty, worn, and shabby fatigue-dress, and off duty). Well, had it had not been for him, neither you nor these big Austrians would have been here!"

Mr MacKenzie's servant during the Peninsular campaign was Robert Murray, a batman. He was a sly, taciturn person, but of determined courage. The 50th and 71st were in the same brigade at the *coup de main* at Almarez, and upon the ladders being placed, Murray and one of the 50th happened to be next each other at the foot of a ladder, when Murray jocularly said, "Well, I suppose the 71st lead the way, as usual," and instantly rushed up. Upon his head appearing above the work, a Frenchman fired, and the bullet went through Murray's bonnet. Mr MacKenzie asked him what he did with the French soldier, and he dryly answered, "I put him out of the way." Murray was shot through the lungs at the battle of Vittoria, when his regiment was almost annihilated. Mr MacKenzie went in search of him, and found him stripped and about to be buried. After examining the body, Mr MacKenzie thought he felt a sensation of life remaining, and got Murray saved from interment. He was long in hospital afterwards.

Our readers may be interested to learn that a descendant of Capt. MacKenzie, whose honourable career is above narrated, is the wife of Mr J. W. Campbell, Bank of Scotland, Stirling.

FAIRS AND MARKETS IN THE STIRLING DISTRICT.

An interesting paper on the markets and fairs of Scotland, prepared by Sir James Marwick, City Clerk, Glasgow, forms one of the appendices to vol. vii. of the "Minutes of Evidence taken before the Royal Commissioners on Market Rights and Tolls." We extract the details relating to the Stirling District, beginning with

STIRLING.

David I. (1124-1153). Pop. parliamentary burgh, 16,001.

Was a member of the Court of Four Burghs established by David I.

By charter dated 18th August, 1226, Alexander II. granted the burgh a weekly market on Saturday and exclusive rights of trading in Stirlingshire, and empowered the burgesses, other than walkers and weavers, to have a merchant guild. Stirling Charters, pp. 9, 10.

By charter dated 20th July 1227, the same King exempted the burgesses of toll and custom of their proper goods throughout the kingdom. Stirling Charters, pp. 9, 10.

A reference to a charter of the fairs of Stirling in 1282. A.P.S., I. 110.

By charter dated 13th July 1386, Robert II. granted the burgh to the burgesses in feu for payment of £16 sterling at Whitsunday and Martinmas by equal portions. Stirling Charters, pp. 21, 22.

By charter dated 25th October 1447, James II. granted a new fair at the feast of Ascension to continue for eight days with the same privileges as at the fair on the Feast of Nativity of the Virgin, and reserved to the burgesses their fairs previously held, as they had been wont to enjoy the same. Stirling Charters, pp. 30-32.

James IV. conferred on the burgh the customs on salt and leather, and the right to appoint a sheriff within the burgh and its liberties. M.C.R. II. 408.

In 1526 Stirling is mentioned as one of the six principal towns of merchandise in the realm. A.P.S. II. 305.

Two annual fairs both in September,—viz., the 8th or latter Lady-day, and the 14th, or Rood-day, being so near to each other were found inconvenient in harvest time. The fair on the 14th of September was accordingly changed to 22nd October, on complaint of the magistrates. 1581, c. 61. A.P.S. III. 239.

Prohibition of fair on 8th September, by reason of the plague, 2nd September 1606. P.C.R. VII, 250.

Charter by Charles I., dated 17th November, 1641, granting weekly markets on Wednesday and Saturday with four yearly fairs, each continuing for eight days: (1) Hallow Thursday, ten days before the Feast of Pentecost, to be called First Fair day; (2) on 20th July, to be called Second Fair day; (3) on 8th September, to be called Latter Lady's day; and (4) on 22nd October, to be called Latter Fair Day, and empowering the town to take double customs at these fairs. Stirling Charters, 124-167.

Act of Parliament ratifying the above charter. 1649. A.P.S. VI. II. 723.

Charter by Charles II., dated 22nd April 1678, confirming the charter of 1641, and promising that no burgh of barony or regality should be erected within two miles of Stirling, nor any weekly markets or annual fairs be authorised to be held within that distance. Stirling Charters 171, 174.

A report to the Convention of Burghs in 1692 states that there were then a weekly market and four yearly fairs, each continuing for one day. C.R. IV. 577.

The same report states that no ships, barks, or boats belonged to the burgh, save two galliots of about 30 tons burden each, and of the value of about 1000 marks each. *Ib.*, IV. 577.

Act of Parliament granting two fairs to John Murray of Touchadam: (1) on the first Tuesday of December, (2) on the last Tuesday of January. 1705. c. 30. A.P.S. XI. 274. App., p. 95.

Against this grant the Commissioner of Stirling in Parliament protested in respect the fairs authorised were within two miles of the burgh and in violation of the charter of 1678. A.P.S. XI. 276. See the Town of Stirling *v.* Murray, 7th February 1706. Morrison's Dict., 4148.

The N.S.A., published in 1845, states that the burgh had a weekly market for grain on Friday, and the other produce of the district, which was well attended. It had also several annual fairs or extraordinary markets for horses, wool, &c., which were held also on Friday. VIII. ii. 432.

Weekly market on Friday. Fairs on the first and third Fridays of February, March, and April, and the first and last Friday in May. Hiring fair on the third Friday of October.

The fairs here are almost defunct, as the marts better meet the wants of cattle dealers.

ABERFOYLE.

Village and Parish in Perthshire. Pop. of Parish *quoad civilia*, 465 ; *quoad sacra*, 409.

The N.S.A., published in 1845, states that three annual fairs are held in the parish (1) in April, for the sale of cattle, (2) in August for the sale of lambs, and (3) in October for hiring servants. X. 1159.

Fairs (1) on third Tuesday in April, (2) Friday before third Tuesday of August, (3) last Thursday of October.

AIRTH.

Village and parish in Stirlingshire. Pop. of village, 487 ; of parish, 1,362.

Charter by James VI., dated 24th December 1597, in favour of John Bruce, erecting the town into a burgh of barony with a weekly market on Friday and two yearly fairs (1) on 24th July and (2) on 8th October. R.M.S., VI. 208, No. 634.

Act of Convention of Burghs, dated 4th July 1498, setting forth a complaint by the Commissioner of Stirling that the laird of Airth has purchased the town of Airth—which had been erected a free burgh—contrary to the privilege of its enfeftments. The convention advised the burgh to insist on a reduction of the erection, and promised their concurrence. C.R. II., 35.

Act of Convention, dated 6th July 1599, applicable to Airth and other towns in the same position engaging to give them aid and pecuniary assistance in resisting encroachments on the liberties of burghs. C.R. II., 54.

Charter by King Charles II., dated 8th February 1678, in favour of Richard Elphingstoun, confirming *inter alia* the lands and barony of Airth, with the burgh of barony of Airth and the port and harbour thereof which formerly belonged to Alexander Earl of Linlithgow ; and authorising a weekly market on Tuesdays and two annual fairs each of eight days, (1) on 14th July to be called , and (2) on 18th October to be called

Act of Parliament ratifying the above charter, 1681. c. 48. A.P.S., VIII. 305–307.

Act of Convention of Burghs, dated 8th Feby. 1719, fixing contributions to be paid by Airth for the communication of trade in the royal burghs. C.R. V., 211.

The N.S.A., published in 1845, states that there was an annual fair on the last Tuesday of July, chiefly for hiring shearers. VIII. ii. 287.

The only fair which now survives, and that merely as a holiday, is held on the last Tuesday of

July. It is popularly known as the "Whistle Fair." No hiring has taken place at it for twenty or thirty years.

Alloa.

Town in Clackmannanshire. Pop. of police burgh, 8,812; of town and suburbs, 10,591.

Charter by James VI. to John, Earl of Mar, dated 27th January 1620, erecting and creating the town of Alloa, and the crofts thereof, called the burgh crofts, with the port and harbour of Alloa, and the pow thereof into a free burgh of barony and regality, with the privilege of free markets, &c.

Charter by King James VII., dated 1st June 1677, to Charles Earl of Mar, of the lands and earldom of Mar, with the liberty and privilege of a burgh of barony and regality at Alloa; the weekly markets belonging thereto; and two yearly fairs (1) on 25th July called , and (2) on 29th October, called St. Mungo's fair.

Act of Parliament ratifying the above charter, 1685, c. 69. A.P.S. VIII. 508. M.C.R. II. 7.

The O.S.A., published in 1793, states that there were two weekly markets, on Wednesday and Saturday, and four annual fairs on the second Wednesday of February, May, August, and Nov. respectively. VIII. 624.

The N.S.A., published in 1845, gives four annual fairs as above, adding that at three of these cattle were sold, but that the fairs were little more than nominal. That held in August was the great fair, where servants were hired, and reapers for the harvest. It was attended by immense multitudes of people from all the surrounding district. VIII. 65.

Weekly market on Saturday.

Fair on the second Wednesday of August.

Hiring servants on second Wednesday of August, and on second Saturday of October.

(To be continued.)

THE MINISTERS OF NORRIESTON.

ROBERT STIRLING,

the first ordained minister of Norrieston, was licensed by the Presbytery of Dunblane in 1763, and being nominated to this charge by the minister of Kincardine, with the consent of the people, he was ordained on the 25th September, 1766. He seems to have been a man of some weight. The old statistical account of Crieff, to which he was translated in 1770, was written by him. In this account he tells us that "about twenty times more tea is used now than twenty years ago. Bewitched by the mollifying influence of an enfeebled potion, the very poorest classes begin to regard it as one of the necessaries of life, and for its sake resign the cheaper and more invigorating nourishment which the productions of their country afford."

Stirling was troubled during his ministry at Crieff by the rise of the sect called the "Bereans." John Barclay, the founder of this sect, was a native of Muthill, and after studying at St Andrews he was licensed and presented to the church of Fettercairn, but his loose views on the subjects of Revelation and Inspiration caused him to leave the church in 1773. There were thirty-seven of his followers in Crieff when Mr Stirling wrote his report. The report goes on to tell us that about the year 1780 female servants and others of that rank began first to wear ribbons. "Conscious of attracting superior notice, superior charity was also displayed."

Of the Seceders he will not speak. To form an idea of them in a religious or political light would perhaps be useless, "but as they do not maintain their own poor," they diminish the ordinary poor's funds supplied merely from church-door collections. He was not acquainted with Gaelic, and thought a Gaelic-speaking catechist would be of some service to him in the parish.

Through the help of a Crieff gentleman I gathered that Mr Stirling had the reputation of being a very austere man, and as ministers were more feared in those days than now, he had great control over the people. When he appeared at the east end of the town, the word was passed—"To your tents, O Israel"—and the streets were speedily cleared, not a soul venturing out till his reverence had passed. He was very strong on the good effects of catechising his people, and caused no end of discomfort to members who had a somewhat hazy conception of the difference between justification and sanctification. In his day the ministers had their stipends paid in grain, and they kept a granary at the manse, where it was stored and sold when prices were high. Mr Stirling seems to have been very exact as to measure. A bushel, when full and rolled over on the top with a piece of wood, will hold a little more if it is kicked on the side. This kick Mr S. never forgot to give. On one occasion, a farm servant was sent from a remote part of the parish with the set number of bushels which fell to his master to pay. On the minister's remeasurement, and with the administration of the usual kick, it was found that a few handfuls were awanting. He insisted that the measure should be full, clinching his argument with the remark that justice should flow like a stream. The servant was annoyed at the deficiency, and begged of the minister not to put him to the trouble of going back all the distance for the small quantity required, promising to make it good next time. Mr Stirling was firm in his demand, however; and there was nothing for it but to go back for the deficiency. When the man returned, it was found that he had brought a very small quantity too much. This, the minister remarked, would not be worth the man's while to take home with him; but the latter appeared to think otherwise, and repeating the minister's words, "justice should flow like a stream," carefully swept up every grain of it and carried it away, to the great annoyance of the divine.

Mr Stirling was very severe in cases of discipline, and administered the public rebuke to the erring with great sternness. In his old age, one of his daughters had the misfortune of being among those who had to be dealt with, and it was said to have broken the old man's heart as he never did much after it. He had a son, Michael, who was settled at Cargill in 1808, and who was a determined champion of non-intrusion principles in connection with the Lethendy case. He died in 1865, universally respected and beloved.

Mr Stirling's grave-stone at Crieff is thus inscribed—

"In memory of the Rev. Robert Stirling, minister of this parish, who died 16th December, 1813, in the 74th year of his age and the 48th of his ministry."

JOHN SNODGRASS,

a native of Paisley, and student at Edinburgh University, was licensed by the Presbytery of Haddington in 1766. He was called and ordained in succession to Mr Stirling in 1772. He laboured here only two years, having been called to the charge of the "Overgate quarter" of Dundee in 1774, from which he was translated to the Middle Church of Paisley in 1781. The Rev. P. L. Burr of Lundie and Fowles, clerk of the Presbytery of Dundee, has examined the minutes of Presbytery carefully for me, and finds "nothing recorded of the sayings or doings of Mr Snodgrass. He seems, however, to have performed all the duties of his office to the entire satisfaction of the Presbytery and of the whole community; for at the meeting when Commissioners from Paisley appeared to prosecute the translation, the Kirk Session of Dundee tried hard to retain his services, and intimated that should Mr Snodgrass leave Dundee, the town would deeply feel his loss. But the pleading of the Commissioners and the better endowment of the Church to which he was called, at last prevailed, and he went to Paisley," to the great grief of the Second Charge or South Church of Dundee.

Mr Snodgrass received D.D. from the College of Princetown, New Jersey, in 1793, and died in 1797, in the 57th year of his age and 25th of his ministry.

The church to which he was called in Paisley was the Middle Church, opened on the 13th Nov., 1781. Mr Snodgrass's stipend was at first £120, but three years after, it was raised to £130 by his Paisley hearers.

His literary productions were a sermon preached before the Society for Propagating Christian Knowledge in Edinburgh, on 29th May, 1794, and two years after his death a commentary on part of the book of Revelation, 592 pages, was published in Paisley.

In the History of the Shire of Renfrew (1782), by George Crawford and William Semple, it is said, "On the east side of the Cart, the proprietors are the Rev. John Snodgrass, heir of the late John Stevenson," and he was a subscriber for the above history. Altogether a superior man, with an extensive knowledge of men and books, he must have possessed a great influence for good during his brief sojourn in this district.

He had a son, Kenneth, a C.B., and a daughter, Margaret, who was married to Major Sullivan of the British and Portugese armies.

Patrick Caldwell

was licensed by the Presbytery of Dumbarton in 1768, and after a probation of five or six years, he was called and ordained at Norrieston. His tombstone is thus inscribed—

"Erected in memory of the Rev. Patrick Caldwell, who was ordained minister of this Chapel of

Norrieston, October, 1775, and died on March 20, 1796.

Remember them which have the rule over you, who have spoken unto you the word of God; whose faith follow, considering the end of their conversation.—Heb. xii. 7."

Mr Caldwell had a bad wife. She had been given to him by a gentleman who got tired of her; and she turned badly to the drink. Once when Mr Caldwell was preaching in the tent at Gargunnock, he was observed every now and then looking anxiously in the direction of Thornhill. He had left his wife at home alone, and he was afraid she might set fire to the manse in his absence. Hence his anxious looks.

During sermon one day, Mr Caldwell observed Mr Lennox, Chapel, asleep as he imagined, so he called upon some one sitting near, "Waken the Cauper there." Mr Lennox was not so far gone as appearances might indicate, for he replied, "The Cauper's no sleepin', sir, jist ye stick to the point."

In 1796, the year in which Mr Caldwell died, John Murdoch, his servant, craved a certificate of church membership, which was refused. Murdoch appealed to the Session of Kincardine, who consulted with Mr Caldwell. He wrote them that he had refused the certificate because Murdoch had shown "disrespectful behaviour to him in person." However, about three months after, the certificate is again claimed on the ground that "no special accusation" had been brought against Murdoch; and probably it was granted.

James Hughes

was licensed by the Presbytery of Edinburgh in 1787. He was called to Norrieston in succession to Patrick Caldwell, on the 1st Sept., 1796. He was greatly troubled with his lungs, and died after a ministry of between three and four years here. In the last church was a board 4ft. by 2½ft., or rather three boards joined and surrounded by a moulding, painted white with letters in black, and inscribed as follows—

This was Erected by
Mrs Hughes in Memory
of her Husband,
Rev. Mr James Hughes,
Who was ordained minister of the Gospel at Norrieston Sept. 1st, 1796, and in that station he labour'd a pious and painful, learned and eminent servant of Christ untill his Lord removed him by death upon March 15th, 1800, in the fortieth year of his age and twelfth
of his ministry, and was
Interred below this pulpit.

This sacred herald whose sweet mouth spread
Gospel light abroad, like Timothy, was but a youth
and yet a man of God.
Soon did this young and ready scribe a friend for
Christ appear, and was among the sacred tribe
a faithful, Godly seer.
Mounting the pulpit from his Bow'r he prayed with
Divine aid, and preached the Gospel sacred truths
with heavenly zeal and strength.
His life and death did both express what strength or
Grace was given, his life a lamp of holiness, his death
a dawn of heaven.
His zealous soul, through heavenly grace, did
Mortal life despise, to feed the lambs around the
Place where now his body lies.
His dying breath triumphantly did that sweet
Anthem sing, Thanks be to God for victory,
O Death where is thy sting.

HUGH LAIRD

succeeded Rev. James Hughes in the charge. His grandson, the Free Church minister of Durris, has furnished me with some information regarding him. He was born at Houston, Renfrewshire, in 1765; studied at Glasgow University, where he gained distinction as a student; was licensed to preach by the Presbytery of Glasgow in 1795. He was called by the parishioners of Norrieston in the autumn of 1800, and was ordained on New Year's Day, 1801. Before this he had been labouring as assistant to Sir Harry Moncrieff, minister of St Cuthbert's, Edinburgh. While he remained here he did some good work. He had a Sabbath school, which Macfarlane of Whirriston attended. He remained here only two years, having been called to Portmoak in August 1802. Macfarlane went to Portmoak to hear him preach, and waited to speak with him at the close of the service. After the usual salutations and chit chat, the minister said, "O! it was a fine place, Thornhill; I could get plenty of respectable men there for elders; here I can get only tailors and shoemakers." "Can you get no Christians?" retorted the democratic Macfarlane. The minister was silent; no doubt he felt caught. Mr Laird visited this place several times after, and stayed with Mr Mackison, Norrieston, a family for which he had great respect. From his translation from Norrieston, Laird was all his life minister of Portmoak. In 1813 he received the degree of D.D. from Marischal College, Aberdeen. "He had a very large family," his grandson says; "fifteen, I believe, and was only once married. His wife was a Miss Blackhall, whom he first met in a house (Drenbog) near Newburgh, Fifeshire, where she was a governess. He must have been married about the time of his ordination." Three of his sons entered the ministry—one was minister of Leslie, another of Braco, and the third at Cupar, who was the Moderator of the Free Church Assembly in 1889. The father and his three sons left the Establishment at the Disruption. Dr Laird was much respected about Portmoak, and is still remembered there. His grandson says he must have been a superior scholar from the fine set of classical books he possessed. His medical knowledge was considerable, and was much appreciated in the surrounding neighbourhood. "I have read," writes Mr Laird, "some of his sermons, but I have no very clear idea of their character." His style was clear, calm, and truly rational. He died in 1849.

JOHN FINDLAY

received license to preach from the Presbytery of Glasgow in 1800. He was called to Norrieston, and ordained in June, 1803. There are no reminiscenses of his sojourn among us—except that an aged parishioner said to me "he was a terrible moderator, him." He was translated to Perth in 1807, got the degree of D.D. from St Andrews in 1839, and died aged 67 years.

There is a tablet in St Paul's Church, Perth, erected by the congregation to his memory, thus inscribed—

"Erected by the congregation of Saint Paul's, in memory of John Findlay, D.D. Inducted at the opening of the church, 19th of November, 1807, died 4th April, 1846, aged 67 years."

"Looking unto Jesus, the Author and Finisher of our faith.

He had the name of being a good preacher and very much respected by his congregation, beyond which he was but little known. He was the only minister in the town of Perth that adhered to the Establishment in 1843.

SAMUEL CAMERON

was licensed by the Presbytery of Auchterarder in 1793 and became assistant at Fowlis Wester. Thence he was called to Norrieston and ordained on the 29th September, 1808. He filled our pulpit only a year, and hence we can say little about him. He was removed to Monzie in 1809. The usual story is told of him "Lie ye there, minister, till Samuel Cameron fecht for himsel'." My informant assures me that the highland blood of him once warmed on a sacramental Monday after dinner to such an extent that it had to be be let out by a hand-to-hand fight in a quiet place with one of his elders. He died in 1836 in his 68th year and the 28th of his ministry. He had several sons and a daughter married to Principal Cunningham's brother, Lord Panmure's factor.

The venerable Mr Omond, Free Church minister of Monzie, was appointed his colleague and successor, and through him I learned that he died between Mr Omond's ordination and introduction. The sermon for introducing the junior colleague was the funeral sermon of the senior. In Mr Omond's first sermon he generously said of him, "he spent his life under a cloud," though it was well known that the cloud was charged with liquor. He and two or three fellow students were returning from college after the session. They came to an inn tired and benighted, and with nothing to pay. In spite of this Cameron induced them to spend the night in the hotel. "I'll make it all right," he said. During the night, he burnt his trousers and made a grievous complaint to the landlord threatening pains and penalties for keeping a disorderly house, and declaring that a £5 note had been consumed with them. The landlord was glad to supply another pair of trousers and let the students away without paying the "lawin'."

JOHN SOMMERS.

There is a stone in the churchyard thus inscribed :—

"Andrew Symers and | Elizabeth Smith— where | lyes inter'd Elizabeth | and Andrew and Jean | and Alexander Symers who | died young children | of theirs Heir lyes | four blosams early pu'd | ever they [came] to their | priem Theirfor do ye | improve weaill while | you have precious time |

1770.

I have reasons for thinking that Mr Sommers was closely connected with this family; at least that he was connected with, and well known in Thornhill before he came as the minister.

The Rev. Mr Sommers had been assistant at St Ninians, and came to Norrieston from Chryston in 1810. He was twice married, and his descendants are too well known to need anything further said about them.

During his ministry, which ended with his death in 1839, the church was rebuilt in 1812, the manse was greatly increased in size and convenience, and the glebe was much improved, for Mr Sommers was a man of the world as well as a Churchman.

There is a good story told of him. He was once asked to intimate a political meeting or some meeting which went against his grain. He refused. The precentor was accordingly asked and consented. After concluding the psalm, this official cries out, "Notice.—A pub——" whereupon down came the big hand of the minister, seized the document, squeezed it into a ball, pitched it down in the bottom of the pulpit, and went up in the usual way of pronouncing the benediction.

He acquired the lands of Little Mill and Chapel. Most of the fine trees round the chapel are due to his taste. He was also possessed of Herre of Boquhapple for about a year, when he sold it to the father of the late Mr M'Queen, grandfather of the present laird.

At the ordination of Mr Watt at Bucklyvie in 1837, he preached from the text he saw inscribed on the church as he rode past. Whether he had studied it before or not is not known. A considerable impression was made by his admonitions to avoid cock fighting at Han'sel Monday. Cock fighting was a recognised game, and furnished a considerable item in the educational revenues of the parish. The dead cocks and the "fugies" became the property of the schoolmaster, who treated the boys, if not the girls also, to a glass of mountain dew in return for their annual benefactions. The brutal sport of cock fighting died hard in this locality. An old native of the district told me that Mr Sommers spent some time every Sabbath before Han'sel Monday in warning the people against it. He was once preaching on Sabbath breaking, and "he began," said my informant, "My dearly beloved, I was reading just before leaving home that the people were out playing shinty on the Lord's day. Alas, alas, my dearly beloved, and where do you think this took place? Just ower by at Greenock." But whether the Greenocks in the neighbourhood or the town "owre by" on the Firth of Clyde, I am unable to say. And mark, while he said this, "the tears were running down his cheeks."

Thornhill. G. W.

LOCAL BIBLIOGRAPHY.

The Farmer's Catechism; or, the Farmer-Field Spiritualized, by way of Question and Answer. Being collected and gathered from Sacred Scripture, very proper for the Instruction of every Reader, but particularly the Farmer; wherein is set forth all the Operations of the Farmer-Field, from his beginning his Field from a state of Nature to a proper Mould. The which Operations are all Spiritualized, and applied to bringing the Heart of the Christian by Grace into a proper Mould. By George Frazer, late Farmer of Rack-Miln, in the parish of Dollar. A new edition, corrected and enlarged. Jeremiah iv. 3: "Break up your fallow-ground, and sow not among thorns." Genesis iv. 9-12: "When thou tillest the ground, it shall not henceforth yield its strength unto thee." Broomedgehall, near Carron, 1785. Printed by Daniel Reid for the Author. 24 pp. 12mo.

The Dove's Flight to a Thicket, for Her Life. An Emblem of Sinners sheltering themselves under the Wings of Christ, or the Flight of a Soul (under a High Sensibility of its Necessity) Flying to Christ's All-sufficiency. Being the subject of a number of Composures collected from that Holy Volume the Sacred Scriptures (and none else) in solitary hours and humbling circumstances. Very proper for every Christian's Perusal. By George Frazer, late Farmer in Rack-Mill, in the Parish of Dollar. Psalm lv. 6: "And I said, O that I had had wings like a dove; for then would I fly and be at rest." Broomedgehall, Carron, 1786. Printed by Daniel Reid for the Author. [This is a curiosity of literature, of which I may give a fuller account some day.]

Adam's Fig-Leaf Righteousness. By George Frazer. [8 pages 12mo., probably printed at the same press. Is in the form of verse, and without date.]

Mary Magdalen Viewing Christ's Sepulchre after His Resurrection. 8 pp. 12mo. To this is prefixed the following note:—Reader, the 252 pages containing the subjects of the Dove's Flight, not being sufficient to contain all that the Author designed to set forth in said book, he therefore begs leave to be allowed to satisfy the purchasers, by giving them an opportunity of seeing the rest of the subjects at the small expense of one penny, and some an halfpenny. [This also is an 8 page poetical "composure," no date, but must be subsequent to 1786, the date of the Dove's Flight.]

The Impropriety of one Farmer coveting or taking his Neighbour's Possession over his Head at a Higher Rent, or any other way. [This, the author says, is a narration of genuine facts, and from the text he himself seems to have been the sufferer from this objectionable impropriety. It is another 8 pages, composed in prose and verse of the most doggerel description. No date, but like the former, must be subsequent to 1786.]

Verses composed on seeing John Reid, late servant at Ratho, brought from the Tolbooth of Edinburgh to be tried for the horrid murder of his own son, a child only eight months old. To which is added Verses on hearing of seven persons being rebuked by the Rev. Mr. M——, minister of the Gospel at N—— M——. With a Description of a Lewd Woman who lived in Ar——ie. By George Frazer. [8 pages 12mo., no date, but as the murder referred to happened on the 2nd December 1786, the pamphlet would probably appear early in the following year.]

A Collection of the most esteemed Farces and Entertainments performed on the British Stage. Edinburgh: Printed for Silvester Doig and William Anderson, Stirling. 1792. 6 vols. 12mo. [Probably William Anderson is the same as the one who figures in the following petition.]

Unto the Right Honourable the Lords of Council and Session, the Petition of William Anderson, Bookseller in Stirling, and John Robertson, Printer in Edinburgh, humbly sheweth, &c., &c. [This is a defence lodged by the petitioners against a bill of suspension and interdict at the instance of some London and Edinburgh booksellers, to prevent the petitioners from printing and publishing an edition of "Blackstone's Commentaries on the Laws of England." The case is one of literary property, and the defence extends to 24 quarto pages, signed Charles Hope, and dated 1st June 1787. It is interesting as showing the enterprise at this early period of the Stirling booksellers, who could venture on the publication in a provincial town of such a work as "Blackstone's Commentaries." William Anderson was Provost of the Burgh in 1793 and 1794, and again in 1813 and 1814.]

Pitcaithly Wells: a Poem in two parts, composed

by Allan Campbell of Falkirk, while attending these Wells for the cure of his sore leg. To which is subjoined, a Description of the Wells, from Mr Heron's journey through the Western Counties of Scotland, in the year 1792. The Third Edition. Falkirk: Printed by T. Johnstone, for the Author. 1805. [This is just an ordinary 8-page chap book, and like most of them, the paper it is printed on is bad, and the poetry (!) worse.]

Life, Adventures, and Moral Sentiments of the Sterling Boy; or, a Spectacle from Human Nature, a Poem, by John Cheugh. Most respectfully dedicated, to the Gentlemen and Tradesmen of Coatbridge, Airdrie, Campsie, Kirkintilloch, &c.

MOTTO.

But some will scan, and say that Man
Was formed good and evil;
Thenceforth amain, God did ordain
A portion to the Devil.

Edinburgh: Printed for the Author. 1842. 24 pp. 12mo.

Original Poems and Songs, chiefly in the Scottish Dialect, by Dougal M'Killop, Stirling. Second Edition.

Go—sally forth thou little Muse,
And may good luck attend ye;
May gen'rous friends thy faut's excuse,
And gently try to mend ye.
But cankered critics let them rage—
Perfection canna bind them;
Their chatt'rin' teeth are aye on edge,
So wha the deuce wad mind them.

Stirling: printed for the author, by J. Fraser. 1824. 40 pages 12mo. [There is little merit in this volume, the songs and poems are, as far as mere words go, a pretty close imitation of Burns and other poets, but still it must have sold, seeing this is the *second* edition. I would be obliged if any reader could give the date and description of the *first* edition, or any particulars as to who Dougal M'Killop was.]

Glasgow. J. I.

FAIRS AND MARKETS IN THE STIRLING DISTRICT.

(Continued.)

C. ALVA.

Town in Stirlingshire. Pop., 4,961.

Act of Parliament authorising Sir John Erskine of Alva, to have two yearly fairs: (1) on June and (2) on the second Tuesday of October. 1707, c. 78. A.P.S. XI. 477. App. 144 b.

No fairs have been held here for a great number of years.

BALDERNOCK.

Parish, Stirlingshire. Pop. 569.

The N.S.A., published in 1845, states that Bardowie fair was held on 6th June for the sale of milk cows, and showing stallions. It was only a parish fair, and had almost dwindled to a shadow. VIII. ii. 175.

No fair has been held here for upwards of 40 years.

BALFRON.

Town and parish, Strathendrick district, Stirlingshire. Pop. of town, 970; of parish, 1,327.

Act of Parliament authorising John Cuningham of Baldindalloch, to have at the Clachan of Balfron a weekly market on Tuesday, and two free fairs: (1) on the third Tuesday of May; (2) on the second Tuesday of October. 1701, c. 43. A.P.S.X. 335. App. p. 104.

A table of the customs exigible at these fairs attested by William Cuningham of Ballindalloch, on 16th May, 1737. Ballindalloch writs.

Formerly three fairs were held here: (1) on the last Tuesday of May for cattle; (2) on the last Tuesday of July for hiring servants; and (3) on the last Tuesday of October.

The fair in May is the only one now held, but is rapidly falling into disuse.

BALGAIR.

Moor in Kippen parish, Stirlingshire.

The N.S.A., published in 1845, states that a large market, chiefly for black cattle, was formerly held here, but had been transferred to the Moor of Kippen, about three miles from the village, and was held in the month of June. VIII. ii. 272.

Fairs: (1) on last Tuesday of March; (2) on 10th May, but if that a Saturday or Monday, then on the following Tuesday; and (3) on Friday before the 26th of June.

BALLOCH.

Village in Dumbartonshire. Pop. 159.

A horse fair in September still belongs to the family of Colquhoun of Luss. Irving's Dumbartonshire, p. 361.

Fairs: (1) on 27th April; if Sunday, then next day, this fair has now become an auction mart; (2) on 15th September, popularly known as the Moss of Balloch. At this fair a large business is done.

BALQUHAPPLE.

King's town of, parish of Kincardine, stewartry of Monteath, Perthshire. See Thornhill.

Act of Parliament authorising Archibald Napier of Balquhapple, to have a weekly market on Thursday, and four free fairs, each to continue for eight days: (1) on 20th October, to be called Margaret's fair; (2) on 14th November, to be called Martinmas fair; (3) on the first Tuesday of March, to be called Lentron fair; and (4) on the third Tuesday of June, to be called Hill's fair. 1695, c. 95. A.P.S. IX. 499. Extract from MS. inventory of the barony of King's Balquhapple.

These fairs and market are all now extinct.

BALQUIDROCK.

Lands and barony of Stirlingshire.

Act of Parliament authorising John Murray of Touchadam, to have two fairs: (1) on the first Tuesday of July, and (2) on the second Thursday of November. 1705, c. 35. A.P.S. XI. 275, 276.

Against the granting of this fair, the Commissioner for Stirling in Parliament protested on the ground that the site of the fair was within two miles of Stirling, contrary to a charter by Charles II. to that burgh. *Ibid.*, XI. p. 276. App., p. 96.

BANNOCKBURN.

Town in Stirlingshire. Pop. 2,549.

Fair on the third Tuesday of June.

This fair is, however, dwindling away.

BANNOCKBURN NETHER.

Stirlingshire.

Act of Parliament authorising Sir Hugh Paterson of Bannockburn, to have a weekly market on Tuesday, and two yearly fairs: (1) on the first Tuesday of October, and (2) on the second Tuesday of June. 1696, c. 77. A.P.S. X. 77.

No place is now known as Bannockburn Nether.

The market and fairs above referred to have fallen into disuse for many years.

Barorach.

Town near the Clachan of Campsie, Stirlingshire.

Act of Parliament authorising John Lennox of Woodhead, to have a weekly market on Thursday, and three free fairs: (1) on the first Thursday of August; (2) on 6th November; and (3) on the last Thursday of April. 1695, c. 122. A.P.S. IX. 502.

Blackford.

Village and parish, Perthshire. Pop. of village, 679; of parish, 159.

Act of Parliament authorising Sir Robert Murray of Abercairney to have a free fair on 22nd June. 1672, c. 29. A.P.S. VIII. 75. App. 18.

Report to Convention of Burghs in 1692 that the yearly trade of the burgh of barony of Blackford was estimated at £500. C.R. IV., 569.

Braco.

Village in Perthshire. Pop. 270.

Fairs: (1) on first Wednesday of January; (2) on last Tuesday of April; (3) on first Tuesday of August; and (4) on the last Tuesday of October.

No fairs are now held at Braco.

Broxbrae.

St Ninians, Stirlingshire.

The N.S.A., published in 1845, states that an annual fair for cattle, held in June at Broxbrae, part of the field of Bannockburn, was fast sinking into insignificance. VIII. ii., 339.

Fair on second Thursday after last Friday of May.

This fair has not been held for upwards of 30 years.

Buchlyvie.

Village and *quoad sacra* parish, Stirlingshire. Pop., village, 319; parish, 789.

The O.S.A., published in 1791, states that five fairs were held here annually. XVIII. 341.

The N.S.A., published in 1845, states that several fairs were held here in the course of the year, but that, excepting two or three, they were poorly attended. VIII. ii., 272.

All these fairs have been discontinued. The last was held about two years ago.

Callander.

Town in Perthshire. Pop. 1,522.

The O.S.A., published in 1794, states that the greatest fair here was held on 21st March, or the 10th, O.S., which is called *Fil-ma-chessaig*, or the *Festival of St Kessaig*. Another great fair was held on 16th May, for black cattle, where the drovers found excellent accommodation for themselves and their cows, and were relieved from imposts and several inconveniences which were met with in other places. There were three smaller fairs for country business. XI. 597.

The N.S.A., published in 1845, states that several fairs were held in the parish, one in the month of May for black cattle, sheep, and horses. The fair is called Cockhill, from its being upon a hill of that name. The stance for this market is given free by Mr Hunter, the proprietor of the land. Another very considerable market is held in March, called *Feill-ma-Chessaig*. There are also two or three smaller fairs for the sale of lambs, hiring of reapers, and the transaction of country business. X. 359.

A weekly market used to be held on Thursday, but has long since been discontinued.

Four fairs—(1) known as *Feill-ma-Chessaig*, or more common "the tenth of March fair," was held on the third Thursday of March, principally for hiring servants; (2) known as Cockhill fair, on 16th May, if Saturday, Sunday, or Monday, then on the Tuesday following; (3) on the third Tuesday of July, generally known as the "Groset Fair," and (4) on the third Thursday of December, known as the "Winter Fair."

The fair *Feill-ma-Chessaig* is said to have been so named by reason of its being held on the anniversary of Saint *Kessaig* or *Chessaig*, the patron saint of Callander, to whom the original parish church was dedicated. *Cockhill* fair is said to have been so named from the facts of its being held on a place of that name situated a mile to the south of Callander. It was formerly a fair of considerable importance, having been resorted to by drovers from all parts of the Western Highlands and Islands. Its popularity was probably increased by the privilege which drovers enjoyed of grazing their cattle by day and night for a week previous to the fair, free of charge, over the whole area of Cockhill, which was a very fine grazing. The origin of this privilege is unknown.

Cambusmore.

Act of Parliament granting to Sir Colin Campbell, of Aberuchill, a free fair, for four days, to commence on 8th August, and be called St Mary's fair. 1686, c. 83. A.P.S. VIII. 649.

No fair has been held here from time immemorial.

Clackmannan.

Town in Clackmannanshire. Pop. 1503.

Charter by James V., dated 18th September, 1542, confirming Letters by him under his Privy Seal, dated 18th April, 1517, granted to Sir David Bruce, of Clackmannan, empowering him to have an annual fair in the town of Clackmannan on the Feast of St Bartholomew (24th August) and the octaves of the same. R.M.S. III. 644. No. 2783.

Charter by James V. in favour of William Menteith of Kerse, dated 26th October, 1542, granting him, *inter alia*, the right of holding a fair in Clackmannan on the Feast of St Bartholomew (24th August). R.M.S. III. 657. No. 2828. The sheriffdom of Clackmannan, by James Wallace, sheriff clerk (1890), p. 93.

Charter by Queen Mary, dated 12th February, 1850-51, to David Bruce of Rait, nephew and apparent heir of David Bruce of Clackmannan, knight, of the barony of Clackmannan, erecting the town of Clackmannan into a free burgh of barony, with liberty to the inhabitants to hold two fairs yearly—(1) on St Bartholomew's day, and (2) on the day of Simon and Jude (28th October). R.M.S. IV. p. 129, No. 572.

Charter by Queen Mary, dated 30th October, 1552, in favour of John Monteith, son and apparent heir of Robert Menteith of Kers, of, *inter alia*, the office of sheriff of Clackmannan, with the profits and dues of the public fairs at the town of Clackmannan, held annually on St Bartholomew's day. R.M.S. IV. p. 129, No. 716. Wallace's Clackmannan, p. 95.

Charter by Queen Mary, dated 8th July, 1565, in favour of John Menteith, son and apparent heir of Robert Monteith of Kerse, renewing the grant of 1552. R.M.S. III. 392. Wallace's Clackmannan, p. 95.

Charter by Queen Anne, dated 28th May, 1708, in favour of Mr William Dalrymple of Glenmure, and Alexander Inglis of Murdeston, merchant in Edinburgh, equally of the lands and barony of Clackmannan, with the office of sheriff and forester of the county of Clackmannan, and the privileges, immunities, and customs of the free fair called St Bartholomew's fair at Clackmannan. R.M.S. Lib. 83, No. 157. Wallace's Clackmannanshire, p. 108.

Fair referred to 12th July, 1556. P.C.R. I. 474. Dispute between Menteith, of West Kerse, and Bruce, of Clackmannan, as to right to hold fair, 22nd August, 1569. *Ib.*, II. 13.

Act of Convention of Burghs dated 7th July, 1613, appointing Perth to charge the inhabitants of Clackmannan to desist from using the trade of merchandise. C.R. II. 403.

An Act of Parliament in favour of Sir Henry

Bruce, of Clackmannan, refers to two yearly fairs as having been authorised by charter, one on St Bartholomew's day, and the other on Simeon and Jude's day (29th October), and changes the latter to 15th June. 1663, c. 21. A.P.S. VII. 465, 630. Wallace's Clackmannanshire, p. 98.

The O.S.A., published in 1795, states that two annual fairs were held here, one in June and the other in September, called Bartholomew's fair, where horses, black cattle, coarse linen, and woollen cloth, and all kinds of hardware and haberdashery goods were exposed. Formerly this last was a great market for wool brought from the south county; of late years, however, very small quantities of that article have been brought into it, XIV. 609.

The market cross of Clackmannan is delineated by James Drummond. R.S.A. Proced. Antiq. Scot. IV. 93.

Fair on 26th June, but if that date happens to fall on Saturday, Sunday, or Monday, then on Tuesday following.

JACOBITE TIMES IN THORNHILL DISTRICT.

Much of the land in this district was owned by the Perth family, and hence we were intimately connected with the Jacobite movements. James, the 3rd Earl of Perth, resided for some time at Burnbank. He was a humble and courteous gentleman, and used to ask any herd boys he met in with during his walks if they had a knife, an awl, stocking needles, horn or ivory combs. When they had none of these useful articles, the Earl gave them money to make the purchase.

His son, the 4th Earl, a prominent adherent of the great Montrose, appears to have resided for some time in this locality. He was a determined Catholic, and made offer of honour and preferment to George Drummond of Blair Drummond if he would give up his Protestantism and become a good Catholic. "My lord," said the laird, "my religion, I see, is better than yours." "Oh, why?" "Because you offer boot with yours, my lord."

The battle of Sheriffmuir in 1715 must have set this place astir. Perhaps, as at Alva, "there was no service in the church to-day, our people being away seeing the battle of Shirramuir."

The attempt of bonnie Prince Charlie to recover the throne of his ancestors made a great stir in this otherwise quiet neighbourhood. As the rebel army was on the march to Edinburgh, they passed through Doune, and Duncan M'Pharic, who commanded a company of Highlanders, lodged a night in Thornhill. The Prince slept a night in Fisher's Inn at Ruskie, now owned by Mr M'Keith; and many saw the quaigh and candlestick used by him during his visit, which were shown in the Glasgow Exhibition by Wm. Fisher, Garchel, a descendant of Daniel Fisher, the innkeeper.

In the house where the piper stands puffing and panting, and suffering the heats of summer and the colds of winter, there lived a man of the name of Ballantyne, of whose father or grandfather I have been told that the rebels took a horse from him which entertained strong Hanoverian principles. Like many more of the Prince's followers, that horse deserted the cause and was home in Thornhill before the army reached the Forth. Lennox, from whom also a horse was taken, had to follow his animal to Leckie, where he found it grazing with others in a field, and recovered it without asking leave.

There is at Moss-side a sword, a well-authenticated gift from Prince Charles to the grandfather of Mr Syme, for the loan of a horse.

In Chambers's History of the Rebellion, there is an engraving taken from an original drawing of the Prince and his followers crossing the Forth at the Fords of Frew, the present Bridge not having been built till 1783; and they dared not cross the Bridge of Stirling. I have heard it said that a piece of ordnance was lost in crossing.

Several students from Glasgow set out to witness the battle of Falkirk. Among them were James and Henry, sons of Robert Grahame, Esq., of Brae Cessintully. They were both taken prisoners, and for a time confined in a barn. They were taken with the army to Stirling, where James escaped, but Henry was carried north by the Highlanders. James was licensed by our Presbytery on 27th October 1747, and ordained at Bonhill in 1756. He died in 1767, leaving a son, James, who was a member of the Merchants' House, Glasgow. Henry was licensed by the Inverary Presbytery in 1752, was appointed assistant to the minister of Irvine and ordained at Cumbrae in 1768. He died in 1798, leaving a son, John, who was a Colonel in H.M.E. I.S.C.

John Stewart, uncle of the late James Stewart, farmer, told how, when the Highland army came near Stirling, persons went from Thornhill to see it. In the words of Stewart's diary, "Laird Lennox's grandfather and Andrew Sommers (whose blossams early pu'd' lie in the churchyard) were standing, as Andrew told, beside a farmhouse looking on, and ere they were aware a wing of the army had them nearly enclosed. They were frightened enough," and the writer goes on to tell how he got a fright at a sham fight at Kincardine when he was a boy.

But those that are frightened can frighten in their turn. The same writer tells us that the rebels on their journey north came to Maccoriston and ordered the mistress to bake some cakes for them. Stewart's grandfather, in order to get rid of them, got two men to go a little way off and "beat on a wecht," while another cried in at the window of the house, "The Duke's com ng, the Duke's coming." They left without their cakes, "unwept, unhonoured, and unsung."

A desertion from the Jacobite ranks took place at the Bridge of Teith. A man of the name of Macfarlane, from the Ruskie locality—a great grandfather or granduncle of Rev. R. Thomson, from whom I had the story, was forced into the service of the rebels. He felt loth to go far from home, sweet home. At the Bridge of Teith he took leg bail. His departure was noticed and a soldier fired at him. With great coolness and contempt he stooped down, and, turning up the posterior folds of his kilt, cried, "Fire awa, fire awa."

In Nimmo's History of Stirlingshire, we are informed that a Captain Campbell paid a suspicious visit at Wester Frew on the night before the Prince re-crossed the Forth. Robert Forrester pointed out the ford west of his house as the probable crossing, thus misleading him. The Captain emptied a sackful of caltrops into it to lame the rebel cavalry. Charles only crossed by this ford, and his horse was lamed.

Robert Forrester's son, John, was curious to see the great man about whom so much of an ado was made; and "though no one showed him to me," he told Rev. Patrick Murray of Kilmadock, "there was something about him which pointed him out among ten thousand as the son of a king."

ROB ROY.

A prominent character about this time was that famous adherent of King Spulzie, Rob Roy. I have failed to find out any connection between this parish and the old Rob Roy, but his sons were in several respects connected with the district. Robert MacGregor's first wife was a Graham of Drunkie, a family which came to this parish and lived at Wester Boquhapple. An old rhyme says of some of them—

> "Ye may ken the Misses Graham,
> Ye may ken them by their runnin';
> They were at the Borland Ball
> Wi' daft Ba'four an' lang Buchanan."

Their descendants are with us unto this day.

The laird of Middleton is a descendant on the father's side of the enemies of Rob Roy, one of whom young Rob shot as he was ploughing in the field. One of the legal gentlemen that were concerned in his trial for the abduction of Jean Key was James Fairfowl, J.P., of Braendam. One of the young MacGregors, being chased from Stirling for circulating the Pretender's manifesto, called at Ochtertyre to buy a horse, which Mr Ramsay sold rather than that he should take him for nothing, which shows us how these gentry were not by any means disposed to stick at trifles.

NORRIESTON, THORNHILL.

Norrieston was at one time a collection of mean hut homes huddled together on the road between the Ford of Frew and the Ford of Lanrick which crossed the Goodie by the bridge at Mill of Goodie. For many years there were Norries in this district. James Norrie, along with Thomas M'Coran, several Spittals and Mackisons, are mentioned in the Exchequer Rolls of Scotland as holding King's lands in 1480. It was not for a hundred years that Knowhead, where the churchyard now is, was known by its new name Norrieston. Each home in the village clustered round the house of Norrie of that ilk, and had its grass falls and corn rigs, its peat stack and midden, owning the laird as superior.

Norrieston is the mother of Thornhill. When Gabriel Norrie, "wis and prudent man," gave the plot of ground for a kirkyard, Thornhill was covered with briars and brambles and yellow broom and whins. The date of Mrs Small's house was 1691, although there may have been several older. Mr Jenkins' house was feued from Archibald Napier, King's Boquhapple, and his wife Annabell Linton, in 1696. After the road between Stirling and the fort at Inversnaid was made, about 1713, the inhabitants of Norrieston began to feu and build on both sides of it, and between 1730 and 1740 an increase of population in the parish is accounted for by the additions made to the village of Thornhill. In 1792, the population of Norrieston was 626. In 1799 the population of Thornhill was

325; Kippen, 380; Gargunnock and Buchlyvie, about 500 each; and Doune, 939.

Near the close of last century the men were employed for the most part in agriculture, while the women spent their time at the loom, knitting and tambouring. A hundred years ago tanning was an important trade here. About 20 men were employed in this industry. James Campbell, whose tannery was where Mr Sand's workshop now stands, got much of his leather made into shoes for exportation abroad. He died about 1773.

The manufacture of malt spirits was carried on to a great extent. This industry was put a stop to by an Act restricting it to stills of a larger capacity than any that could be profitably set to work in the village. Thornhill whisky was famous in Edinburgh and Glasgow. The water of a well on the farm of Middleton was carried to Edinburgh to make a choice kind of liquor. There were seven licensed houses in the village when Rev. Christopher Tait wrote his statistical account. He complains "these seven houses produce very pernicious effects, especially when the innkeepers are low persons," and he connects the traffic in drink with "a want of veracity and respect for the law, intemperance, fraud and pilfering, and the habit of defrauding the government."

In 1695, there was an Act of Parliament authorising Archibald Napier, King's town of Balquhapple, to have a weekly market on Thursday and four free fairs: (1) on the 20th October, (2) on the 14th November, (3) on the first Tuesday of March, (4) on the third Tuesday of June.

Before 1760, the houses were miserable huts, holes without windows or glass, at least. In 1790, all the houses in the village had glazed windows. The first slated house was the present post office. In these early days the church even was thatched. The minister of Kincardine at the close of last century tells us that the villages "have become a little more attentive to cleanliness than they were formerly, but there is still too much room for improvement in this article with respect to their persons, and still more with respect to their houses." "A cart of peats cost 6d in the moss, and a cart of coals containing 7 or 8 cwts. cost 1s 7½d at Bannockburn, and the carriage to Thornhill is 3s." This was a hundred years ago. At a more recent date there were 40 looms in the village, 6 or 8 shoemakers, 9 tailors, 2 coopers, a saddler, 3 or 4 nailers, and as many smiths, while the horner came for a few days periodically and sold his wares in Thornhill and surrounding district. In 1837, "letters arrive every Monday, Wednesday, and Friday, and are despatched on Monday, Thursday, and Saturday afternoon at one in winter and five o'clock in summer."

The Public Hall

was built about the beginning of the century as a place of worship for the "new licht" anti-burghers. This body never had a settled ministry here, but was content with occasional supplies. It was at the same time used as a school, and a Sabbath School was conducted in it. The burgher and anti-burgher new lichts joined in 1820, and the worshippers at Thornhill were absorbed in the Bridge of Teith Church. The hall was then bought as a school by some that were dissatisfied with the teaching of Mr Junkine. As a school it had a very successful career. It was called the Grammar School or the Easter School, in distinction to the other or Wester School. It was never denominational. When the Education Act was passed, the school was handed over to the public for a village hall.

The First of the Norries of Norrieston.

Robert Norry was confidential servant of James I from 1429 to 1437. He was steward of the household during the minority of James II, and the faithful personal attendant of the King till his death in 1454. In 1446 he rode to Caithness on the affairs of the King. One can see how Robert would be rewarded for his faithful services. At one time he receives the "fermes" rents of Torry, at another time the rents of the lands of Frew. For riding to Edinburgh with the news that an heir was born to James II (afterwards James III), he receives the lands of the ward of Gudy in Menteith and Queenshaugh in the Sheriffdom of Stirling. At his death in 1454, the lands of the ward of Gudy and Queenshaugh passed into the hands of the Queen (Mary of Gueldres.) Just before his death, the King gave him the lands of Buchquhopill in exchange for the lands of Frew. Robert died, however, before the bargain was concluded, for we read, "granted to the deceased Robert Norry." These lands remained with his heirs.

Thornhill. G. W.

FAIRS AND MARKETS IN THE STIRLING DISTRICT.

(Continued.)

C. DENNY.

Town in Stirlingshire. Pop. of town proper, 2823; of town and suburbs, 4080.

Act of Parliament authorising John Earl of Wigtown to have a weekly market on Wednesday; and four annual fairs: (1) on the last Wednesday of April; (2) on 22nd of June; (3) on 4th August; and (4) on 5th November. 1705, c. 22. A.P.S. XI. 272. App., p. 95.

The N.S.A., published in 1845, states that two fairs were held annually in the parish on about Whitsunday, and the other about Martinmas. VIII. ii. 138.

Fairs: (1) on the Wednesday before the 12th of May, and (2) on the Wednesday after 11th November. These fairs are rapidly falling into disuse.

DOLLAR.

Town and parish in Clackmannshire and Perthshire. Pop. of town, 2014; of parishes, 2500.

Act of Parliament authorising James Earl of Perth to have a weekly market on Wednesday; and two annual fairs: (1) on second Tuesday of June, and (2) on second Tuesday of October. 1686, c. 100. A.P.S. VIII. 653.

Grant to Archibald Earl of Argyle of two free fairs: (1) on 8th of June; (2) on 8th October. 1701, c. 30. A.P.S. X. 331. App., p. 103.

The N.S.A. published in 1845, states that four fairs were stated to be held in Dollar, but that only two deserved notice—those, namely, in May and October. In both cattle were chiefly sold, horses and sheep being seldom seen there. At the May fair, the chief transactions were the sale of cattle that had been kept during the winter on straw and turnips. At the October fair, young cattle chiefly were sold to farmers and others who required manure, and were resold at the May market. VIII. ii. 119.

Two fairs: (1) on the second Monday of May, and (2) on the third Monday of October.

They are of little importance.

DOUNE.

Village in Perthshire. Pop. 996.

Charter by James VI, dated 17th April, 1611, in favour of James Earl of Murray, of the lands, lordship, and earldom of Murray, and specially, *inter alia*, of the burgh of barony of Doune *alias*

Douncampsie, with the privilege of a weekly market on Friday, and

Two free fairs yearly (1) on 24th July on the parktownmoor of Doune, and (2) on 6th October on the Castlehill of Doune. R.M.S. VII. No. 465.

Act of Parliament in favour of Alexander Earl of Murray, ratifying the above charter. 1661, c. 376. A.P.S. VII. 349.

Act of Parliament in his favour referring to the above grant of a weekly market and fairs; altering the market day from Friday to Thursday; changing the fair day from 6th (16th) October to 15th December; and authorising the fairs formerly held at Kilmahoug and Kilmadock *(q.v.)* to be kept at Doune in future. 1669, c. 134. A.P.S. VII. 663.

Report to the Convention of Burghs in 1692, that the yearly trade of the stewartry and city of Doune was estimated at £8000, C.R. IV., 569.

Act of Convention of Burghs, dated 11th December, 1705, authorising communication of trade to Doune. C.R., IV., 381; 8th February, 1719, C.R. IV., 211.

The market cross of Doune is delineated and described by James Drummond, R.S.A. Proced. Antiq. Scot. IV. 113, 114.

The O.S.A., published in 1798, contains interesting information in regard to the Falkirk Tryst and to this fair. IX. 595, 597. It also states that six fairs are annually held here at Martinmas, Yule, Candlemas, Whitsunday, Lammas, and Michaelmas. The fairs at Michaelmas and Martinmas are large cattle markets, little inferior to the famous trysts at Falkirk, XX. 80.

The N.S.A., published in 1845, gives six annual fairs: (1) Candlemas fair on 11th February, for grain and general business; (2) May fair on second Wednesday of May, for milch cows and cattle for grazing; (3) July fair on 26th July, for hiring shearers and general business; (4) the Great fair, called the Latter fair, on the first Tuesday and Wednesday of November, for sheep on Tuesday, and for black cattle on Wednesday; (5) on the fourth Wednesday of November, this fair is next in importance to the Latter fair, and (6) Yule fair, on the last Wednesday of December, for fat cattle, grain, and general business. X. 1242.

Fairs were subsequently held here: (1) on the second Wednesday of May; (2) the last Wednesday of July; (3) on the first Tuesday and Wednesday of Movember, known as the Latter fair, and (4) on the fourth Wednesday of November.

The only fairs now held here are those in July and November.

DRYMEN.

Village and parish in Stirlingshire. Pop. of village, 234; of parish, *quoad civilia*, 1431, *quoad sacra*, 764.

Act of Parliament authorising William Buchanan of Drumakill, to have a weekly market on Thursday, and two annual fairs: (1) on 10th May, and (2) on 15th October. 1669, c. 131. A.P.S. VII. 662.

Act of Parliament confirming two fairs, called St Colmes days, in use to be kept; (1) on 9th June, and (2) on 23rd August. 1670, c. 19. A.P.S. VIII. 20.

Act of Parliament changing the fair authorised to be held on 15th October from that date to 29th October, and other fairs and weekly market confirmed. 1681, c. 165. A.P.S. VIII. 440.

The N.S.A., published in 1845, states that there used to be a fair almost every month, but that of late years they had been reduced to four, chiefly for the hiring of servants. VIII. ii. 110.

No weekly market has been held here from time immemorial.

For many years four fairs have been held annually; (1) on the last Wednesday of April, for grazing cattle and sheep; (2) on the day after Callender, in May, for cattle, sheep, and horses; this is the old *Shandon fair*, and was brought down from the Muir, north of the town, 30 or 40 years ago, to the square in Drymen; (3) on 21st May, but if that Saturday, Sunday, or Monday, then on the Tuesday following, for hiring servants; and (4) on the first Friday in November, for hiring servants. About eight years ago an additional fair for cattle and sheep was commenced and held on Friday before the first Doune market in November. There are thus, now, five yearly fairs here.

DUNBLANE.

Town and burgh of regality, in Perthshire, Pop. 2186.

The city of Dunblane and the lands of the bishopric erected into a free barony in favour of the bishop. 1442, c. 8. A.P.S. II. 58.

Formerly a bishop's see, situated within the barony of Cromlix, the superior of which, Lord Kinnoul, formerly named a bailie, who resided in the town. M.C.R. II. 38.

Fair on 10th August, referred to in an Act of the Privy Council, dated 28th May, 1611. P.C.R. IX. 182.

Act of Parliament authorising a weekly market on Thursday.

Three annual fairs, on Whitsunday, Laurenceday, and Hallowday, referred to as having existed from time immemorial; and a new fair granted to Lieut.-General William Drummond and his heirs, to be held on 1st March yearly, and called St. Monance fair. 1669, c. 9. A.P.S. VII. 557, 558.

Report to the Convention of burghs in 1692 that the yearly trade of the regality and city of Dunblane was estimated at £8000. C.R. IV. 569.

The fairs and markets above referred to are not now held.

ELPHINSTONE.

Village in the parish of Airth, Stirlingshire.

Charter by King Charles II, dated 1st February, 1673, in favour of John Lord Elphinstone, of the lands, lordship, and barony of Elphinstone, and erecting the town of Elphinstone, viz., Overtown and Nethertown thereof, commonly called the Saltpans, into a burgh of barony, with power to him to erect a market cross therein, and to have a weekly market on Tuesday, and a free fair for three days annually, commencing on 9th September.

Act of Parliament ratifying the above charter. 1681, c. 156. A.P.S. VIII. 430.

A fair is held here on the last Tuesday of July annually.

THE MINISTERS OF KINCARDINE-IN-MENTEITH.

In Roman Catholic times the parishioners were supplied with religious ordinances by the monks of Cambuskenneth Abbey, and after the people of Scotland threw off the yoke of Rome ministers and readers were placed to fill the place of the former clergy. According to Hew Scott, the parish of Kincardine was supplied by Alexander Anderson, Reader, in 1574; David Hay, Wm. Stevenson, and Michael Lermonth, who was presented to the living by James VI, in 1584. Lermonth was succeeded by Rev. Wm. Stirling, who was translated from Kincardine to the Port of Menteith, in 1597.

In 1599, John Aissoun was ordained and inducted. He seems to have been a man of means, for he left ten merks to build the library of Glasgow College. On the death of Aissoun, in 1636, David Ouchterlony succeeded. He filled the pulpit for 14 years. His widow, Christian Aissoun, probably a daughter of the previous minister, had her house plundered, and "the utensils and domicills, sua farr as war not robbed, spulzied and taken away by the enemy," were valued at ten pounds.

We come next to a "hame owre" name, Thomas Forrester. He seems to have been a most conscientious man, for we find him refusing the test—an oath to own the Headship of the King in ecclesiastical as well as civil causes, to renounce the Covenants, to discountenance all Assemblies held without the royal sanction, &c. To all which Thomas Forrester refused to swear, and in consequence was removed from the pulpit. He could demit his charge all the more readily, because he possessed property of his own.

His place was filled by John Cameron. Cameron was of the Lochiel branch of that famous clan, and warmly espoused the cause of his chief. Too warmly, for the Privy Council, on 29th August, 1689, removed him; "for not reading the proclamation of Estates, for not praying for their majesties, for employing one who prayed for King James, not observing the national thanksgiving, for not reading the proclamation for the collection, bringing down the rebels to rob his parishioners, and saying, 'If God would not give amends of them, he would make the devil do it.'" This rabid Jacobite lived till 1719, and died in Edinburgh, aged 65.

Rev. John Cameron, Dunoon,
Brother of the 16th Lochiel.

John C., Principal of Glasgow University.	Thomas.	Archibald.
	Thomas.	

Rev. John of Kincardine.

Died 6th June, 1719, aged 65; married, 1682, Margaret Barclay, and in 1701, Elizabeth Lucklow, a lady in whose veins flowed the blood of the Scotts of Balwearie, the Montrose Grahams, and the Drummonds of Perth.

His son, Dr Thomas Cameron, born 1704, practised medicine in Worcester, and left a numerous colony of "Cameron men" there.

A young practitioner apologised for being late in keeping an appointment with him by saying, "I've been so busy." Replied the Doctor, "When, sir, you have as much to do as I have, you'll learn to be punctual."

One of the Wallace line succeeded—Matthew Wallace, ordained in 1695. He was "remarkable for his great appetite, and for being able to drink a great deal without being the worse of it. He used to say that a man that could not hold a pint must content himself with a chopin." He had a son who was famous in his day, Dr Robert Wallace of Edinburgh.

It was during his ministry that the village of Thornhill began to be built, a circumstance which gave an impetus to the population. We owe it, perhaps, most of all to Mr Wallace that we have a church in the west end of the parish. He arranged with his co-presbyters of the Port and Kilmadock to preach once a fortnight time about with them. But these two brethren soon tired of the extra work. Mr Wallace, however, continued, and, doubtless, his services were much appreciated. I cannot find that there was any church specially built for these services. Perhaps they held worship in the open air in the kirkyard, already begun to be covered with gravestones, or, perhaps, in some commodious shed or large room in the immediate vicinity of our present kirks.

Matthew Wallace died in 1727, aged 55, his son being at this time minister of Moffat.

John Smith came as minister in 1728. After his ordination, an examination was made into the state of the parish, at which it was found that Mr Murray was a sufficient session clerk and schoolmaster. There were "two or three private schools in other corners of the parish, particularly at Thornhill." The Earl of Perth, the patron of the parish, had mortified 2000 merks for the teacher's salary (now known as the Perth Mortification.) Quarterly school fees, 20d for Latin pupils and a merk for English. Some dozen Bibles were got from Edinburgh, and distributed among the poor scholars by the session. Mr Smith seems to have been highly esteemed in the parish, and to have had a fair share of common sense. He was not much more than a year settled when he told the session that he did not incline to keep up sermon at Thornhill "each fourtnight by himself, unless the ministers of Kilmadock and the Port join him." Besides, there was generally a "slack attendance" when he preached there. He was decidedly opposed to the erection of the Chapel of Ease at Norrieston. There had been a proposal made as early as 1650, when Forrester was minister, to get this wester end of Kincardine and outlying parts of Kilmadock and the Port of Monteith united for religious purposes. The ground was perambulated by order of Parliament, in 1653, although no steps of a practical character were taken to further the object till 1720.

In 1729 it was reported that an aliment had been secured by voluntary contributions for two or three years for a preacher to the west end of the parish. Mr Smith opposed the Thornhill people. "If they had taken the measure he first proposed," says the session record, "they might have met with a soft answer." "The minister reported that now the gentlemen of this and the neighbouring parishes had taken alarm at the design of those people in trying to secure a preacher, that they had appeared personally and by proxy before the Presbytery to oppose them, and the Presbytery would not venture to let it go to a higher judicatory, but would rather dissuade the people to desist than irritate the whole gentry and nobility who were joined unanimously to withstand the proposal."

One of the nobility referred to in the above minute of kirk session was Lord Napier of Ballinton. "His ideas were very much English." We quote from Ramsay's "Scotland and Scotsmen." "Whilst the affair of Norrieston Chapel was in agitation, he wrote the Presbytery signifying his disapprobation of settling a *curate* there." The brethren were very wroth because their ruling elder had used a word so entirely and exclusively English and Episcopal. Even his cousin, good Archibald Napier, could not defend him." The good Archibald, his cousin, was son of the laird of King's Boquhapple and minister of Kilmadock. [He who removed the Kilmadock Church East to the village of Doune in 1746, and who owned King's Boquhapple in succession to his father.]

Despite such violent and influential opposition, the parishioners gained their point. A new church was built in 1728, and was opened in March 29 by Rev. Mr Duncan, Tillicoultry. At this service Mr Duncan caught a bad cold. The weather was tempestuous, and there was a severe fall of snow. Suffice it to say, he met his death in May following, at the early age of 31. Mr Duncan was a man of wit, and a volume of expositions on the Epistle of the Hebrews proves his ability.

Norrieston secured preachers at length, and for a list of their names Dr Scott has again to be thanked.

Henry Moir.

Robert Wingate, afterwards of Abdie. He was licensed by the Dunblane Presbytery in 1746, and ordained at Abdie in 1752; died 1788. After

Wingate left, John Bruce was appointed in 1744, and continued here till he died, in 1758. David Carmichael, afterwards ordained in Pittinain; and, last of all, John Knox, who was called to Slamannan. This brings us up to 1766, at which date we have a line of ministers of our own to follow out.

Mr Smith was troubled with the Secession, and a great many of his parishioners left him. "Many Seceders," says Ramsay, "refused his ministrations because he had homolgated the defections of the judicatories!"

Mr Smith's communion roll contained 800 names, an increase upon that of Mr Forrester, which in 1651 numbered 450.

Some of Mr Smith's sentiments do him honour, *e.g.*, on appointing the Sacrament of the Lord's Supper, he prayed that God "would beautify His own ordinance with much of His merciful and gracious presence." He died in 1768, having served the parish for the long period of 40 years.

SCOTTISH CUSTOMS AND FOLK-LORE.

SHIRES OF STIRLING AND DUNBARTON.

In former times funerals were conducted on different principles from those in fashion to-day. In the neighbourhood of Campsie when the head of a family died, the custom at one time prevailed of issuing a general invitation to the parishioners to attend the fnneral. The guests were usually accommodated in a b..rn, where refreshments, consisting of cake, bread and cheese, ale and whisky, were served in no stinted way. The proceedings began early in the forenoon, but the "lifting," as the removal of the coffin from the house was popularly styled, did not take place till well on in the afternoon. As a rule the coffin was carried to the place of interment on hand-spokes.

Till within recent times sturdy beggars, "sorners" as they were often called, were the special bugbears of kirk-sessions and burgh officials. An entry in the session records of St Ninians parish, under date 1665, tells of the appointment of a constable to stand at the style on Sundays for the purpose of turning back vagrants, with authority, if they proved refractory, to put them in the stocks or in the steeple. There are also references to vagrancy in the "Extracts from the Burgh Records of Stirling"—a series of documents throwing much light on social life in by gone days.

From that source we learn that in the 17th century the town was so infested with vagrants that in 1699 steps were taken to abate the evil. For this purposes badges were given to the resident poor, and those not so qualified were expelled from the burgh. Four years before the Magistrates and Council sought to relieve the necessities of the poor by ordaining that the church bells should be rung at funerals on their behoof, the amount paid for the ringing of the bells to be received by the kirk-session for distribution among those requiring and deserving such help. About sixty years earlier a velvet mortcloth was brought into use in connection with the funerals of guild brethren. An entry of the time records that "na gratis gildbreither, ather bygane or to cum, sall have no benefit of the same to cover their corps, bot that the same clyth sall pertene only to the use of the gildbreither, present and to cum, quha hes payit and payis for their libertie allanerlye." The custom of ringing a hand-bell in front of a funeral procession was long maintained. We learn that in 1747 the Treasurer of the Council was instructed, on account of the insufficiency of the dead bell then in use, to order a new one, the old bell to be given in part payment for the same. A piper was employed by the burgh to accompany the town drummer on his rounds morning and evening. He had a fixed salary and a free house, and in addition was authorised to play at penny weddings within the burgh territory. Certain abuses seem to have crept in in connection with such festive gatherings, for in 1680 the Magistrates and Council issued an order that in future "noe person exact nor receave, within this burgh and territorie, noe laweing nor pryce exceiding eight shilling Scottis frae each persone, under the payne of twentie pundis Scottis money for each transgressien."

Chapmen formerly held a more important position as distributors of merchandise than at present, when greater facilities for travelling allow people to do their own shopping. There was an incorporation of such retail traders in Stirlingshire, as elsewhere, and liberty was granted to the members to elect a Lord-Chapman and other officials for the proper regulation of the Society. A chapmen's race was run in the burgh, and in 1733 a gold ring of the value of a guinea or thereby was offered by the Town Council as a prize. Other races were at one time popular in the town. We read that in 1673 the Magistrates and Council arranged that a horse race should take place on the Bridge Haugh 15 days after Cupar Race. In connection with it they recommended that a silver cup should be provided as a prize. Notices of several races occur under date 1706, viz. :—"A goose race to be ryden for by the maltmen of this burgh, upon the Saturday immediately befor Whitsunday next, as also ane horse race for ane fyne saddel and furnitur, to the value of xii. lib. 14s, . . . as also ane foot race . . . for ane pair of new stockines, ane pair of new shoes, and ane blew bonnet." Archery was also a favourite sport. In May, 1679, the town treasurer was instructed to provide a silver bow and arrow as a prize to be shot for by the archers in the Friars Yard. The morals as well as the amusements of the burghers were attended to by the civic authorities. In 1701 the Magistrates and Town Councillors recommended that a Court should be held every Saturday to investigate cases of alleged profanity and Sabbath-breaking, with a view to the punishment of the offenders. Functionaries, styled private censurers, were to be appointed in every quarter of the burgh. Their duty was to supply information to the magistrates, and as a reward for their diligence and fidelity they were to receive a certain proportion of the fines.

About a century before attempts had been made to put down duelling. From an entry of date 1604 we learn that it was ordained "that quhatsomever gild brother wretis cartallis to uther that the wretar of the cartell sall pay the soume of —— and tyne his fredome, and the resavar of the cartell that acceptis the provocatioun sal be under the lyk paine gif the same be not revelit be the said partie quha acceptis the same." In troublous times the guild brethren had to act as a town guard, and were accordingly required to have arms at hand to be in readiness for any emergency. Even in our own days the itinerant doctor is not unknown. He may still be seen occasionally in our streets on the outlook for patients among the passers-by. Such practitioners were formerly more common. In Stirling, in 1710, a certain Mr Francis Clerk, "practitioner of physick and chyrugerie," was allowed to erect a stage in the public street on condition that he should not receive patients till after one o'clock on market days.

In the 17th century Dunbartonshire was known as the "shyre of Dun-Britton." This spelling gives a clue to its etymology, since the name means the "fort of the Britons." The fortress, anciently called *Alcluth—i.e.*, the "rock of the Clyde," was the capital of the kingdom of Strath-Clyde, extending from Cumberland and Westmoreland through the counties of Dumfries, Peebles, Ayr, Lanark, and Renfrew into Dunbartonshire. Rydderch Hael, the friend of Kentigern, became king of Strath-Clyde in 573. Dunbarton was several times besieged. In 756 it was captured by the Angles under Eadbert, and in 870 by the Norsemen, under Olaf the White, King of Dublin. The town was created a royal burgh by Alexander II. in 1222. Till the beginning of the present century the houses had a quaint, old-world appearance, and were marked by the number rather than by the size of their rooms. During the 17th century the Magistrates seem to have been specially active in looking after the welfare of the burgh. They fixed the price of provisions, saw that strangers did not remain within the town without having their antecedents inquired into, tried witches, and otherwise performed the duties at that time incumbent on civic authorities. Since 1292 the castle has been a royal fortress. During the War of Independence it was associated with the exploits of Bruce, who died at the neighbouring castle of Cardross. The county was formerly known as *Levenach* or Lennox—*i.e.*, the "district of the Leven." In 1175 Dunbartonshire and part of Stirlingshire were formed into the Earldom of Lennox by William the Lyon, and granted to his brother, David. The picturesque glen through which flows the Fruin on its way to Loch Lomond was in 1603 the scene of a bloody fight between the Colquhouns of Luss and marauding bands of Macgregors. On account of their conduct on this occasion, the Macgregors incurred the vengeance of James VI., and their clan name was proscribed by Act of the Privy Council a few months later. Another severe statute was passed against them in 1621, but these Acts were repealed in 1775. Till the latter date members of the clan usually took the name of various landed proprietors. Thus the famous Rob Roy, who died in 1736, was called Campbell after the family name of his patron, the Duke of Argyll.

In Roseneath, parish marriage rites used to be more elaborate than they are now. Crowds assembled at the ceremony, and for several days thereafter the newly-married couple, accompanied by a piper, went from house to house to visit their friends. In the early part of the present century shinty was a specially favourite game in the parish. A match was held annually on New-Year's Day, and many hundreds gathered to witness or to take part in it. There were music and banners on the occasion, and the day usually ended with a ball. On the farms round Gareloch some old harvest customs lingered till about sixty years ago. These had to do with the cutting of the last sheaf, "the maiden," as it was called there, as in some other parts of Scotland. "The maiden" was usually decked with ribbons and hung up in the farmhouse, where it was allowed to remain for months, and sometimes for years.

As is well known, the Forth and Clyde Canal joins the latter river at Bowling. The construction of the canal was begun in 1768 by a company having as its chairman Sir Laurence Dundas, after whom the district of Port-Dundas was named. The expense was found to be greater than was expected, and the canal was not finished till 1790, £15,000 having meanwhile been granted by Government to aid its completion. The formal opening was made quite a festive occasion. The committee of management, accompanied by the Magistrates of Glasgow, sailed along the entire length of the canal, and a hogshead of water brought from the Forth was poured into the Clyde to symbolise the union of the two rivers.

J. M. MACKINLAY.

VISIT OF ENGLISH ARCHÆOLOGISTS TO STIRLING.

On Wednesday, 12th August, 1891, the members of the Royal Archæological Institute of Great Britain and Ireland had an excursion to Stirling.

INSPECTION OF THE PARISH CHURCH.

The Parish Church was visited under the direction of Mr G. Washington Browne, architect, Edinburgh. The following are Mr Browne's notes on the building, as printed in the official handbook to the places visited :—

The Church consists of nave and choir, with a space between, which may have formed transepts, but which has been so modernised as to destroy all traces of its original form. Both nave and choir have side aisles; the east end of the choir terminates with the polygonal apse (an irregular semi-octagon) of frequent occurrence in 16th century churches in Scotland; the tower is at the west end of the nave, its north and south walls prolonging the line of the nave arcades.

The nave and choir are of different dates. They were divided by a partition wall erected in 1656, and are now separated by a corridor, vestries, &c., into east and west churches. The choir was erected in the early years of the 16th century, say 1507-23. From the Register of Dunfermline Abbey we learn that on 3rd May, 1507, indentures were made between the abbot and convent of the abbey, and the provost, bailies, council, and community of the burgh of Stirling, "in maner and forme eftir following, that is to say that the saidis provest, ballies, counsale, and communite of the said burgh has takin apon hand to big and compleitlie edifye and end ane gud and sufficient queyr conformand to the body of the peroch kirk of the said burgh or bettir, and sall deliver to the saidis abbot and convent, the said body of thair peroch kirk of Striveling frely to remane with thame as ane queir ay and quhill the said queyr now to be biggit be fullely completit and endit; for the quhilk biggin of the said queyr to be biggit and compleitlie endit be the saidis provest, balyeis, counsale, and communite of the said burgh of Striveling." The abbot and convent on their part undertook to contribute the sum of 200 pounds Scots, and to furnish the ornaments for the high altar; and further, to pay 40 shillings yearly towards the upholding of the same; and in the Stirling burgh records, under date 27th April, 1523, is entered the deliverance of "the somme of xl pundis in pairt of payment of ane mair somme for temyr to the queir of the kirk of the said burgh."

The walls are dressed of stone, inside and outside; the side aisles are groined in stone, and covered with a flat roof, above which rises the clerestory. The central aisle of the choir has an oak roof, the timbers of which are hidden by modern lining, and the apse is covered with a ribbed stone vault of pointed section, and roofed externally with stone flags.

The windows of the aisles and apse are tall, and filled with tracery, all modern, except the two side windows of the apse, which retain the original stone. The eastern end of the choir, with the apse, forms a very effective piece of architecture, especially from the outside, where the falling ground gives additional height to the walls of this part of the church.

The date of the nave, which is earlier than the choir, can be determined with nearly the same accuracy. It is obviously a 15th century building, though the massive cylindrical piers of the arcade, and the semicircular headed windows of the clerestory over, might seem at first sight to claim a much greater antiquity. The details, alike of mouldings and carvings, are clearly not of early date, and similar cylindrical piers are found in the nave of Dunkeld Cathedral, the foundations of which were laid in 1406. In the Chamberlain's account for the year 5th July, 1413, to 27th June, 1414, occurs the following entry:—"The Chamberlain discharges himself of the issues of an ayre (an itinerant court) held at Stirling, because it was granted to the work of the parish church which had been burnt." References in the register of Dunfermline Abbey show that a church existed in Stirling from an early period in the 12th century, and it probably occupied the site of the present parish church, but from the entry last quoted it is evident that building, or a successor of it, was burnt, and the parish church was rebuilt in 1413-14. This date coincides with the style of the present nave, and the cylindrical piers find their counterpart in their contemporaries at Dunkeld.

The nave is five bays long; the side aisles are vaulted in stone, the central aisle has an oak roof, under which an imitation groined ceiling in plaster has been introduced and should be removed.

The church was dedicated to the Holy Cross, and references are found in pre-Reformation times to no fewer than nineteen altars besides the high altar, viz., St Lawrence, St James, St Thomas, Holy Bluid, St Katerine, Our Lady, St Luke, St Matthew, St Michael, St Ninian, St John the Baptist, St Mary, St Andrew, St Salvator, St Stephen, St Anne, the Virgin, SS. Peter and Paul, and the Trinity. The consecration crosses are to be seen incised on walls and piers both in nave and choir; and in connection with the dedication of the church to the Holy Cross or Holy Rood, it is interesting to notice upon the surface of hundreds of stones, both outside and inside the nave, the incision of five minute circles arranged to form the points and intersection of the arms of small crosses, varying in size from $1\frac{1}{2}$ inches downwards, thus:—

∘
∘ ∘ ∘
∘

Beyond the walls of the nave aisle, on the north side, were two chapels, which have been identified as the Laird of Garden's aisle and Duncan Paterson's aisle. The latter is traditionally known as Queen Margaret's chapel, said to have been erected by James IV. in honour of his queen. The style of architecture coincides with the period, and the rose and thistle carved upon the arch leading into the chapel give colourable support to this tradition. Beyond the south aisle wall, in the eastmost bay, was Bowey's aisle or the Puir's aisle, afterwards the Earl of Stirling's aisle; and projecting from the second bay, from the west end on south side, was a porch or "bourock." The jambs of an earlier door are still to be seen built up under the cill of existing window in this bay. The tracery in all the windows of the nave was inserted about 1820, and at the same time the door through the tower was wholly destroyed by being partially built up and partly demolished to lower the cill of the window over it.

The tower to the level of the ridge of the nave roof seems contemporary with the nave. At this level the stone employed changes, but the architecture does not indicate a long interval of time between the lower and the upper stages. A water table built into the east wall of the tower indicates an intention of raising the nave roof some 8 feet, but this has never been carried out. The tower contains four bells, one of pre-Reformation date, to which the Rev. G. Mure Smith (minister of the West Parish Church) has already publicly called attention. I am indebted to him for a rubbing of the inscription, which is as follows:—"+ Ave Maria gratia plena dominus tecum benedicta tu immulieribus et Benedicta." The legend stops thus abruptly, there being no room for its completion within the circumference of the bell.

Treasurer Ronald of Stirling has recently published, in pamphlet form, two lectures read by him before the Stirling Natural History and Archæological Society, containing particulars of much interest regarding this church, a publication to which reference has been made in the preparation of the above notes in supplement to *Charters relating to the Burgh of Stirling*, and *Records of the Burgh of Stirling*, published in 1884 and 1887 respectively.

Mr Browne, in addressing the party in the Church, laid great stress on such points as supported his theory that the nave was not erected before the beginning of the 15th century. It was a fair assumption that the parish church which had previously existed occupied the same site, but no such remote antiquity could be claimed for the present fabric. The semicircular arch was in Scotland no evidence of antiquity; it was by no means sure to be Norman, but was quite as likely to be 15th or 16th century work. The date 1413 coincided with the appearance of the nave and the large cylindrical piers. There were no Norman features in the building; he had disposed of the only two which he thought superficially claimed to be considered on their merits. With regard to the piers, he said the sections of the caps, the sections of the mouldings, and their relation to the width of the piers, conclusively satisfied an architect that the Church was not Norman but belonged to the 15th century. They would notice a change in the section of the two pillars at the east end of the West Church. These were not cylindrical but fluted and clustered, and the theory was that originally there was no choir to the Parish Church, which was terminated by a chancel equal to the nave itself, and that a rood screen at that time existed between these clustered piers. Calling attention to the incisions in the form of a cross, he wished to emphasise the fact that they were found equally in these clustered piers which those who claimed Norman antiquity for the fabric admitted were 15th century. He thought they might take it that the work upon which these crosses were found—they were not found in the choir or East Church—was contemporary. There was no reason to claim for simple cylinders an earlier date. The carvings on the caps of these piers were obviously late work. It had been suggested that possibly these were carved at a late period, but carved out of what? There must have been stone there which could be carved, and that stone would not have been a Norman cap. He thought they were shut up to the conclusion that there was no Norman work now in the building, and that 1413, when the church was built up after the fire, was the date of the earliest work. The aisles were vaulted in stone, very much like St Michael's in Linlithgow, and as there, the nave vault was only a base imposture, and was very unworthy of the fabric. Above that there was the old timber roof of oak, and it would be much better if it was exposed instead of this plaster vaulting. The tracery in the windows of the aisles was about 1820, and doubtless it followed the lines of the original tracery. The buttresses outside, which resisted the pressure of the stone vaulting of the aisles, did not seem to him to be banded in with the nave aisles. The courses of the stone were not horizontal, and this almost suggested that the buttresses were an after consideration. He did not suggest that they were of later date, but they might have been formed while the work was in progress. The tower at the west end had a very fine stone vault, similar to that in St Michael's, Linlithgow. The space between the nave and the choir had been spoilt by modern work, and whether there was originally a transept there or not there was now no means of ascertaining, the old work having been obliterated. Passing into the East Church, Mr Browne called attention to the mural arcade, which was called an Easter Sepulchre, and referred to a change in the design of the chancel, which accounted for its present appearance. He also pointed out the great arch above the gallery, and the small vesica window near the roof. In reply to a remark of one of the party, Mr Browne said that the great massiveness of the central piers suggested at once an intention of erecting a central tower. Outside the building, Mr Browne directed attention to the various points mentioned in his "Notes" given above.

Visit to the Castle.

The party then went through the Cemetery, reaching the Castle Esplanade by the flight of steps at the south-west corner. The Castle was inspected under the direction of Mr Thomas Ross, architect, Edinburgh, whose "Notes" we subjoin:—

Stirling Castle, in a military point of view, has always been one of the most important fortresses in Scotland—forming, as it does, the key of the passage by land between south and north. Its history is thus mixed up with the general history of the country throughout.

The foreworks of the Castle consist of a moat, defended by batteries. That on the east side commanding the town is said to have been erected by Mary of Lorraine, and the other, connected with the outer gate, was erected by Queen Anne, and bears her initials. Beyond these is the entrance way, with its two drum towers, probably the work of James III. (1460-88). It contains a central passage and two narrow side passages, all three having a portcullis and folding gates. The towers, which contain the guard-rooms, are now greatly reduced in height, having originally been finished in the style of the gateway at Falkland, and the towers at the north-west corner of Holyrood. The curtain wall, continuing westwards from the gateway, abuts upon a square keep-like tower, which probably formed the angle tower of the Castle wall before the large building adjoining it (the Palace) was built.

Inside the outer gateway is the lower courtyard, with the Palace on the left hand, and the great hall in front; and beyond these is the inner courtyard, from which the hall enters.

The general design of the hall corresponds with that of the English halls of the period (James III.), having two fine oriels at the dais end, roofed with groined vaulting. The hall itself had an open timber roof, which was removed at the beginning of this century, when the building was reduced to the disgraceful state in which we now see it; enough of its details is, however, left in its two beautiful oriels and its deeply recessed windows to enable us to say that this must have been one of the grandest castle halls in Scotland. It measures 125 feet long by 36 feet 6 inches wide. It has a vaulted underfloor, containing kitchen, offices, and guard-rooms.

The Palace forms a complete square of about 122 feet by 108 feet, with a central courtyard. The entrance is from the north-west angle of the inner courtyard, and leads into a corridor running along the west side. The first room on the north side was probably a reception room leading to the audience chamber, with the King's private rooms beyond. The corridor conducts to a suite of rooms running along the south side, which appear to have been the more private reception rooms of the Palace. These apartments were all of them richly decorated with wood carvings, which were taken down in 1777. Some remains, however, of these decorations, known as the "Stirling Heads," are preserved in the Smith Institute in Stirling, and in the Museum of Antiquities at Edinburgh, and one or two are in private hands.

The basement floor is arched, and contains the kitchen and offices along the south side. The upper floor contains many good rooms lighted by dormer windows, on some of which is the date 1557, with the initials M. R., which may refer either to Queen Mary herself, or to her mother, who was then Regent.

The exterior of the Palace is fantastic, and is probably the earliest example showing the influence of the Renaissance style in Scotland. It is adorned with baluster-shaped columns supporting grotesque figures carved in rude imitation of antique models. Some of those on the south side are worthy of attention as representing soldiers of the period. One appears bending a cross-bow, and another taking aim.

The date at which the erection of the Palace was begun is marked by an entry in the accounts of the Lord Treasurer, recording a payment on 8th June, 1496, to Walter Merlyoune, mason, on occasion of making the contract "for bigging of the Kinge's hous," and the accounts contain many payments to successive masters of work in relation to this building. The date, 1557, already referred to, shows that it was long in being completed, and probably the tradition that it was erected by James V. is substantially correct.

The north side of the inner courtyard is the Chapel, erected by James VI. in 1594. Its exterior is very plain, and the interior has been entirely destroyed. A chapel existed here in the 12th century, which appears to have been rebuilt early in the 15th.

While going through the Castle, Mr Ross did little more than point out the portions mentioned in his paper. He objected to the name of Parliament House, or Parliament Hall, being given to what was simply the Great Hall of the Castle, although by accident a Parliament or two had been held there. It was quite illegal, he said, to hold a Parliament in a King's Castle. The view from the Douglas Garden was much enjoyed by the visitors, the weather being very favourable for seeing a long distance.

THE AGE OF THE PARISH CHURCH.

A two days' inspection of our Parish Church convinced Mr Browne that it was a mistake to suppose any part of the edifice was older than the fifteenth century, and the emphasising of this opinion seemed to be the chief object of the remarks he made in the Church on Wednesday. Our readers are aware that Treasurer Ronald, who has given every detail of the building the closest study, considers the nave the work of the thirteenth century, while the Rev. Mr Mure Smith, who is also entitled to be considered an authority, has little hesitation in dating some parts of the work a full century farther back. Into this interesting controversy we do not propose to enter, but we wish to point out, with all deference to Mr Browne, certain circumstances which, to our mind, somewhat detract from the value of his unqualified decision so confidently given.

Having airily disposed of the two Norman features of the nave which, as he says, "have a superficial claim to be considered on their merits," by a reference to Dunkeld Cathedral, which may be a later work, Mr Browne fixes upon an entry in the Exchequer Rolls of date 1413-14 as probably determining the period when the present Church was erected. The entry in question attracted our attention ten years ago, when the fourth volume of the Rolls was first published, and we brought it under the notice of the Rev. Mr Mure Smith, by whom it was quoted in his first paper on the Church. It is from this excellent paper that Mr Browne has taken the interesting item. But the view we took at the time, and we have seen no cause to change it, was that the ancient Church was not destroyed by the fire to which the entry in question refers, and that the work towards which the "issues of a chamberlain-ayre" were granted, was not a re-building of the sacred edifice, but merely repairs. The churches of the period were built strong enough to withstand both fire and siege, and it is not probable that any fire so completely destroyed the Parish Church of Stirling (whose existence in the first half of the twelfth century cannot be disputed) that re-building was necessary. Besides, the fees of a Circuit Court would not go far to rebuild a church—the very entry from which Mr Browne quotes bears that the Court held at Montrose barely paid expenses—and if such an important work had been carried through after 1400, it is certain we should have had some better evidence of it than a single entry in the Exchequer Rolls.

Even in his own province of architecture, Mr Browne gives cause to question his ability to decide the age of our Parish Church. He asserts, for example, that the nave roof was never higher than it is at present, and that the water table inserted in the tower shows an intention that was not carried out. Anyone who looks at the hood mouldings of the clerestory windows in the south wall, and observes how the gurgoyles press down upon them, will be convinced that the roof has been lowered, and the gurgoyles also; and if he ascends the tower, as we did under the able guidance of Treasurer Ronald, he will find indisputable evidence that the original roof was as high as the water table. In the first place, there is no water table for the present roof, which is a proof that it, at any rate, is not in the original position; and, in the second place, there are distinct marks of a stair leading up to the opening in the tower from which access was had to the roof when it was at the height of the water table, a height which, according to Mr Browne, was never reached! Again, in speaking of the tracery of the windows in the West Church, Mr Browne said it followed the lines of the old tracery, but the plate in Treasurer Ronald's work, showing the windows as restored in 1797, proves that the tracery inserted in 1818 was entirely different from the old lines. It is surprising that with Mr Ronald's book in his hands, Mr Browne could have fallen into this error. More astonishing than all, however, was his mistaking Collie's arch above the gallery in the East Church for part of the original work of the choir, thus falling into the snare which the president of the architectural section of the Archæological Institute pointed out was constantly being set by the ingenious restorer. Here again Mr Ronald's book would have kept him right. Mr Browne was also wrong in saying that the outside buttresses of the West Church are not banded into the church wall. Anyone can see for himself that the original buttresses are banded into the wall. In the face of these and other mistakes that might be mentioned, Mr Browne will pardon us for saying that we altogether decline to accept his opinion as the last word on the age of the Parish Church, and until we have better evidence, both architectural and documentary, than he adduced, we shall continue to regard the matter as an open question.—ED.

AN OLD WILL.

The following is a copy of the will of a Stirlingshire farmer who died in 1580, viz., John Mitchell, in Bandeath. The will, which we reprint from the *Scottish Antiquary*, is interesting as giving an insight into the value of farm stock, &c., in the 16th century. The spelling is in a modernised form.

The testament testamentar and Inventory of the goods, geir, sums of money, and debts pertaining to unquhile John Mitchell in Baddindeth, within the Sheriffdam of Stirling, the times of his decease who deceased in the neth of May, the year of God 1580 years, faithfully made and given up by himself as concerning the nomination (?) and debts owing by him, and presently made and given up by Janet Johnston his relict, and Alexander

Young, baker, in Stirling, his son-in-law, as concerning the Inventory of his goods and geir, whom he nominated his Executors in his latter will underwritten of the date at his dwelling-place of Baddindeth the 26th day February, the year of God 1579.

Item, the said unquhile John Mitchell, had the goods, geir, sums of money, and debts of the value and price of the following pertaining to him the time of his decease; viz:—A grey horse price, £14, 13s. 4d.; Item, another white grey price 20 marks; Item, three mares, two black and one grey, price each £10, total, £30; Item, an old grey mare, price £4; Item, a Stag of a year old, price £4; Item, two fillies, price each £8, total £16; Item, two old oxen, price each £6, total £12; Item, three Stots of two years old, price each £4, total £12; Item, ten cows of which five old farrow cows with stirk, and five young cows with calves, price each 10 marks, total 100 marks; Item, three young cows of a year old, price each 30s., total £4, 10s.; Item, a Stot of a year old, price 30s.; Item, forty-six old sheep, price each 16s., total £36, 16s.; Item, twenty hoggs, price of each 12s., total £12; Item, sown on the ground forty bolls of oats 'estimat to ye third corne extending to VI^{xx}' bolls of oats, price of the boll with the foddes 40s., total £240; Item, more than ten bolls of wheat sown, 'estimat to ye ferd corne' extending to forty bolls of wheat, price of the boll with the foddes £4, total £160; Item, more than ten bolls of peas and beans sown, 'estimat to ye ferd corne' extending to 40 bolls peas and beans, price of the boll with the foddes, £3, total £120; Item, more than ten bolls beir sown, 'estimat to ye ferd corne,' extending to 40 bolls, beir price of the boll with the foddes 5 marks, total 200 marks; Item, in utencils and domiciles with the 'abuezements of his body', (clothes) Estimated to 50 marks.

Total of the Inventory, £914 2s 8d.

No debts owing to the dead.

Follows the debts owing by the dead.—

Item, there was owing by the said unquhile John Mitchell to Thomas Moderall in Cambuskenneth of borrowd money, £30; Item, to Duncan Randal in Papiltreis, of borrowed money, £22 14s 4d; Item, to John Mitchell, Elder, his son in Alloway, £23 6s 8d; Item, to Thomas Mitchell, his son in Stirling, for 'geir' furnished to the horse by him the time of the defuncts sickness, £15 14s; Item, to Andrew Stevenson in Craignigelt for the rest of the price of a horse, £6; Item, to

David Robeson, weaver, £4; Item, to James Mitchell his son of borrowed money, 4 marks; Item, to Malie Murray for ale the time of his sickness, £4; Item, to Thomas Watson, merchant in Stirling, 33s; Item, to John Muirhead, smith, 20s; Item, to Alexander Brown, pedlar, £4 6s 8d; Item, to my Lord of Mar for his rent of the ground, in the year 1580 years, £17; Item, to William Stevenson, for his fee, £9 13s 4d; Item, to Richard Kedstoun, £4; Item, to Janet Johnston, £3 10s; to John Archibald, 12s of fee; to James Johnston, 22s of fee.

Total of debts owing by the dead, £151 4s 8d.

Rest of the geir the debts deducted, £762 18s.

To be divided into three parts the dead's part is £154 6s.

Whereof the total is compounded for £8.

Follows the dead's legacy and latter will.—

Upon the 26th day of February, the year of God 1579 years, which day the said John Mitchell made his legacy and latter will as follows, viz.:—the said John Mitchell nominated and made Janet Johnston his spouse, and Alexander Young, baker, in Stirling, his son-in-law, his Executor, and referred the making and upgiving of the Inventory of his goods and geir unto them; Item, he ordained and made the said Janet Johnston his spouse only intromissative with his goods and geir; Item, he ordained and made John Myllas, bailie of Stirling, 'overman' to the said executors; Item, the defunct left and disposed of the free geir that pertained to his part, to his daughter Isobel Mitchell, 100 marks money, the remaining free geir that pertained to him he left and disposed to Janet Johnston his spouse. This was done at his dwelling-place in Buddindeth before these witnesses, John Myllas, bailie of Stirling, Duncan Ranald in Papiltries, and Alex. Schort in Blackgrange, 'w^{t} vyis dues sic subscribitur. Ita est,' Patricius Gillespie, Minister of the word of God in the church of Kirkton, etc., etc.

Janet Johnston, his relict during her lifetime, and after her decease William Mitchell her son, and Christian Wyild his spouse, had a tack of half the lands of Bandeth from the King (on the forfeiture of the Earl of Mar), on the payment of seventeene pounds usuale money of this realm, at twa terms in the year Whitsunday and Martinmas in winter, in equal portions, together with six capons at the term used and wont only at Holyrood House, 3 Oct., the year of God 1584.

KINCARDINE-IN-MENTEITH IN OLDEN TIMES.

THE CARE OF THE POOR.

One of the duties of the Kirk Session was to keep the aged and destitute from starvation. There was a "box" for the relief of paupers. Funds came from church-door collections, fines or mulcts upon transgressors, mortcloth dues, and private charities. When this end of the parish began to walk on its own feet, the other end thought we should look after our own poor. On 31st January, 1730, a meeting was held to pay out poor's money, at which it was resolved that "nothing should be allowed for the poor in the west end, in regaird there was no elder appeared to represent the case of their bounds, and no more to be given them till such tyme as the elders there give an account how they distributed the last they got." One unfortunate account "for weiring and glassing the new Kirk of Norrieston, in all £14 12s 8d," was paid under protest, in "disposing the poors' money in that way."

When a premature parent felt reluctant to sit on the black stool, in the place of repentance before the congregation, he or she might offer "a guinea to purge the scandal." The almighty guinea found its way to the box, and the scandal was thereby purged. You remember Dumbiedykes, "Jeanie, woman; Jeanie, woman; dinna greet: it's sad wark, but siller will help it." Quite true; the money was effectual. Such items of information are common in the old records of Kincardine.

Our ancient forebears were brotherly men. In 1728, at a meeting of Session, sums of money were given to "John Lamond, a Highland gentolman in Argyleshire, who had all his goods destroyed by ane axedentall fyre, hardly escaping the flames himself." "To a poor blind man in Dunkeld; to a poor woman in Dunblane, having her arm to cut; to Wm. Mitchell in the west end, in great distress; to ane poor distressed man, having his house and goods, with his wife, burnt by ane axedentall fire; to Malise Graham, in Thornhill, to help to get winter fyre to his family; to a dead-coffin to Patrick M'Arthur, his wife in Norrieston, £3 Scots. Collection for suppression of popery in the paroch of Ennie, in Rivun of Baidynoch; popery has increased and come to a great height there, 10 pounds Scots" (price of three coffins, not a bad collection for the Enzie), "and £6 to help to build ane ane harbour at Banff." Well done, Kincardine. "To a minister's son, who lost his goods at sea," and so on.

The collections were not very large, and sometimes ill-conditioned worshippers cheated the box with a button or lead penny. In 1775, the parish assessed themselves for the maintenance of the poor at 11/6 per cent. In 1775 there were only 12 on the roll; in 1795 only 3, so that the assessment was dropped. At this date the Session funds included the collections at Norrieston, which amounted to about £24 in the year. The Rev. Christopher Tait, in the statistical account of the parish from which I got some information, says, "the less deserving are the more clamorous!" Door to door begging was disapproved of, and an officer called "buff the beggar" was appointed to drive off the sorning and vagrant class of the community. I don't need to tell you why this official got this name. We all know what a well "bufft" sheaf of oats is, and no doubt the buffing would at times be very amusing, especially were the fugitive to turn round on the "buffer." Our policemen do the duties of these "buff the beggars" as well as those of the baton men. Mr Sands and Mr Andw. M'Kenzie were our village baton men, and probably their baton, the symbol of their office, may yet be preserved.

In 1795, a petition for relief for Walter Doig was handed in from Thornhill, but our Eastern neighbours would not entertain the prayer of the petitioners, and recommended them to apply to their own Mortcloth Society. They then examined the state of the funds at the chapel of Ease.

The Mortcloth Dues.

The fund for relief of the poor was partly kept up by the mortcloth dues. The minute book of the Society commences in 1813, but the Society was in existence long before that. A code of rules and list of members was then drawn up, and this list is valuable as a record of the old inhabitants of the village and neighbourhood. Some of these names are highly interesting, *e.g.*, A. C. Adams, gardener, Boquhapple, which tells us of a time when ripe and rosy apples hung from the trees in the orchard west of our village. Among the early members of the Society were Rev. Robert MacLaurin, U.P. minister of Coldhingham. He was a native of the village, was son of the baker whose oven was behind the house west from the police station, and had a son, one of the U.P. ministers of Glasgow. He was born 1783 and died 1848, in the 41st year of his ministry.

In 1829 Mr Andw. M'Kenzie got a Bible for collecting money to build the churchyard dyke. In 1848, Mr Mackison drew up a new lair book and was rewarded with a Bible; and Mr M'Kenzie again gets a pair of silver spectacles for uplifting lair assessments. In 1859, it was agreed that the officer should ring the bell for the space of three minutes half-an-hour previous to the uplifting of funerals—a custom which emphatically ought never to have been discontinued. Sums of money were frequently given by the Society to the poor. It may be interesting to note that the silk velvet mortcloth cost 38s a yard, in all £17, besides making and mounting in 1814; and that a bag for keeping bones concealed from public gaze at interments was at one time used.

The Mortcloth Society's minute book contains also the names of farms and cotteries now well nigh forgotten, as for instance, Loig, Carpenter Hall of Murdieston, Balindornock, Gourlayston, The Bourtree, Syoch and Skioch.

FAST DAYS.

At the communion season several days were set apart from ordinary work and recreation for self-examination and humiliation and thanksgiving. The Fast day as known to us is usually spent part in devotion and part in diversion. But such was not the case by any means a hundred years ago. For our grandparents "the fast-day" often meant literal abstinence, simpler fare and strict religious exercise. The Rev. Mr Caldwell would eat nothing till the services of the day were over. There is a complaint in the Kincardine Session records of date 1730, that the people of the west part of the parish do not keep the Fast day; but this was because they wanted a Fast day of their own, which they soon got.

In 1797, Benjamin M'Ewan, tenant in Daldoran, raised a *fama* against himself by causing his servants to work on the Norrieston fast day, because although not a member of the church here, he was living "within the perambulated grounds." Benjamin compeared, tried to justify his conduct, and quarrelled with the Moderator. However, about two months after, he confessed his fault and was duly absolved.

Mr Mackison, the multurer, was among the first in this quarter to grow turnips for feeding cattle on during winter to be sold fat in spring. One year he made the sale of his stock on the same day as the Kilmadock fast. He would have been pretty severely dealt with had he not taken the wind out of the sails of his vengeful persecutors.

He made a point to call on Dr Murray on the day after the sale, exclaiming, "O Dr, I've made a great mistake. I'm ashamed an' rael sorry for what I've done. Do ye ken, Dr, I made my roup on the Kilmadock fast day, and me living in the parish." What could Dr Murray say to this frank confession? and Dr Murray was a farmer as well as a minister; so he said, "Weel, weel, laird, an' had ye a good sale?" "I had," replied the multurer, "a rael good sale." "Man, I'm glad to hear it. Come in to the manse and tak' a bite o' dinner wi's." Here the matter ended. G.W.

AMATEUR ANTIQUARIANISM.

While the publication of the Stirling Burgh Records has had the effect of stimulating and materially assisting local research, there is reason to fear that it has also tended to encourage what for want of a better name we may call "amateur antiquarianism." As illustrations of the wise and scientific use of these Records, we can point with pleasure to the valuable papers on "The Parish Church of Stirling," and "Old Landmarks," which Treasurer Ronald has contributed to the Transactions of the Stirling Natural History and Archæological Society, while as samples of amateur antiquarianism, we are sorry to have to refer our readers to the essays read before the same Association by Mr W. L. Shirra. To this gentleman credit is due for the trouble he has taken in compiling papers of local interest, but his method of working cannot commend itself to anyone who has the true antiquarian spirit. We have sometimes thought that even Treasurer Ronald, with all his care and caution, had been led astray by relying too much on some entry in the Burgh Records, but we have no hesitation in saying that Mr Shirra has altogether misused them, and that his ingenuity, both in attacking old traditions and in constructing theories to replace them, is entirely misdirected. We frankly admit that in antiquarian, as in all other kinds of research, there must be something of putting this and that together—indeed, the chief pleasure of the study consists in the fitting of one fact into another—but Mr Shirra's assumptions are out of all proportion to his facts, and his papers are more adapted for a debating society than a learned body such as our Archæological Society professes to be. To those who know how many errors have been made by former writers of local history, and how difficult it is to establish the truth, it is really vexing to find an intelligent member of the community like Mr Shirra, with the best motives in the world, rather increasing than diminishing this difficulty by using the very materials intended for our enlightenment to darken our understanding and make confusion worse confounded. The Stirling Records, to be rightly and profitably used, must be read in connection not only with history, but with charters, titles, and other deeds, and Mr Shirra fails precisely because he trusts too much to the Records, and from an entry here and another entry there, draws conclusions which a wider acquaintance with record work would have greatly modified, if not entirely changed. We have no wish to be severe on Mr Shirra, we rather desire to treat him impersonally as the representative of a style of writing which, in our opinion, it is not advisable to encourage; but having reflected upon his method of research and his imaginative conclusions, we feel bound to adduce proofs in support of our antagonistic attitude towards what we have styled amateur antiquarianism. For this purpose, although we might easily enlarge the scope of our observations, we intend to confine ourselves to the latter part of Mr Shirra's interesting paper on "The Hospitals of Ancient Stirling," which is to be incorporated in the Transactions of the Archæological Society.

First, in regard to Colonel Edmond's almshouse. "Clement" Edmond we take to be a misprint, and only mention that it may be corrected in the Transactions. Mr Shirra states that in 1603 the work of rebuilding the old almhouse was gone about with expedition, and before the end of the year the house was ready for occupation. This circumstantial statement is admittedly made on the strength of a minute of the Town Council of 9th October, 1603, appointing six persons to be placed in the Hospital for their lifetime, but it is, nevertheless, quite untrue. The rebuilding of the almshouse was only in progress in 1609, in April of which year the Dean of Guild, the Treasurer, and a member of the baker's incorporation were appointed to be "maisteris of the wark of the hospitall and receave the money appointit to big that wark and see the depursing yrof and to mak compt yrfoir as apperteins." How long time was occupied in building, we cannot state, but it was not until March 1613, that the accounts of Treasurer (then Bailie) Allan in connection with the work were audited. Our readers will see how far a single minute of the Town Council has misled Mr

Shirra, who would have had to recast his account of Colonel Edmond's almshouse if he had known the facts. Mr Shirra says quite candidly, "I have never been able to make out exactly the extent of Colonel Edward's benevolence." We can give him the exact sum. It was £1019 18s 8d (Scots.)

If Mr Shirra's mistake in regard to this comparatively small matter were all we had to found on as evidence of his peculiar method of conducting antiquarian research, we would have taken no notice of his paper. But, proceeding on the same lines, he makes a rather startling assertion with regard to the foundation of Spittal's Hospital. And here we must quote his exact words:—

"The Nether Hospital, the last of these houses with which we have to deal, has a special importance, as it was the root out of which has grown the existing institution which by long usage has come to be known as Spittal's Hospital. I say 'by long usage,' I do not think it has any better title to the name. I suppose I am guilty of a mild kind of heresy in venturing to call in question what is not only the popular, but the official belief on this matter, but in these days articles of belief, the most ancient and venerable, have to stand or fall by the evidence which can be produced in their support, and I can find no proof that Robert Spittal ever founded a hospital in Stirling, or that he had any part in the establishment of the one that now bears his name."

We share Mr Shirra's healthy scepticism, and we only wish he had been more mindful of his own *dictum*, which he will allow us to extend to the assertions he himself makes, as well as to ancient and venerable traditions. After disposing of the local inscriptions relating to Spittal in a somewhat contemptuous fashion—we confess we cannot follow him in his distinction between "is founded" and "was founded"—and identifying the building known as "Queen Mary's Palace" with the original Nether Hospital, Mr Shirra says—"All through the history down to this time, [1628], the house is called simply the Nether Hospital or the Almshouse. Robert Spittal is never mentioned, his name first occurs in the Great Charter of 1641, one hundred and ten years after the supposed foundation of the Hospital." These assertions of Mr Shirra's are much too strong and unqualified, unless he has exhausted every source of knowledge. The history of Spittal and the Hospital is not confined to the published volumes of the Stirling Records, which alone are the foundation for the statements so confidently made by Mr Shirra. It is only within recent years that anything definite regarding Robert

Spittal has become known; scarcely twelve months have elapsed since it was possible to fix the year of his death. In these circumstances, it would be extremely rash for any writer to assert what Spittal did or did not do, and it seems to us that to write a paper, "vamped up" from the Stirling Records, with the view of showing that he did not found the Hospital so long connected with his name, is to show a very slight acquaintance with the proper method of antiquarian research.

We may say at once that we are glad—and we are sure Mr Shirra will share our satisfaction—to be able to vindicate the truth of the ancient tradition, and to restore to Robert Spittal the enviable reputation of which Mr Shirra has sought to deprive him. A document exists whose genuineness will not be disputed, although it is not included in the published Stirling Records, which at once disposes of Mr Shirra's argument against Spittal and of the theory which has fascinated him in regard to Queen Mary's Palace. This document is of date 1614, and is a charter (with the old burgh seal attached to it) by the Provost, Bailies, and Town Council, granting to the Hospital an annual rent from a house in the Castle Wynd, which formed part of the endowment of St Laurence's altar in the Parish Church. It is only necessary to quote the description of the Hospital contained in this important deed:—*Domus elimozinarii olim per quondam Robertam Spittel super lie Gowanhillis ex parte borealis burgi de Stirling fundat*—the almshouse founded in past times by the late Robert Spittal on the Gowanhills, in the north part of the burgh of Stirling. This statement in a formal deed of the Corporation, within seventy-five years of Spittal's decease, is conclusive evidence that he was the founder of Spittal's Hospital, and that the original almshouse was not Queen Mary's Palace, or any house in St Mary's Wynd, but was situated on what are elsewhere called the "little Gowanhillis," that is, in the locality of Irvine Place.

It is quite unnecessary to add anything to this unimpeachable piece of evidence,* but in further illustration of the nature of the process of getting up antiquarian papers against which this article is a protest, we may say a few words as to Mr Shirra's "pious opinion" of Queen Mary's Palace. He finds in the Records a minute of an agreement dated 1665, between the Earl of Argyle and the Town Council, for the purchase by the former of the old Hospital, and he surmises this must be the

*The charter has been presented by the writer to the Stirling Town Council.

Palace. He is aware of the tradition that this house once belonged to John Cowane, but he has a strong suspicion that the story was invented to explain the letters "J. C." and "A. C." which were carved in a stone above the lintel of one of the upper windows. It is strange that although Mr Shirra is a "Son of the Rock," he never saw this stone, and stranger still that never having seen it, he should not only attempt to describe it in a paper for submission to an Archæological Society, but found upon it a pious opinion that the letters "A. C." do not stand for Alexander or Agnes Cowane, but for Archibald Campbell, Earl of Argyle. A glance at the stone itself (there are really two stones), which Mr Shirra might have easily obtained by applying to the Misses Satchwell, would have at once knocked his "pious opinion" on the head, for it bears the date "1633," exactly 32 years before the house was purchased by the Earl of Argyle, if it ever was in his possession! We are pleased to see Mr Shirra interesting himself in local history, but if he is to do any good he must change his method of working, and beware of "fascinating theories," which only lead astray. We look to the Archæological Society to see that the paper on "The Hospitals of Ancient Stirling" is not embodied in their Transactions without a qualifying and correcting "Note," giving the information set forth in this article, to which they are heartily welcome.—ED.

THE JACOBITE LADIES OF MURRAYSHALL.

Bank of Scotland House,
Stirling, 20th November, 1891.

SIR,—In reply to the enquiry by your correspondent in the *Sentinel* of the 11th inst., I am pleased to be able to supply the information wanted.

The paper entitled as above appeared in the May number of the *Cornhill Magazine* of 1869. It was written by Miss C. H. Callander, daughter of Randal Callander, Esq., of the family of Craigforth.

The Wilsons of Sands (a place situated somewhere on the banks of the Forth) were prominent Jacobites, and at the '45 had to part with their property. The eldest son of the last laird of Sands, William Wilsone, was a Writer to the Signet in Edinburgh. He married (May 3, 1729) Lillias Haldane, daughter of John Haldane of Lanrick, another noted Jacobite family, and by her had many children. From the troubles of the rebellion and the years which followed, Mr Wilsone, in all probability, finding Edinburgh too hot for him, took refuge with his wife, family, and three sisters at Murrayshall, an old residence of his wife's kinsfolk, the Murrays of Touchadam and Polmaise. Murrayshall is beautifully situated at the base of the crags which rise abruptly behind it to form the far-famed Gillieshill. It was built as a residence for the eldest son of a laird of Polmaise, who, I think, married a famous heiress, Anna Gibson of Durie, about the middle of the 17th century. Mr Wilsone acted as factor to the then laird of Polmaise.

One of the three maiden sisters was for long in delicate health, and her three neices, Marion, Janet, and Lillias, took it in turns to sit up at night with her, and while thus attending their sick aunt, these three ladies (the Jacobite ladies of Murrayshall) wrote each a romance. The one written by Miss Janet, entitled "The Earl of Tankerville," is still in existence in manuscript. Miss Janet died during the great snow storm of 1823; her eldest sister Marion had died in 1821, and the last, Miss Lily, died in March, 1829, in her 91st year. As in years long past they had carefully tended their invalid aunt, so were the wants of their own declining years carefully ministered to by their own neices, one of whom will be remembered by a few Stirling people as Miss Wilsone of Graham's Court, Broad Street.

The Jacobite ladies of Murrayshall were, I need hardly say, staunch Episcopalians, and when the penal laws were in force, Murrayshall was one of the places where furtive services were held, and I think there can be little doubt who the three old ladies were who are referred to in a memoir of Bishop Gleig, thus—"There were two or three old ladies, Jacobites to the heart's core, who, long after the regular church was built, continued as often as the Royal Family were prayed for to shut their books with a slam, rise from their knees, and yawn audibly."—Yours, &c.,

J. W. CAMPBELL.

OLD PLACE-NAMES IN AND NEAR STIRLING.

[BY THE EDITOR.]

The following notes are meant to be supplementary to Treasurer Ronald's valuable paper on "Old Landmarks, &c., in and around Stirling."

BISSET LANDS.

These lands, Mr Ronald believes, were so called from the name of a former owner. He is quite correct, and it is interesting to learn that the name dates from the time of Robert the Bruce. A charter of Robert I. (of which, unfortunately, we are unable to give the date) grants to William Biset of Vpsetlington the lands of "Fuleth, Hwytemyr, Suthfeld, Welcroft, Goscroft, and Torbrekis, *ac omnia burgagia*, which belonged to Henry of Maleville, and which he gave up to the King, *per fustum et baculum*." (Reg. Mag. Sig.) The family of Bisset, Byset, or Bisert (according to Anderson's "Scottish Nation," came into Scotland about the reign of William I. and settled in two branches, the one in the province of Moray, and the other in Berwickshire. From the territorial designation of Upsetlington, we may infer that William Bisset belonged to the Berwickshire branch, of which the chief members had to fly to England in 1242 on account of their implication in the murder of the sixth Earl of Athol at Haddington. Prior to this time, however, a Walter Byset was one of the witnesses to the important charter by Alexander II. incorporating the Stirling Guildry, the date of which is 18th August 1226, not 1117, as erroneously inscribed on the Guildry seal. Among the Scottish Barons who capitulated to Edward I. at Irvine in 1297, was "William Biset, son and heir of the deceased Robert Biset," and it is probable that this was the same person who was Sheriff of Clackmannan in 1304, and who was appointed Sheriff of Stirlingshire by the English King in 1305. He was also constable of Stirling Castle, in which capacity his name occurs in a writ of Edward's (dated 20th October, 1305,) referring to the repair of Stirling Bridge—a most important local record, showing as it does the state of the Bridge at that period. It may be assumed with some confidence that before Robert the Bruce collected his forces for the decisive struggle with England's power at Bannockburn, Sir William Bisset had renounced the service of Edward and rejoined his patriotic countrymen; and it may have been for services rendered during the war of independence that the Scottish King gave Sir William a grant of lands in and near Stirling. The Henry de Maleville whom Bisset succeeded was probably the son of John de Maleville, who was a Baron of Scotland in 1296.

A great part of the lands which Sir William Bisset obtained from Robert the Bruce retains the names by which they are designated in the charter in his favour. Southfield, Goosecroft, and Torbrex are as familiar place-names now as they were at the time of the battle of Bannockburn. Fuleth, Hwytemyr, and Welcroft, were probably the lands which were afterwards called Bissetlands (now Viewforth, Springbank, Viewfield, and Annfield.) Welcroft may signify an extension in the direction of St Ninians Well Green, connecting the rest of the property with Goosecroft, and there is reason to believe that the two Livilands were also included in one or other of the remaining names. Whitemyre had still its distinctive name in 1359, in which year Robert Erskine, Sheriff of Stirling, accounts for five shillings as rent of "Wychtmyre." (Exchequer Rolls.)

In 1357, we find Sir Thomas Bisset, the son, or grandson, of Sir William, among the nobles who were present at the Parliament which agreed to the ransom demanded by the English for David II., and his name appears as a witness to a number of charters during that King's reign. He seems, indeed, to have been a special favourite of the King. In 1362 he married Isobel, the twice-widowed Countess of Fife, and was created Earl of Fife, the charter giving succession to his heirs male by Isobel, whom failing, the earldom was to revert to the King. Before the celebration of the marriage in St Andrews Church, Sir Thomas Bisset executed a charter giving Lady Isobel in liferent the barony of Glaschune in the county of Perth, and parts of Airth and Slamannan in the county of Stirling. He died in 1366 without issue, and the Countess resigned the earldom to Robert, Duke of Albany who was the brother of Walter Scott, her second husband, who died young without issue. The barony of Glaschune was in 1369 resigned by Thomas Bisset, son and heir of the Earl of Fife, and granted by the King to John Herying. The Airth property continued in Bisset's hands, and came to be called Erth-Bisset.

After this we lose sight of the Bisset family for more than a century. In 1485, Thomas Bisset of Quarrell witnesses a charter of James III., and on 14th July, 1492, he, or his son, appears in a case before the Lords of Council. The lands of Quarrell were in the barony of Herbertshire, and on the death of Thomas Bisset, they were granted by

James IV. (August 29, 1512) to Alexander, Lord Elphinstone, and annexed to the barony of Elphinstone. The Bissets, however, seem to have retained the designation "of Quarrell," although they had no longer the property of that name. The next reference to the family we find is the one which Mr Ronald has extracted from the Stirling Records, and is of date 17th July, 1520. In this extract there is mention made of "xxx Aikaris" as belonging to Thomas Besat of the Quarrell, but as will be seen below, there were two places of this name, Bisset's property (now part of Forthbank) being distinguished as "Easter Thirtie Akeris" or "Bisset-akeris."

In the reign of James V., Robert Bisset of Quarell disposed of the greater part of the landed property belonging to the family in this locality. Goosecroft was probably the first to go, though we have no record of its sale; then Torbrex, or at least part of it—the lake and bog. It had been held by James Binney, burgess of Stirling, and was in 1533 transferred to Duncan Nairn in Bannockburn and Margaret Scott his spouse. The charter defines it as lying between the lands of Cammysbarron, Newpark, Lovylandis, the Kirkland, and Southfield. In the following year Robert Bisset sold to James Cunyngham of Polmaise and Margaret Aytoun his spouse, the whole of Bissetlandis, also Easter Thretty Akeris, called Bisset-Akeris, the lands of Huddisfield, the fourth part of Levilandis, and the lands of Torbrex. Bissetlandis, it is important to note, had previously been divided into two, one half being occupied by Annabella Duncanson, relict of Alexander Craig, and the other by James Lang. Huddisfield we have not as yet been able to identify. The fourth part of Livilands sold to Cunningham of Polmaise, was occupied by William Geythane, or Gichane. In 1542 Robert Bisset sold a fourth part of what remained to him of Livilands to Ninian Bruce, son and heir apparent of David Bruce of Kinnaird. After this the connection of the Bissets with this part of their old property seems to cease altogether, although they continued to hold other lands in the neighbourhood of Stirling.

James Cunningham of Polmaise left five daughters, who were his co-heiresses, and in February, 1559-60, Jonet Cunyinghame sold to John Cunyinghame of Drumquhassil and Isobella Cunyinghame (probably cousins) half her share of the inheritance. This comprised half of the half of Bissetlands (Craig's part), half of Easter Thretty Akeris, half of Huddisfield; half of the other half of

Bissetlands (Lang's part), half of the fourth of Livilands (Geythane's part), half of Torbrex, and a fifth of the other property belonging to her father, including a fifth of another quarter of Livilands. Cunyinghame of Drumquhassil also acquired part of the share of another of the sisters, viz., Agnes, wife of William Murray of Polmaise, and this included half of Huddisfield, half of the Easter Quarter of Livilands, and half of the "tua Bissetlands," without prejudice to the right of Margaret Aytoun, relict of James Cunyinghame of Polmaise. Mrs Murray of Polmaise appears to have regained possession, not only of part of what she had given to Drumquhassil, but also of her sister Jonet's share, for in 1583 she granted a charter in implement of a contract between her son, John Murray of Touchadam, and her daughrer, Jonet Murray, which she sold to John Murray, along with two-fifths of other properties, two-fifths of the fourth of Levilands, the half of Bissetlands, Easter Thirty Acres, Huddisfield, the other half of Bissetlands, the other quarter of Levilands (Gichane's part), and Torbrex, reserving to herself during her lifetime (*inter alia*) half of Easter Thirty Acres and Huddisfield, half of the half of Bissetlands (Lang's part), half of the quarter of Levilands (Gichane's part), and half of Torbrex, with 14 salmon yearly from the "*proficuis partes*" of Bissetlands, occupied by John Wawane, and called Wawanis-maling. (This last we have not been able to identify. The name was afterwards corrupted to "Wallanlandia.") At the death of Mrs Murray of Polmaise, about 1588, her charter to her son was confirmed by James VI. There is a very interesting charter by the same sovereign (22nd December, 1602), which indicates that the Murrays of Touchadam and Polmaise had not been allowed the peaceful possession of their estates. It runs, in our rough translation, that the King for service to himself by John Murray of Touchadam from his infancy, and for service rendered to James III. by the late John Murray of Touchadam, great-great-grandfather (*abavum*) of the said John (*familium et domesticum dicta regis*), and because during the troublous times the said John was excluded from a great part of his property, which neither he nor his successors recovered, and a great part of the titles of the lands underspecified, held blench, having been stolen and others lost, grants of new to the said John and Jean Cockburn, his wife, the lands and barony of Boquhadrock (viz.—the town and lands of Boquhadrock, the Wester Thirty Acres, called

Pardovan [not identified], Bennie's Croft, Busbie's Orchard [now Allan Park], also two-fifths of Polmaise, Bissetlands, both halves, Easter Thirty Acres, Wawain-lands, Huddisfield, one-fourth of Livilands (Gichen's part), and Torbrex. The John Murray mentioned in this charter was succeeded by his son Wiliam, and William's son John is retoured as successor to his father in all the lands above specified, the date of the retour being May 13, 1643.

We have thus clearly, though necessarily in a somewhat tedious manner, traced Bissetlands from the time of the Scottish Baron whose name the property has preserved, down through three centuries, and its after history may be dispcsed of in a few sentences. It was purchased by the town of Stirling, at what date we have not yet ascertained, but certainly it was in possession of the burgh before 1734, for in that year the treasurer was appointed to pay eight pounds Scots as the town's proportion out of the lands of Bennie's Croft and Bizet lands for rebuilding the steeple of St Ninians. In 1782, Bissetlands was divided into feus, and sold by the Town Council for £750, but it is understood that the superiorities still belong to the burgh, although they do not appear in the Town Chamberlain's accounts.

Goosecroft and Claycroft.

As we have seen, Goosecroft was included in the original grant by Robert I. to Sir William Bisset. The reddendo, or annual rent to the Crown, was a pound of pepper, which, although it may appear strange nowadays, was not an unusual payment at that period, the object at first being to supply the Royal household with luxuries not easily obtainable. By and bye, this and other "blench fermis" were converted into money. In 1391 the value of a pound of pepper was 1s 6d (Scots); in 1455 it was 3s 4d. In the table of conversions of blench duties in use before the Union, its value is fixed at £1 10s (Scots.) By whom Goosecroft was acquired when it was sold by Sir William Bisset's descendant, we have not discovered, but it is probable that the purchaser was Forester of Garden, as in 1508 we find James IV. confirming a charter to Sir William Forester of Torwood, son of Duncan Forester of Garden, which includes *inter alia* the lands of Gusecroft and Claycroft, with meadow of the same, incorporated in the free barony of Gardene-Forester. In 1528, James V. grants to David Forester, son and heir-apparent of Sir James Forester of Garden, the lands and barony of Garden-

Forester, including Guyse-croft and Clay-croft, with meadow lands, and in 1542 they appear in a confirming charter to David Forester and his wife, Elizabeth Sandilands. In 1603, James Forester of Garden succeeded to the property, but whether it was from this family or a later proprietor it was acquired by the burgh, we are unable to say.

SHIPHAUGH.

The earliest notice we find of Shiphaugh is of date 1374, in which year Robert II. confirms a contract between Sir Hew of Eglinton, his brother, on the one part, and Sir Hew of Aldiston on the other, whereby the latter held himself bound to the former for the sum of £80, which he received while in great necessity, and "impignorated" or assigned to Sir Hew Eglinton the lands of Cambusbarron, Inveraloun, and Schephalch. Shiphaugh appears to have afterwards reverted to the Crown. Mr Ronald conjectures that it may have been granted to William Murray of Polmaise by James II. in 1455, but the grant really belongs to the reign of James III. In January, 1474-5, that monarch gave to his "familiar esquire," John Murray of Galwamour, the lands of the barony of Touchaldam with the following "annexes," viz. :—Kepmad, Polmais-Weland, Newpark, Schiphalch, and Wikitschaw. In 1533, it was in possession of John Murray of Touchadam, and in 1569, James VI. confirmed a charter of William Murray of Touchadam in favour of his wife, Agnes, giving her in liferent the barony of Touchadam, "excepting the piece of land commonly called the Shiphaugh." In 1603, James VI. regrants to John Murray of Touchadam and Jean Cockburn, his wife, the barony of Touchadam, including Schiphaugh. It was doubtless from the Murrays that the property was purchased by Cowane's Hospital in 1655.

WINCHELHAUGH.

This is not such a modern name as Mr Ronald supposes. It occurs as far back as 1502, a century earlier than the date given by the Treasurer, and even then it must have been an old name. Of course, it was only a part of what is now called Winchelhaugh, which includes several lands that had formerly distinctive names, such as St Laurence Croft, or Ferry Croft, the two rigs of St James the Apostle, &c. Among the good deeds done by James IV. as penance for his share in the rebellion in which his father was slain at Beaton's Mill, was the founding of a chapel dedicated to St. Roche, a saint who was popularly credited with the gift of healing diseases. This chapel was erected at the south end of the Bridge of Stirling, and in the absence of evidence to the contrary, we suspect that it is the chapel which appears in the Council Records of a later period under the strangely-corrupted name of "St. Marnock's," or "St. Marock's Chapel." We know that owing to the mistakes of transcribers of the old writings, "St. Roche" was changed to "St. Ruth," and also to "St. Rachell," and it is within the range of possibility that if "St. Marnock" was not a re-christening of the chapel, it was just another misreading by some careless scribe. Undoubtedly, as shown on Mr M'Donald's plan, St. Marnock's Chapel occupies the exact site on which we should place the chapel of St. Roche, judging from the deed of foundation, and we do not think it likely there would be two chapels near the same spot. By a charter dated 4th December, 1502, the King granted for the maintenance of daily mass and a chaplain in the chapel of St. Roche, the lands of Wynschelhalch, extending to eight acres or thereby, in the Roploch, near the Castle of Stirling. It consequently appears that the description "Lands of Winshell Haugh and St. Ruth," on Mr M'Donald's plan, is doubly wrong, and should read "Winshellhaugh *or* St. Roche." In 1561, Queen Mary, just before her return to Scotland, signed a charter at Joinville in France, in which she figures as patroness of the chapel and altars of St. Roche, at the Bridge of Stirling. This document confirms a charter of Sir John Wilson, perpetual chaplain, granting in feufarm to David Ramsay of Corscaple, the lands called the Wynschellhauch, extending to six (*sic*) acres or thereby, lying near the Bridge of Stirling, between the lands of Roploch on the west, the lands of the chapels and altars of SS. Laurence and James in the Church of the Holy Cross on the north and east, and the water of Forth on the north. The reddendo was £5 6s 8d (Scots) for the previous and customary fermes, or dues, and 3s 6d in augmentation of the rent. Into whose hands Winchelhaugh fell after Ramsay of Corscaple, or his heirs, we cannot tell, and it is not until 1695 that we again come upon a trace of it. A retour of that year informs us that Alison Justice, relict of James Stirling, Mill of Keir, heiress of Margaret Justice, daughter of the late Patrick Justice, burgess of Edinburgh, succeeded to half of the lands of Winshellhaugh, and fishings on the river Forth, both salmon and other, extending to six acres or thereby, from the

Chapel of St. Roche at the Bridge. Perhaps by this time St. Laurence Croft was included under the name of Winchelhaugh. Two years later Mrs Stirling was succeeded by her son James, surgeon-in-chief of Maitland's regiment. Here our information ends for the present.

Chapelcroft.

As we have already indicated under the head of "Bissetlands," the croft belonging to St Ninian's Chapel was probably included (although not under that name) in the original grant by Robert I. to Sir William Bisset. Perhaps the chapel itself was not in existence at the time. Mr Ronald has doubtless good authority, although he does not cite it, for saying that the revenues of Chapelcroft went into the coffers of Dunfermline Abbey, but one thing is clear, that the patronage of the chapel did not belong to the Abbey. It formed a pertinent of the barony of Airth-Bisset, which, as we have seen, was for centuries in the possession of Sir William Bisset's descendants. A charter by James IV., dated 14th July, 1459, grants to James Sandilands of Calder, and Margaret Kerr, his wife, the barony of Erthbissate and lands of Bannockburn with advocation (or patronage) and gift of the chapel of St. Ninian. A descendant of this Sandilands, John by name, succeeded, along with his wife, Margaret Bertoun, to the barony in 1533, and while the patronage of St Ninian's Chapel is included in the charter, it is also mentioned that it went by the name of Tibermasko. Of this curious name we can offer no explanation. When, in 1567, the barony of Airth-Bisset passed into the hands of Robert Drummond of Carnock, the patronage of the chapel went along with it, and it is also mentioned in James VI.'s charter in favour of Drummond's son and successor. Later charters of the same King, dated 1601 and 1608, show that it was afterwards annexed to the barony of Elphinston. The lands of Chapelcroft were in the possession of Alexander Forester of Garden in the beginning of the seventeenth century, and there can be little hesitation in holding that they became the property of his ancestors about the same time that they purchased Goosecroft. We are therefore confirmed in our opinion that what we now call St Ninians Well Green, formed part of the lands originally granted to Sir William Bisset. We have not met with any record showing at what time the Chapelcroft became burgh property. (*Vide* "Goosecroft.")

THE FIRST HISTORY OF STIRLING.

The original of the subjoined forms part of "The History, Ancient and Modern, of the Sheriffdoms of Linlithgow and Stirling," which was published in 1710. The companion "History of Fife and Kinross" was reprinted about a century later, but the smaller and more locally-interesting work has never been reprinted. In 1892 a Stirling firm issued in quarto form a reprint of the section of the folio volume relating to Stirlingshire. Notices of Stirlingshire are to be found in writings prior to Dr Sibbald's, but he was the first to give what may be called a scientific description of the county. He was a man of great learning, and his style seems somewhat pedantic to the modern reader, but as he described what he saw, his observations are of peculiar value, and his accuracy, as compared with other old writers, has frequently been established by later historians. What Sir Robert Sibbald has to say regarding the "City of the Rock" is not uninteresting, and in reproducing his remarks, we have preserved the author's orthography and punctuation throughout.

This Town in old Writes is call'd Strivelin, and that, as the Inhabitants say, by reason of the striving of three Streams, viz. Forth, Teath, and Allan; all three joining in one a little above the Bridge of Stirling. It may also be called Striveling, upon another account, because it being the Pass betwixt North and South, the two Principal Divisions of the Kingdom, when any trouble happens, there uses to be a striving about this Town which of the two contending Parties shall get Possession of it.

This town although it be but the fifth in order in the Rolls of the Royall Burghs, yet may be reckoned as the strongest Town within the Kingdom, by reason of its Situation and Fortifications added thereto. For it stands upon the Descent of an Hill; and from the West end of the Town to the Gate, called the Burroughs Gate on the East end, it hath a strong Wall built upon the edge of the declining Rockie hill; and from thence to the River of Forth it being a soft ground, there either is or was, or may be, a deep Fossa or ditch, which may secure the South, and South east part of the Town. The East part is secured by the Windings and turnings of the Water of Forth, which is in no place thereabouts foordable, even when the Tyde is out, and the Water at the lowest Ebb. And this reaches to the Bridge, which is of hewn Stone, consisting of four Arches, and at the furthest end of it is a Port with an Iron Gate: From this Bridge up to the Gastle, is a Ridge of Hills, declining towards the Town, but in many places almost perpendicular, towards the North. These hills are commonly call'd the Gowan Hills, or as some say the Gowling Hills, because the People made a great Gowling or Lamentation, when Duke Murdoch was beheaded there. But Hawthornden in his History of James the first, seems to say the Contrary, in regard the people, as he says, were very well pleased with the Execution.

The Town consists of severall Streets; as, the High Street, the Back-Row, the Baxter's wind, the head of the Baxter's Wind, St Mary Wind, the Tolbeoth wind, &c. The Church stands at the upper part of the Town, towards the West, it is a stately Fabrick, and is divided in the Middle by a Stone wall, and may very well serve two Ministers Preaching at the same time, without the least disturbing of one by the other. It has an high Steeple; King James the 4th got it to be erected into a Collegiat Church by Pope Alexander the Sixth.

In this Church July 29th 1567, James the Sixth was crowned, and anointed King by the Bishop of Orkney, assisted by two of the Superintendents. The Sermon was made by John Knox, The Earl of Morton and the Lord Home took the Oath for the King, that he should maintain the Religion received, and minister Justice equally to all the Subjects. This King being born in the Castle of Edinburgh, on the nineteenth of June 1566, was Crown'd being only 13 Months and ten days old.

Within few paces of the Church-Porch is the entrie to Cowans Hospital, a Fine convenient Fabrick built upon the top of the Rock at the West end of the Town; it has a very fine Garden adjoining to it, which has on the South side of it, the Town Wall, from whence and from the House it self, there is a very pleasant Prospect to the Kings Park, as also to the Countrey East, South, and West. This Hospital was founded by a great Summ of Money, left by John Cowan, (or Colhown) a rich Merchant in Stirling, for the supply and maintaining of decay'd Merchants there. The Affairs and Revenues thereof are managed by the Magistrats and Minister of Stirling, who have purchas'd severall Lands, which now belong to it, and by vertue of some of these Lands, the Hospital is in the roll of the Free-Holders of the Shire, and as such, the Masters of the Hospital, *pro tempore* have a Vote in the Election of a Commissioner to the Parliament.

There is also near the St Mary-wind-Port, another Hospital, call'd Spittals Hospital, founded by Robert Spittal, Taylour to King James the fourth, for the relief of decay'd Merchants and Tradesmen. This is also managed by the Magistrats of Stirling. The same Robert Spittal also built the Stone Bridge at Down, over the Water of Teath.

The High Street of Stirling is very broad, especially at the East end where the Cross stands, where they have two weekly Markets for all sorts of provisions brought thither from the Countrey, upon Wednesdays, and Frydays. On the South side of the Street near the middle of it, is the Trone, and to the South of it, the Tolbooth, where the Town keeps their Courts; as also the Sheriff, Commissary and Justice of Peace Courts; and other publick meetings of the whole Shire are kept: It hath a stately Steeple on the North end of it with a publick Clock fronting the Street. On the West end of this Street, the Earl of Mar has a stately House of hewen stone, of curious Architecture, the Front of it is like a Port entering to a City, and adds much to the beauty of the Town: the Rooms are large, from several of which, the whole large Street may be seen, it standing on the Highest part thereof: from thence also may be seen, the windings of the River of Forth towards the East & a great part of the Countrey that way, affording a pleasant Prospect. The Windings and Turnings of this River being so many, that from the Bridge of Stirling to the Toun of Alloway, it is 24 miles by Water, and but 4 by Land, from whence arose the common Saying, that The Crucks of Forth are worth an Earldom in the North. This House was built by the Earl of Mar, in the Minority of King James the sixth. On the second or third Stories of it are stones placed resembling great Guns, because at the time when the House was building, Lord Claud Hamilton having intelligence of the security, wherein the Regent (Matthew Earl of Lennox and Grandfather to the King) with the Nobility, lived at Stirling, and how, as in a time of settled Peace, they did not so much as Keep a Watch by night, took Resolution to invade them, and was therein greatly encouraged by Captain George Bell (a man born in Stirling and one that knew all the Passages and Streets) who made offer to put him and the Company he should bring with him, safely in the Toun. This he communicated to the Earl of Huntly, Walter Scot of Bacleugh, and David Spence of Wormerton, who were all content to joyn in the Enterprise. The second of September, anne 1571, they went from Edinburgh a little before Sunsetting, accompanied with 200 Foot and 500 Horse, to ease the Foot-men, they took all the Horses they could purchase, and came to the Town about the Dawning of the day, September 3, and finding all things quiet, they went to the Noble-men's Lodgings, and finding little or no Resistance, save by the Earl of Morton, but fire being put to the House, he rendered himself to the Laird of Bacleugh. The Regent was taken with less adoe, as were the Earls of Glencairn and Eglinton. The Earl of Marr hearing the noise, issued forth of the Castle with 16 Persons only, and entering the back of this new Lodging, which was not then finish'd, played with Muskets upon the Street, so that he forc'd them to quit the same. The Towns-men and others, upon this taking Courage, gathered together and put the Enemy to flight, pursuing them so hotly, as they were constrained to quit their Prisoners, and some to render themselves to those they were leading Captive. The Regent, who was Wormerton's Prisoner (for to him he had rendered), being carried a little without a Port, when they saw the rescue coming, was shot by Captain Calder, and with the same bullet, Wormerton (who did what he could to save the Regent) was stricken dead. The Regent being laid in bed and his wound dressed, his Bowels being cut, died some hours after. There fell at this time on the Regent's side some 24, among whom the most eminent were George Ruthven, Brother to the Lord Ruthven, and Alexander Stuart of Garliess on the other side, as many were slain, and divers taken Prisoners, among whom were the two Captains Bell and Calder, who were executed as Traitors. The Lord Claud Hamilton with the Earl of Huntly and the rest escaped.

The Earl of Marr is said to have kept a very great Port in this House, which occasioned one of the Stirling merchants, who had been merchandizing on the Baltick, to say when he came home, that the Earl of Marr kept a greater House there, than the King of Denmark either did, or could keep. Sure I am, on the part of the House, which looks to the back Court, there is this Inscription,

ESSPY . SPEIK . FVRTH . AND . SPAIR . NOTHT
CONSIDDER . VEIL . I . CAIR . NOTHT.

A little further in the High Scool or Castle-wind, there is another fine House, of a newer

Architecture and Contrivance, with several Apartments and Gardens; (it was at first built by Sir William Alexander, Principal-secretary of state to King Charles the first, and by him created Earl of Stirling, anno 1633), it now belongs to the Duke of Argyle.

A little from this towards the Castle, is the High-school, in which there is a principal Master, and under him two Doctors or Ushers, the first for teaching the Rudiments, Vocables, &c., and the other for teaching English and Writing. Hard by the School there is a large space of ground called the Valley, in which the Scholars recreate themselves, in it there is a great Fair yearly, September 8th, wherein are sold many young Fillies brought from the Highlands. This Fair is call'd also the Riding-fair, because frequently at it, the Town ride in a great Parade to the end of their Jurisdiction beyond the Bridge: They have also another great Fair, on the 22nd of October, for Cows, as also some other Fairs which I need not particularly mention.

There are many other fine Houses in this Town, which I shall not notice, save one which furnishes me with Particulars worthy the noticeing: viz., the Minister's Manse. It stands near the east end of the church, and looks Eastward to the Street called the Back-row, wherein the Fleshers keep their Market. It is three Stories high, in the lowest whereof, is a Stable, and Coal House: together with a Bake-house and Brew-house, furnished with necessaries at the expences of the Reparation Box, for in this Town they have a Laudable Custom not used in other places, viz., At the Church door on the Lords Days, they have two several Persons appointed to collect Peoples Charity, the one is allotted for the Poor, the other is called the Reparation; and out of this Money so collected, the Church, Manse, and Belfrey are repaired; as also the Servants belonging to the Church and Belfrey with severall other things relating thereto, are satisfied and payed. Upon the East end of this Manse, severall years since, but whether it be defac'd by continuance of time I know not, were placed the Baxters Arms, viz. three Piels, and I was told that the House was either built or enlarged by one Colonel Edmonds, who was a Baxters Son in this Toun, and being a young Boy, upon some occasion or other, which I cannot particularly remember, he run away and went over to the Low Countries, and there took on to be a Soldier, when he behav'd himself so gallantly, that at length he was advanced to be a Colonel; after this being in company with some fellow Officers, a man came to him, and speaking Scots the Colonel asked him, what news from Scotland, the Scots-Man expecting to get some large Reward from him, reply'd your Cousin, my Lord —— is very well, your Cousin, Sir John —— &c., are all well, with severall such Answers. The Colonel then told his fellow Officers, that he knew this man was a Scots Man by his Language, but he was but a base Sycophant, and therefore pack'd him out of his presence, telling his Comerads that he was noways related to those Lords and Gentlemen, he himself being the Son of an honest Baxter in Stirling. I have seen a pair of Colours which the Toun made use of in their publick Rendevouzes, which they said was given or sent to them by this honest Colonel. I was also told then, that once when he came back to Stirling, the Magistrats and others went out to meet him and conduct him to his Lodging, he would not go to any House, but that where his old Father and Mother dwelt in, as also that when the Earl of Marr invited him either to Dinner, or Supper he refus'd unless his Father and Mother came with him, and were plac'd at Table above him.

The Town is govern'd by a Provost, and four Bailies, Merchants. Their Town Council consists of one and twentie Persons, viz. The Provost and four Bailies, the Dean of Guild, the Thesaurer, seven other Merchants; Seven Deacons of Trades, viz. the Hammermen, Baxters, Fleshers, Skinners, Shoe-makers, Weavers and Taylors; out of which seven Deacons of Trades, one is chosen Deacon Convener by the rest. All those one and twentie Members of Council are chosen yearly at Michaelmas, and the Dean of Guild is always Præses of the Town Council; which is contrary to the Custom of other Towns, wherein the Provost is always President.

The Seal of the Town carries on the one side, the Bridge with a cross in the middle of it and armed men on each side of it, with this Inscription,

Hic Armis Bruti, Scoti stant hic cruce tuti.

And on the other side a large strong Castle in a Wood, with this Motto,

Continet hoc in se Nemus et Castrum Strivlingense,

that is,

The Britains stand by force of Arms
The Scots are by this Cross preserv'd from Harms
The Castle and the Wood of Stirling Town
Are in the compass of this Seal set down.

The mention made here of a Wood, argues the great antiquity of the Seal, for now there are small, if any remains of the Wood.

The famous Poets, John Johnston, and Arthur Johnston, have written Elogies of the Towns.

That of John Johnston's on Stirling is thus,

Regia sublimis celsa despectat ab arce,
Pendula sub biferis mœnia structa jugis
Regum angusta parens, Regum metricula natis
Hinc sibi Regifico nomine tota placet.
Hospita sed cuivis, quovis sub nomine amicus
Sive es, seu non es, hospes an hortis item
Pro lucro cedit damnum ; Discordia tristis
Heu quoties procerum sanguine tinxit humum !
Hoc uno infelix, at felix cætera, nusquam
Letior aut cæli frons, geniusve solis.

Arthur Johnston's is thus,

Sterlino quis digna canat ? cunabula Reges
Hic sua securis imposuere jugis,
Aura salutifera est, facit hoc vicinia Cæli,
Nec datur a sævo tutior hoste Locus.
Adspicis hic geminas structas in rupibus Arces ;
Tectaque Tarpeii turribus æqua Jovis,
Fortha triumphales hic, dum fugit, excipit arcus,
Cogitur & curvo subdere colta jugo.
Haud aliter Phrygiis ludit Mæander, in oris,
Sæpe fluit, trepidans sæpe recursat aqua.
Orbe pererrato levis, huc vestigia flectens
Advena, miratur Ruris & Urbis opes.
Admiranda quidem sunt hœc & carmine digna
Plus tamen hic virtus Martia laudis habet :
Non semel Ausonius Sterlinum reppulit Euses
Limes & Imperii quem bibit, amnis erat.

The Romans had a Station here, where some of the Legio II. abode, and this, 'tis like might have given rise to the Town ; as Roman Stations have done to many in this Island.

It is thought that Julius Agricola first laid a Bridge ever the River here, it was for a long time only of Timber, but in later times it was built of Stone.

The Town is well fitted for Trade and Commerce, and is the best pass from the North parts to the South. There are many Salmon taken in the River of Forth. The Town of Stirling is Heritable Bayly of this River, from the Drip-Coble above the Bridge, to the Abbacy of Cambuskenneth, Eastward from the Town, neer to which there is an Haven belonging to the Town, whereto Ships of small burden come up.

The Town of Stirling kept the Standart for the Jugg, or Pint, Chopin, &c., for all Wet Measures within the Kingdome ; as the Town of Linlithgow kept the Standard for Dry Measures, viz., the Boll, Furlet, Peck, &c.

This Town had always one Commissioner to represent them in the Parliament or Convention of Estates; but since the Uunion the Burghs of Innerkeithing, Dumfermling, Queensferry, Culross, and Stirling, being in conjunction, send only one Member to represent them in the British Parliament.

Mr Sletzer in his Theater has Prospects both of the Town and the Castle.

The Castle stands at the head of the Town towards the North-West; It hath stately buildings in it, raised by King James the fifth. In it there is a spacious and stately Hall, which may serve for the receiveing, and entertainment of Foreign Ambassadors, and other Royal Solemnities. King James the sixth built a flue Commodious Chapel, wherein his eldest Son Prince Henry was solemnly and in great State Baptized August 1594. by Mr David Cunninghame, Bishop of Aberdeen. The Ambassadours from the Queen of England, the King of Denmark, the Duke of Brunswick, Megelburgh, with the Estates of the United Provinces, being present. vid. Spotswood. Page 406.

The Earl of Mar is Hereditarie Governouer of the Castle, which is furnished with Cannon, and other Warlick Provisions, being one of the chief Magazines of the Kingdom, standing upon a considerable part, near the Center thereof. The South part of it stands upon a high Rock almost Perpendicular, and beneath it is the Royall Park, being very large, and surrounded with a good Stone Wall, on the North-East part of which Park, there is an Orchard, and the vestiges of a large and spacious garden.

INTERESTING DISCOVERY AT BLAIR CASTLE, BLAIRLOGIE.

In the year 1890 Blairlogie estate was purchased by Lieut.-Colonel Hare, who altered and extended the ancient mansion-house on the estate known as Blair Castle, or "The Blair," and picturesquely situated on the table-land at the foot of the Ochils. On removing the plaster ceiling of the hall, or as we call it now, the dining-room of the old house, the joiner observed that the oak beams which formed the original ceiling of the apartment were still *in situ*, and that they were decorated with curious antique designs. We paid a visit to the place, and at our request, Councillor Small, who has a special knowledge of ancient architecture, afterwards inspected the ceiling, and he has furnished us with the following description:—It consisted of about a dozen oaken beams about six inches square, with the boards of the next floor resting on them. These oaken beams had all been decorated in the style prevalent at the end of the sixteenth century. They were all painted in white, the various ornaments were coloured in red, yellows, and blues, and outlined and slightly shaded by lines in black. On seven of the beams the ornament could be distinctly traced, although it was sometimes necessary to pick it out from several of the repeats. There was the familiar guilloche ornament of the period in red and green dots outlined on black. It may be mentioned here that the ornaments covered the three visible sides of the beams, but there evidently had not been any on the under side of the flooring between them. The fleur-de-lis in yellow, and red circles between, occupied another beam; conventionalized pears and leaves a third, while an elaborate design of flower, fruit, and leaves in yellows and blues was depicted on a fourth. Another carried a series of yellow rings joined together with a band, while the sixth was covered with what we might call a rude representation of serpents with their tongues protruding and their tails twisted up, somewhat similar in design to what we see in old oak carvings of this period. The last one that could be deciphered was divided by red bands every twenty-four inches or so, and the space between filled with a pot and a flower, conventionally treated. Similar examples of this treatment of Jacobean ceilings are to be met with in Dalcross Castle, near Inverness, in which the three sides of the beams are painted, also remains of similar decorations on the walls and ingoings of window; at the Bishop's Palace, Elgin; at Greyfriars, Elgin, where the proprietor has carefully preserved the decorations on the beams of his dining room; and at the Palace, Culross, and other places. The examples at the Palace, Culross, are well worthy of a visit. In some of the rooms the whole walls and ceilings are covered with this painted decoration. In Blair Castle the aumbry in the hall has a very prettily panelled oak door, with characteristic iron drop handle and hinges of the same period as the paintings. Colonel Hare was duly informed of the discovery, but preferred a more modern ceiling for the room than the old oak beams, and they have again been concealed from view.

A few notes on Blair Castle may be interesting. The late Dr Rogers, in his "Week at Bridge of Allan," says that from a date inscribed on the top of a window above the entrance, and near the roof, it would appear that the Castle was reared in 1513. There is a date on the east side of the house which looks like 1513, but the figure 1 is so peculiarly made that it may stand for some other numeral. There is another date, and also a peculiarly interesting mark on the walls, which Dr Rogers does not notice in the excellent work referred to. On the pediments of two windows to the west are the fleur-de-lis and thistle ornaments, with the initials A · S and E · H, and the date 15 6. The third figure has been worn away, but if we filled the blank space with a 4, we should probably come near the real age of the building. The mark 4XX X on one part of the Castle walls indicates that its builder was a merchant, and it is pretty safe to say that although the adopted seal of the Stirling Guildry (a mere modern invention) shows the figure reversed, the owner of Blair Castle was a Stirling merchant. Dr Rogers, writing in 1851, mentions that the Castle contained several antique articles of furniture, of which the most interesting was a small oak cabinet, which, originally fixed to the wall of one of the upper apartments, served to conceal a secret entrance to a staircase conducting to a turret on the top of the structure. This is not the aumbry described by Mr Small, but another cabinet which has disappeared. It opened (says Dr Rogers) by the touching of a spring which no stranger could discover, and shut with equal celerity by the operation of some mechanism within, so that any one acquainted with its construction, and desirous to escape, could readily gain his end without the detection of his hiding-place. The contrivance, it is said, was made use of by a monk of Cambuskenneth, who from some unknown cause had lost confidence in his personal safety.

The Spittals were an old Stirling family whose history has already been sketched by the present writer, and there is no necessity to go over the same ground here, although we are now able to fill up blanks and correct inferences in our previous paper. The most eminent of the Spittals was Robert, Court tailor in the time of James IV. and Queen Margaret, and founder of Spittal's Hospital in Stirling. It was probably through his influence that his kinsman (perhaps his brother) James, merchant, and one of the bailies of Stirling, obtained a grant of Blairlogie, which was part of the ancient dowry of the Queens of Scotland. The exact date of the grant we are unable to fix to a year, but it must have been prior to 1508, in which year, as shown by an account of the King's rental in the Exchequer Rolls, Blairlogie was claimed in feu-right by James Spittale. It had been previously claimed both by James, his father, Patrick, and the widow of an earlier James Spittal, probably his uncle. The revenue previously derived by the Crown from this part of the royal property amounted to £4 (Scots) per annum, with one chalder of wheat and one of malt. In 1513, Robert Spittal, "servant to the King," secured for himself a charter of feu-ferme of the lands of Easter Coldoch, and before 1528 both James and Robert had purchased or obtained extensive lands in the neighbourhood of Doune and Thornhill. James Spittal of Blairlogie had two sons, for the younger of whom, Archibald, he amply provided by conveying to him, in 1528, a large part of the family property in the Stewartry of Menteith. This Archibald is doubtless the same who was a Bailie of Stirling at a later period. James Spittal's elder son was named Henry, and was a merchant burgess of Edinburgh. In 1527, James V. granted to Henry, for good service, a house and field in Stirling which had fallen into the Crown, and in 1530 he succeeded to Blairlogie on the death of his father. His wife's name was Elizabeth Forbes. She seems to have had no family, as on the decease of her husband about 1541, he was succeeded in Blairlogie by his cousin Alexander, his charter of succession being dated 12th December, 1543. It is probably the initials of Alexander and his wife which are inscribed above the west windows of Blair Castle. Alexander Spittal was succeeded by his son Adam in 1580. On the 20th April, 1583, we find, from the Stirling Register of Sasines, Adam resigned a tenement in Stirling to Jean Foulis, his future spouse in liferent, in fulfilment of part of their marriage contract, and at the same time he gave her possession of half of the lands of Blairlogie, with manor-place, &c., for the days of her lifetime. This Adam is mentioned in the Stirling Town Council Records as being in possession in 1592 of part of the family property in the Backraw. William Shaw, of Knockhill, seems to have been the laird of Blairlogie in 1597, and in 1600, Thomas Erskine of Gogar, for services rendered in connection with the Gowrie conspiracy, obtained from James VI. a grant of Blairlogie, which was incorporated in the barony of Corntoun.

ED.

FAIRS AND MARKETS IN THE STIRLING DISTRICT.

(Continued.)

FALKIRK.

William IV. (1833.) Pop. parliamentary burgh, 13,170.

Charter by King James VI. in favour of Alexander Lord Livingstone, dated 13th March 1600, erecting Falkirk into a burgh of barony. By this charter privileges of merchandise as in other free burghs were conferred and Lord Livingstone was empowered to create burgesses, to hold a weekly market on Thursday, and to have two fairs annually in the burgh: (1) on 29th June, and (2) on 26th October. R.M.S. VI. 342. No. 1031. M.C.R. I. 431.

Charter by King Charles I. in 1646, in favour of the Earl of Callendar, erecting Falkirk into a burgh of regality, to be called the burgh of Falkirk. This charter authorised a market cross to be erected and burgesses to be created with power to sell all staple goods and others imported from within or without the kingdom, to hold two weekly markets and four free fairs. This charter was ratified by Parliament on 27th March 1674. M.C.R. I. 431.

The estate of Callendar passed to Alexander Lord Livingstone, who in 1663 obtained a charter from Charles II., which recites that of Charles I., and of new erected the town of Falkirk with the pertinents into a free burgh of regality.

Act of Parliament authorising James Earl of

Linlithgow and Callendar to have two yearly fairs: (1) on 20th January, and (2) on 10th September. 1701, c. 31. A.P.S. X. 331. App., p. 104.

Acts of Convention of Burghs, authorising communication of trade to Falkirk, 12th June 1705. C.R. IV. 363. 12th July 1705. C.R. IV. 372. 11th December 1705. *Ibid.*, IV. 381. 8th February 1719. *Ibid.*, V. 211.

The town continued to hold of the family of Livingstone till the attainder in 1715 of the Earl of Linlithgow and Callendar, when his estates and superiorities became vested in the Crown. In 1720 the estate was purchased by the York Buildings Company, from whom it was acquired by William Forbes of Callendar in 1783. It still remains in his family, M.C.R. I. 431.

The O.S.A., published in 1792, states that there was a market every Thursday, besides several fairs in the year and three trysts. At these trysts 60,000 black cattle were on an average exposed for sale. As most of them were of the small Highland breed, the medium price might be fixed at £4 each. Thus, at these meetings, it was supposed £400,000 sterling were put into circulation. Horses and sheep were also disposed of at these markets. XIX. 23.

The N.S.A., published in 1845, states that there were seven annual fairs for buying and selling horses and cattle, and two for hiring servants. The markets and fairs were held uniformly on Thursdays. VIII. ii. 37.

Weekly market on Thursday.

Six fairs: (1) on the last Thursday of January, (2) on the first Thursday of March, and tryst on the last Tuesday of March, (3) on the Thursday before the third Friday of April, (4) on the third Thursday of May, (5) on the second Thursday of July, and (6) on the Monday before.

Hiring fairs the first Thursday of April, and last Thursday of October.

Falkirk-Tryst

On Stenhousemuir, parish of Larbert.

The O.S.A., published in 1792, contains interesting information in regard to this tryst under the head of Crieff. IX. 595–7.

The N.S.A., published in 1845, states that this tryst is held on a dry sandy level moor or heath (the property of Sir Michael Bruce), on the second Tuesday of August, September, and October. The first market is only for black cattle, the two last are much more numerously attended. At each of these markets there are about, *first* tryst, 4,000 black cattle, 400 horses and ponies; *second* and *third* trysts, 17,000 black cattle, 20,000 sheep, and 700 horses and ponies. The tryst is of considerable advantage to the country, as it occasions a demand for grass and foggage. The second crop of clover is generally let for the two last markets, at the rate of £2 per acre; and a great deal of money is also circulated among the keepers of publichouses. VIII. ii. 377.

Nine trysts, viz: (1-5) on the last Tuesday of March, April, May, June, and July, (6) on the second Tuesday in August and the day after, (7) on the second Tuesday of September, (8) on the second Tuesday of October and the day before and after, and (9) on the Monday before the first Tuesday of November.

Hatton of Fintry.

Village and parish in Stirlingshire. Pop. of parish, 414.

Act of Parliament authorising John Napier, of Culcreoch, to have a weekly market on Wednesday; two fairs: (1) on the last Thursday of June, and (2) on the second Thursday of December. 1705, c. 26. A.P.S. XI. 273, 274. App., p. 95.

Three fairs are said to have been held here on the first Saturday of February, April, and December respectively.

No market or fair is now held here.

Gargunnock.

Village and Parish in Stirlingshire. Pop. of village 261, of parish, 698.

Charter by King Charles II., dated 1 June 1677, to Charles Earl of Mar, of the new erection of the burgh of barony of Gargunnock, with power to hold a weekly market on Thursday; and two free yearly fairs, each to endure for days, (1) on the second Wednesday of June, and (2) on the second Wednesday of October.

Act of Parliament ratifying the above charter. 1685, c. 69. A.P.S. VIII. 508.

No market or fair is now held here.

Gartmore.

Village and *quoad sacra* parish in Perthshire. Pop. of parish, 375.

Act of Parliament in favour of Sir William Graham, of Gartmore, granting a weekly market on Wednesday; and four free annual fairs: (1) on 5th May to be called Beltane fair, (2) on 16th July to be called St Mark's fair, (3) on 8th October to be called Gartmore fair, and (4) on 28th December to be called St John's fair. 1681, c. 169. A.P.S. VII. 441.

Kilmadock.

Parish in Perthshire. Pop. 3,012.

An annual fair at the kirk on 31st January, called St Mittan's day, possessed by the Earl of Murray. Kal. S. S., p. 408.

Thirty years before 1669 the fair came to be held at Doune, and the change was authorised by 1669, c. 135. A.P.S. VII. 663. *See* Doune.

C. Kilsyth.

Town in Stirlingshire. Pop. 5,405.

Erected a burgh of barony by charter from George IV., dated 7th August 1826. M.C.R. II. 106.

Fairs on the second Friday of April and third Friday of November.

But they have become almost extinct.

Kingshouse

Balquhidder, Perthshire.

A fair held at the Kingshouse in the month of May is called "Feill Aenais." Stuart's Sculptured Stones of Scotland. II. 33.

Fair on Wednesday after the second Tuesday of August.

Kippen.

Village and parish in Stirlingshire and Perthshire. Pop. of village, 330; of parish, 1,449.

Act of Parliament granting to the heritors and parishioners two annual fairs, to be held at the kirk of Kippen, on the first of May and first of October, each for days. 1663, c. 50. A.P.S. VII. 484.

Act of Parliament authorising William Leckie, of Deshoars, to have on the Castlehill of Deshoars, a weekly market on the first, second, and third days of December; and three free fairs yearly, each for three days: (1) on the first Tuesday of January, (2) on the third Wednesday of April, and (3) on the 6th of September. 1686, c. 96. A.P.S. VIII. 652.

The days on which the first two of the fairs authorised by the Act of 1686 were held seem to have been afterwards changed (1) to the first Wednesday of January, and (2) to the second Wednesday of April.

Larbert.

Village in Stirlingshire. Pop. 831.

Fair on the last Wednesday in April.

This fair was originated by Sylvester Douglas Stirling of Glenbervie, Larbert, in 1843. For 25 years after its establishment it was the largest fair in the district. Since then, however, it has rapidly diminished, and at the last fair not a single beast was shown.

PORT OF MONTEITH.

Hamlet and parish in Monteith district, Perthshire. Pop. of parish, *quoad civilia*, 1,175; *quoad sacra*, 654.

Erected into a burgh of barony by charter of James III., dated 8th February 1466-67, in favour of the Earl of Monteith. R.M.S. II. 189. No. 902.

Charter by Charles II., dated 2nd May 1680, in favour of James Marquess of Montrose, erecting the lands therein specified into a free regality, and the port into a free burgh of regality, to be called the Burgh of Regality of Monteith, with a weekly market on Wednesday, and two free fairs yearly: (1) on the second Wednesday of June, and (2) on the first Thursday of October.

Act of Parliament ratifying the above charter. 1681. c. 17. A.P.S. VIII. 254.

† No market or fair has been held here for a very long time.

NEWMARKET.

Parish of St Ninis· popularly St Ringans, Stirlingshire. Pop. of ...sh, 10,423.

The N.S.A., published in 1845, states that an annual fair held at the east end of Newmarket, in the neighbourhood of Bannockburn, was rising in importance, and that a large number of cattle, especially milk cows, and also of horses, were exposed for sale. The market was attended by dealers from Edinburgh, Glasgow, and the country around. VIII. ii. 339.

*† An annual fair is held on the third Tuesday of June, and is the only fair now held in the parish.

POLMONT.

Village and parish in Stirlingshire. Pop. of village, 519; of parish, *quoad civilia*, 3,955, *quoad sacra*, 3,861.

Charter by James VI., dated 17th August 1611, in favour of James Marquis of Hamilton of the lands, lordship, and regality of Abbotskerse, erecting the town of Polmont into a free burgh of regality, with a weekly market on Monday and yearly fairs on 26th July for eight days. R.M.S. VIII. No. 560.

Charter by Charles II., dated 8th January 1668, to Anna Duchess of Hamilton, of the lands, lordship, and regality of Abbotskerse, with the burgh of Polmont as the head burgh of regality.

Act of Parliament ratifying the above charter. 1669, c. 44. A.P.S. VII. 578.

Act of Parliament empowering the Duke and Duchess of Hamilton to have a weekly market on each Wednesday of June and a yearly fair on the last Wednesday of October, at "the Redding, in a moorish place within the barony of Polmont." 1672, c. 27. A.P.S. VIII. 74. App. 18.

No market or fair has been held here during the present century.

DUNBLANE AND ITS CATHEDRAL.

THEOPHILUS—What town is this?
ARNOLDUS—Dirty Dumblain; let us pass by it, and not cumber our discourse with so inconsiderable a corporation.

So wrote in 1658 Richard Franck Philanthropus, who seems to have stalked through "Dumblain" with hankerchief at nose. "Pittiful pedling corporation," he says, "no scavengers amongst them; and for their housewifery, let that alone, for if you touch it you sully your fingers."

The "inconsiderable corporation" of Dumblain has had other eminence than that of narrow streets and dirty houses, and can even boast of more than "the reliques of a ruinous heap of stones facing the mountains" which once were a palace and a cathedral. The auld place is a town with a history. During the period of Catholic supremacy in Scotland, Dumblain was the cathedral city of a famous See; in the great days of Macbeth and Malcolm Canmore it was a rich Culdee settlement; in the lifetime of St Columba it was a mission station of the early Church, lying within the Rath Maol (Ramule), or ruined fortification; and within speaking distance of Galgacus and Agricola there stood, looking down the Allan from the western edge of Holmhill, the Dun Blaan [Alwen, Alauna, Vlaan, Blaan], or Fort of the Allan. Such eminence and such antiquity should satisfy any "pittiful pedling corporation" in the land.

Yet, far from being content, Dunblane is consumed by a secret ambition for the fame of still greater antiquity. The title of which it is proudest is neither "Cathedral City" nor "Town of Blane," but is "Auld Dumblane." Its sons know little and care less about the true sources of its fame—the stately church and Jessie the Flower o' Dumblane—but they croon contentedly and vaguely over its mysterious ancientness. Its song laughs to scorn the pretentions to age of all places of note and glorifies "Auld Dumblane;" indeed, throws it bodily back into the days of the Roman, and places it grandly among stricken fields and Roman camps, with an air of naive pomposity, as if there never was a time without a Dumblane. Of course, nothing is improbable when verything is unknow.. There may have been Roman camps aboun Dunblane when the Roman road was being made past the east side of Holmhill. There may have been sharp skirmishes belween Caledonii of Dunblane and the Romans. There may even have been a little fort on Holmhill. But, except in probabilities of a somewhat shadowy kind, there is no foundation for the pious belief that Dunblane rejoices in an antiquity which makes the year one a mere modern date.

The first city of Dunblane—distinct from the Dun which may have been a Roman legacy, and from the town which grew up round the Cathedral as a nucleus—was the little Kirktown of St Blane, the "Dulblaan" of the Picts and Scots. This town was situated on the "Home Hill," whose steep sides and capacious summit made it an ideal place for a fortified home. It looked down Allanwards on the bogs and wellus of Petzsawock, and on the thickets and straggling marshes of the Ald Menych. At the foot of the hill, to the east and south, lay the great morass of Monthamyr and the swamps of Ochlochy. To the north, at "the back of the town," was the black moor of Ramule. The town consisted of a fortified enclosure—the Rath of Dulblaan, afterwards the Rath Maol, now Ramoyle—within which were placed, as in all early ecclesiastical settlements, the church, the houses of the clergy, the common kitchen, and the hospitium for the reception of strangers. Outside the rampart, probably a little to the east, there stood a little cluster of farm buildings—the cowhouse, the stable, the barn. Behind the fort were huddled together the huts of the Pict converts. In front of the town, on the southern slope, lay the kirk garden, cornfield, and pasture. The Kirktown of St Blane continued until the year 857, when the Britons of Strathcluyd marched up the old Roman road from the frontier fort of Stirling, stole past the Pict outpost on the Drumcastle of Kippenross, burst through the thickets of the Ald Menych, and destroyed the houses and church of Dulblaan.

The Kirktown of St Blane came into existence towards the end of the sixth century. St Blane, the founder, was bishop and head of a religious community at Kingarth in Bute. Inspired by the missionary enthusiasm of St Columba, he headed a band of disciples, and went forth to preach the gospel in the wilds of Pictland. After many wanderings they pitched on the banks of the Alwen, and settled down at Dun Blaan to the "measure of work" and the "measure of prayer" until the tears came, which was the rule of the Columbian Church. With their own hands they built a church, perhaps on the site of the old Dun. They erected houses, reclaimed land, dug peats on the moor, sowed corn, lived lives of self-denial and hardship, were in all things "diligent in business, fervent in spirit, serving the Lord." In a few years the town within the Rath of Dunblaan became known as St Blane's "chief city." Of Blane's further connection with the city which he founded there is little known. It is probable that, after seeing the church built, he returned to Bute, where he died and was buried, Fordoun, however, tells a strange story. He says:—"The Church of Dunblan has a just right to the lordships of Appilby, Congere, Troclyngham, and Malemath in England, which were gifted by an English Prince, whose son St Blane raised from the dead, and baptised Columba. Both were wonderful in life and miracle; they were buried, Columba in Dunblane, and Blane in Bute." There is little known of the work of the saint's disciples and their successers in the Kirktown. They enjoyed 150 years of prosperity, and then they languished through a century of decay They were oppressed and they were delivered, and then oppressed again. Their rule came to a violent end just when, in the last stage of weakness, the Britons destroyed the Scoto-Pict village of Dunblaan, in the middle of the ninth century, and left the church a blackened ruin, its priests dead or fugitive, and its lands at the mercy of any who could value them.

The people of Dunblane have always been singularly apathetic and unambitious. Whatever fame the town has had, has never been won by the efforts of its sons, but has been thrust upon it by the energy of strangers. Strangers have always been its most prominent men—its clergy and men of affairs. It is very probable, therefore, that the canna-be-fashedness of its natives would have allowed Dunblane to pass out of existence after 857, had not the Culdees taken up the work of the Columbian clergy and made the town again a centre of religious influence. The Culdees seem to have been the ancient lay evangelists of Scotand, perhaps the first of the street-preaching fraternity in the land. Like their kindred in the present day, they believed that priest was but hypocrite "writ small," and that a converted "churl" or "villein" who felt an inward call to preach needed no ordination from the hands of men. The Culdees flourished in Scotland from the ninth to the thirteenth century, but the date of their settlement in Dunblane is unknown. We learn, however, from the Chartulary of Cambuskenneth that there were Culdees of Dunblane at the close of the twelfth century, and from the statement of Bishop Clement to the Pope that from the year 1000 the Culdees of Dunblane were busily engaged in making themselves, their wives, and children comfortable by appropriating the lands and revenues of the earlier Church. Yet the Culdees of Dunblane must not be written down only as ecclesiastical thieves. When they were poor they built a Church. When they were rich they built a tower, which still stands. Both in riches and poverty they revived and increased the city of Dunblane. Culdees continued at Dunblane till the thirteenth century—acting as the Bishop's chapter from the middle of the twelfth—and saw the foundation of the great Cathedral. They were among the last of their kind in Scotland.

During the Culdee period, Dunblane could hardly have been worthy the name of town. It was in the transition stage from the fortified Kirktown of St Blane to the unwalled Cathedral city, and was slowly and timorously scattering its houses over the lower ground beside the river. The church seems to have stood on the small plateau between Holmhill and the high wooded bank of the Allan, where the Cathedral was afterwards erected. Conveniently near the church would be the houses of the prior and brethren, in which they lived with their wives and families, each house surrounded by its garden and cornfield and pasture land. On Holmhill lay the deserted and dilapidated Rath, now known as Ramule, and behind it, on the site of the ancient Pict village, would probably be the miserable huts of the Culdee slaves. As the Culdee population grew, provision had to be made for it. Houses would dot the hill, each on its croft. The bog of Petzeawoch would be drained and cultivated. The marsh on the lower ground of Ald Menych would disappear, and a few huts be scattered over the site of the present High Street and Mill Row. The streets would be paths and mud-puddles, and the population of the village clergy, crofters, and slaves.

With the reign of David I., in the twelfth century, there began a new era in Dunblane. In it the rustic priest became a Bishop, his brethren dignitaries, and handicraft gave place to statecraft. The little church swelled out into a stately Cathedral, and simple ceremonies were superseded by a splendid ritual. The city stepped out from the hill and crept together from the scattered crofts, its huts became tenements, and the prior's house a palace. In the reign of David I. there occurred the great event in the history of Dunblane, its erection into a bishopric of the Romish Church.

The diocese of Dunblane was never very extensive or very rich, indeed it was the smallest and poorest in Scotland at the time of the Reformation. The territory of the See was taken out of the more ancient diocese of Dunkeld, and lay for the most part west and north-east of the Cathedral. Its limits were Cambuskenneth on the south, Inchmabone on the west, Inchaffray on the north-east, and perhaps Forteviot on the east. Yet within these narrow bounds there were forty-three parishes, and Dunblane itself was the centre of much local religious activity. In the glen of Kilbride there was the Church of St Bridget, an appanage of the Abbey of Inchaffray; in and near the Doune of Menteith the two Chaplainries of St Fillan, and other "churches, benefices, and chapels" at no great distance; on the lands of Keir the Chaplainries and Hermitage of Lupno; two miles south the churches of Lecroft and Logie; and the churches at Callander, Kippen, Leny, the chapels of Stirling and the Abbey of Cambuskenneth within walking distance on a Sabbath morning. The revenue of the See was derived from the free lands of the earlier Church for the first hundred years, and afterwards from Church lands and a fourth of the tithes of all the churches in the diocese. During the first period the bishops were nearly starved, one of them complaining that his income was hardly sufficient for six months; and in the second period the revenue decreased from £507 in 1250 to £313 in money and one chalder of wheat, eleven of bear, fifty chalders one boll of bear, nine chalders twelve bolls of oats at the time of the Reformation. The Church lands of the See from which the income of the officials of the Cathedral was mainly derived included Over, Middle, and Nether Cromlix, Kereblane, Over and Nether Auchinlays with the grain and walk mills, Blew-Buthirgask, Barbusk, Crosschaple, Classingallmore with the lands of Bridgend and Romule, and between forty and fifty crofts in the city of Dunblane; the grove, fisheries, and "Chaplainry lands of Sauchinthome, *alias* Deanstoun;" the lands of Auchin-by (to the north of Kippendavie), which were granted in 1592 to Stirling of Keir, with right reserved to the clergy and citizens of Dunblane "to pass with draw and cairtis for peattis, turffis, hadder, duffetis, and other portable things of weight;" Claveg with the mills, woods, and fisheries; Classingalbeg and Drumdewlis which in 1546 were held of William Bishop, of Dunblane, for "sex scoir laidis of petes within the palace," 3 horses for one day's carriage of cement from the Forth, and the service in time of war of one horseman and one foot soldier; and Dean's Lundies, in the parish of Kilmadock, which in 1739 was held of the King for one penny Scots, if asked only, and a proportion of the stipend of the minister of Kilmadock. In addition, there were annual rents from tenements and houses in Dunblane, and properties in at least the parishes of Muthill, Crieff, and Comrie, besides four merks of annual rent from Petlour, eleven merks from Eglesmagrill, six merks from Aulich, forty shillings from "Eister Culyns," and six shillings and eight pence from Monyvard, Moyhe, and Kelty. But as these revenues had to be divided among not less than thirty-four clergy, including eleven chaplains of the choir, it may be presumed that some at least would think themselves passing rich on forty pounds a year.

The Cathedral of Dunblane, which in its time of glory was "a brave kirk," we owe in great measure to the labours of Clement, who ruled as Bishop from the year 1233. "Such was the forlorn condition of the See," wrote the late Joseph Robertson, in "Scottish Abbeys and Cathedrals," "at the accession of Friar Clement in 1233 that—we give his own words—its rents were barely sufficient to maintain him for six months; there was no place in the Cathedral where he could lay his head; no chapter; only a rustic priest saying mass thrice a week in a roofless church. Such was Dunblane when the learned and eloquent Dominican came to its rule; the chronicles tell us that he left it, after a pontificate of fifteen years, 'a stately sanctuary, rich in land and heritage, served by prebendary and canon.'" The chronicles and the Bishop, however, tell us something more. They tell, indeed, that before Clement's day there had been erected at Dunblane a part of the Cathedral. Fordun says that Clement "found the cathedral of his bishopric in so great disrepair through the indifference of his predecessors that in it, as in a rural chapel, divine services were celebrated scarce three times a week," which dilapidated cathedral he "made a stately sanctuary." The great Bishop himself speaks of "a roofless church," and of there being "no place in the Cathedral where he could lay his head." And the chronicles tell also that the whole edifice was completed before the year 1256. It is generally agreed that Bishop Clement built the nave perhaps in seven years as the tradition affirms, and it seems probable that the choir was "the roofless church" of 1233. The general style of the whole edifice is early English, which was the rule till about 1270. The choir is simpler than the nave, less florid and exuberant, which character implies an earlier rather than a later date. The nave is built on and added to a gable wall, which belongs to the choir, and an earlier choir is thus necessary. In the choir there is tracery on a sepulchral niche which belongs to the thirteenth century, and there are mouldings of pillars which are of a more antique form than those in the western part of the Cathedral. It seems probable, therefore, that Clement roofed the neglected choir and added a nave, thus leaving behind him at his death in 1256 "a stately sanctuary, which he gifted with lands and possessions and dignified with Prebends and Canons." As the See was vacant from 1223 the choir must have been built before that date, possibly by money derived from the benefaction of Gilbert, Earl of Stratherne, which seems to have mysteriously disappeared. It may be objected that the carefully-finished stones in the walls of the choir suggest a later date than the rough rubble of the nave. But may not the rough rubble of the nave signify haste rather than age? It is exceedingly probable that Clement greatly desired to see his Cathedral finished, and hurried on the work, but that the earlier bishops, who had no such hope, were content to build leisurely, not for their own glory but for the glory of God. There is certainly reason for believing that the Cathedral of Dunblane was so far finished before 1256 as to leave only decoration and ornamentation to be done in later centuries.

It is not generally known that there were at least eight altars within the Cathedral. These were the High Altar, the Trinity Altar, Our Lady Altar, the Altars of St Blais, St Blane, St Michael, St Stephen the Martyr, and St Nicholas. The Great or High Altar was endowed after 1500 by George Newton with a sum of money which in 1532 yielded £12 of annual rent. Newton was Archdeacon of Dunblane, and the author of the

"Acts of the Cathedral." Our Lady Altar was assigned in 1573 to John Burdon, minister of Balquhidder, for part of his stipend. Its income was xxx merks. Our Lady Altar may have stood in the east end of the low building on the north side of the Cathedral, which is often called the Lady Chapel. The Trinity Altar was situated in the south-western corner of the nave, and as late as 1662 possessed "rents, emolumentes, and deuties." In the "yle" next but one to the "yle" of Trinity Altar there stood St Blane's Altar. This Altar in 1680 was granted by the Kirk-Session of Dunblane to "Alexander Whythead, chirurgion in Stirling," for a burial; and it was probably in the vicinity of St Blane's altar that, in 1793, Slezer saw the painting which represented the Countess of Stratherne and her children kneeling to St Blane, clothed in his Pontificial habit. The altar of St Blais was erected "in finali et boreali partibus" of the cathedral, which location may signify the north-west corner of the nave. To this altar there belonged in 1572 the Columbarian croft, and in 1671 the kilncroft, the longcroft, and Waterstoun's croft. After the Reformation St Blais' altar passed into the possession of the Drummonds of Cromlix. The altar of St Stephen the Martyr was in the patronage of Bishop Leighton during his tenure of office in the cathedral. Leighton presented its rents to his "friend and trusty" John Graham, Commissionary Clerk of Dunblane, who in his turn gave them after the Bishop's death to the Bibliotheca Leightonia. Of two altars within the cathedral which were in the patronage of the Stirlings of Keir, St Michael's altar was one, the other being unknown, and may have stood in the north-eastern bay of the nave, to the north of the "great queere doore" which was known as the Keir yle. The altar of St Nicholas was placed "between the south entrance door and the choir," and was served in 1532 by Robert Aikinheid, chaplain. In 1509 this altar was endowed with rents of "the lands of Ester and Mydil Camshyny," and with three tenements and a house in the city of Dunblane. The endowment was given by Dean Walter Drummond "for the support of one chaplain to pray daily for the safety of the souls of the King, the Queen, Prince Arthur, John Lord Drummond his brother, and Elizabeth the wife of the said John, and the late John Drummond, Dean of Dunblane." The patronage of St Nicholas' altar was sold in 1582 by Patrick, Lord Drummond, to his brother James, the Commendator of Inchaffray

Most of these altars were destroyed in the early days of the Reformation. "On a morning towards the end of June, 1559," says the Book of Perth, a body of 300 burgesses of St Johnstone, with swords in their hands, "Johne Knox into their heids," and halters round their necks, marched along the Ramule, through the arched Nether Port and down the Canongate towards the cathedral. Within the cathedral early mass was being said, but that was no hindrance to these reformed warriors. Into the edifice they stamped by the western portal, bustling the worshippers into the aisles, and advanced towards the choir in two lines, the one headed by the Earl of Argyll and the other by the Prior of St Andrews, Lord James Stuart, who became afterwards the famous Earl of Moray. As soon as a halt was made, the Dean advanced to the balustrade between the space in front of the high altar and the body of the church, and demanded the reason of such an unseemly demonstration in the house of God. "We come, Dean," replied Argyll, "to set forward the Reformation, and to purify this kirk." And, added the Prior, "Therefore shall we execute just punishment till ye desist from your open idolatry and cruel persecution of God's saints." "But," urged the Churchman, "we are here in the peaceable exercise of our holy religion, and if there be persecutors within these walls they who violate the sanctuary are the men." "Peace!" interrupted the Prior, "we are not here to wrangle. Say if ye and your brethren are willing of your own consent to remove these monuments of idolatry." "Alas!" replied the Dean, "we that are here are but servants or menials, so to speak. Our beloved Bishop is even now conferring with the Queen-Regent. To him your request shall be made known, and by his orders we shall abide and act." Upon this Argyll took the Prior aside for a few moments and then made known their decision. "We cannot trust William Chisholm," he said. "This, however, we will do—we will not advance beyond this barrier, nor disturb those assembled within it, but with our own hands will we cast down the images and destroy the altars." Then ensued a wild commotion. The shrines were entered and destroyed, the images were displaced and trampled under foot. "To the brook with them," shouted the Prior, and the armed multitude, rushing out at the western door, bore the relics to the banks of the Allan, and cast them into the rapid stream. Then, before the spectators had recovered from their stupefaction, the band was again marshalled and on its way to Stirling.

So began the deformation of the cathedral. Its bishops and priests for a few years made attempts to say mass within its walls, but after the bishop had been pursued in the General Assembly, and four priests had been bound to the "Mercate Cross of Stirling, and pelted with eggs and other villanie for a whole hour," none were bold enough to raise the sound of devotion under its roof. Soon, indeed, the cathedral was unfit for anything but a quarry. Its treasures disappeared, including "the mikill candlesticks of silver;" the choir was dismantled, and the great altar ruined, the roof of the nave was broken up and its beams used for firewood, and the whole building was so thoroughly gutted that in 1588 the Kirk petitioned the King to save Dunblane from utter destruction. But by that time there only remained "the reliques of a ruinous heap of stones that lean over the verge of a river facing the mountains."—*Scotsman.*

Being under the impression that Logie was, during the old *régime*, connected with the altars in Dunblane Cathedral, we applied for information to Mr Troup, Session Clerk of Logie, who has very obligingly sent us the following interesting particulars:—

"The Prebend of Logie, in the old Cathedral of Dunblane, dates from an early period. In 1275, the tithe attached to it amounted to 14s 10½d Scots. It is stated in a description of the Parish of Logie, written in 1627, that 'The minister at Logie is callit the Prebendar of Logie, bot knawis of no rent belanging thairto, howbeit that zeirlie he pays tuo merkis to the titular of the Trinitie altar of Dunblane.' The last payment by the Kirk Session of Logie for the maintenance of service at the Trinity altar was at Martinmas, 1689, when the sum of £1 6s 8d Scots was paid 'to Harie Blackwood in Dunblane his years salary for serving at the Trinity altar.' If, as stated by the writer of the article on the old Cathedral of Dunblane, the Trinity Altar possessed in 1662, 'rents, emolumentes, and deuties,' it would be interesting to know the source or sources from which these were derived. The emoluments attached to the several altars varied according to the munificence of their patrons. That of St Mary, or Our Lady Altar, which was 'founded in the north aisle of the nave of the Cathedral,' possessed considerable endowments bestowed by the patrons, the Stirlings of Keir. In 1509 it was served by two chaplains, viz., Sir Thomas Myllar and Sir Archibald Balcomy. On 3rd February, 1549, William Blakwod was presented to the chaplaincy, then vacant by the resignation of Sir John Forfar. Sir James Stirling of Keir, in 1574, presented his son, James Stirling, 'for his support at the schools, to the chaplaincy of Our Lady Altar, then vacant through the failure of Sir William Blackwod, the last chaplain, to compear before the Superintendent, to give his attestation of his faith and obedience to the King.' In the then new order of things, the endowments reverted of course to the original donors—the Stirlings of Keir."

A HIGHLAND EPITAPH.

We are all acquainted with epitaphs, elegant, quaint, or eccentric; it is seldom, however, that we meet with one which, in place of the old-time doggered rhyme, or the more modern and decorous text from Scripture, teaches history and enters upon the domain of philology. An inscription of this kind is, however, to be seen in the churchyard of Balquhidder. The stone, or rather stones, for there are two, one upright, the other horizontal, are apparently of recent erection. They are placed a few yards west of the grave of the "brave Rob Roy," under shadow of the ivy-clad walls of the ruined Kirk of Balquhidder. The minute genealogical particulars remind one of the example given by old Camden of Welsh patronymics,—Thomas Ap (*i.e.* son of) William Ap Thomas Ap Richard Ap Hoel Ap Evan Vaghan. The epitaph referred to reads:

> Sacred to the Memory of Mr John Maclaurin, of Lechscridan, the son of Duncan, the son of Finlay, son of Donull MacLabhrainn, of Auchleskine, who departed this life the 20th December, 1788; and of his Spouse Janet MacGregor, Daughter of Mr Hugh, the son of Duncan, the son of John MacGregor, of Auchtowmore (all in this parish of Balquhidder) who died in October, 1797, aged 50, whose mortal remains, with those of Janet, Robert, Margaret, Christian and Cathrine, 5 of their children, who died in infancy; together with the remains of many of their kindred, are here interred. The Auchleskine branch of the ancient Clan Labhrainn, or the children of Laurin, are deposited near this spot. In Memory also of Duncan Maclaurin, of Lombard Street, London, Gentleman, eldest son of the above John Maclaurin and Janet MacGregor, who died at Walthamstow, near London, the 21st November, 1828, aged 53, Beloved by his family and justly respected by all who knew him, and where a

handsome monument to perpetuate his memory has been raised over the vault containing his mortal remains.

This ancient patronymic evidently derived from the Dalriadic chief Laurin of Laurin in Argyle, whose decendants and kindred at an early period of our Scottish history were numerous and powerful in the districts of Monteith, Lennox, Strathern, and Balquhidder, has of late (by Scoto-Saxon transcribers, ignorant alike of Gaelic orthography and its proper pronunciation) been corrupted to MacLaren, and MacLarin, and thus by the mere omission of the single vowel U, equivalent to BH in the Gaelic found in the original spelling of the proper name the identity of this modern name with the ancient and euphonick *(sic)* name of Maclaurin is almost entirely destroyed to the mere Gael. This modern corruption of an old clan name is entirely unknown, whereas the proper name is well-known and never pronounced otherwise in the Gaelic than "MacLabhrain," and in the English, "MacLaurin."

The author of this ponderous epitaph is right in pointing out the affinity of the surnames Maclaurin and Maclaren; although it is open to question whether a tombstone, in a remote Highland churchyard, is the proper place for contentions of such a nature. It is too late in the day, however, to expect the original, and more correct, form of the patronymic to supplant the less correct; more of the sept have been known as Maclaren than Maclaurin; the former, indeed, has long been the more common of the two forms. The imperfection of the Anglicized form of Celtic patronymics is observable in other sept names; and is not in any way peculiar to that of the sons of Laurin. Most probably this clan sprung from the Scoto-Irish settlers on the western sea-board of Scotland; and the fact of their having at an early period held territory in Argyle, lends probability to the contention of those clan-historians who hold that Laurin is identical with Loarn or Lorn.

The horizontal stone already referred to, lies at the foot of the one the inscription on which has been quoted above; on its two sides are inscribed:—

In Memory of the Clan Laurin, anciently the Allodian inhabitants of Balquhidder and Strathearn. The chief of whom in the decrepitude of old age; together with his aged and infirm adherents, their wives and children, the widows of their departed kindred, all were destroyed in the silent midnight hour by fire and sword by the hands of a banditti of incendiarists from Glendochert. A.D. 1558.

Erected by Daniel MacLaurin Esquire, of St John's Wood, London, Author of a Short History of his own Clan and for the use of his clansmen only. October 1868.

"For the use of his clansmen only!" For generations the Maclaurins, who are stigmatised in an Act of the Scottish Parliament as among "the wickit thevis and lymmaris of the clans," were exposed to the savage enmity of their neighbours the Macgregors; faction fights even took place within the sacred walls of Balquhidder church, a clergyman of the Maclaurin name being slain in one of these unseemly brawls. The massacre mentioned in the above inscription is the one referred to by a writer on the Highland clans:—"On one single occasion, the sons of Clan Alpine murdered no fewer than nineteen householders of the Maclaurin name, with (frightful to relate) the whole of their families, 'wyvis and barnis.'" The crime remained uninvestigated for forty-six years; when, apparently quite incidentally, it came to light in connection with another tragedy; the perpetrators were acquitted. This terrible deed is, unhappily, not without parallel in the history of the Clan Laurin, and, indeed, in that of many other septs. J. W. S.
—*Scottish Notes and Queries.*

OLD PLACE NAMES IN AND NEAR STIRLING.

(Continued.)

St. Laurence Croft.

In connection with our note on Winchelhaugh, the following minute of the Privy Council, dated 10th May, 1610, may be printed here:—

Complained by Thos. Soirlie, burgess of Stirling that on 2nd inst. the provost and bailies of the said burgh caused him to be committed to ward in their tolbooth, where he is still detained in "strait prisone and captivities" without just cause,—charge had been given to James Schort, provost, Walter Cowane, Johnne Scherar, John Cunynghame, and John Henderson, bailies, to appear and produce the complainer; and now Scherar and Cunynghame, appearing and producing Soirlie, [at Edinburgh] also produce an act of court of their burgh, dated 2nd May, and subscribed by Johnne Williamsoun, notary public and clerk of the said burgh. It bears that complainer had been called before the said magistrates for closing up "ane slop and entre" of the town's old passage to their fishing on the Foirth through St Laurence Croft, and thereby debarring the town not only from their fishing, but also from the way by the said "slop" to the building and mending of their bridge, and also from watering their horses in the Forth. It further bears that for complainer's "unreverent" speeches against the provost on this occasion—*e.g.* his saying that he had built up the said "slop" at the command of the Laird of Randifurd, his master, and that the provost had better have no dealing with the laird, because that laird's father "brak ane baillie's heid of Stirling named David Foister [Forester] of Logy, that they micht haif turned thrie fingaris in the wound of his heid,—complainer had been amerced in £10 and ordained to remain eight days in ward in the tolbooth. The Lords accordingly find that complainer had been very deservedly punished and therefore assoilzie the defenders; but as complainer has now been eight days in prison, they ordain him to be released and remit the question of the building up of the "slop" to the proper judge.—P.C. Reg. viii. 459.

Queenshaugh.

It is probable that this place received its name from being part of the dowry of the Queens of Scotland. We find it so called in the reign of James I., the Exchequer Rolls showing that in 1434 John Sympill, of Perthwic, was paid an annuity of 4 merks from the lands of Qwenishalch. By a charter dated 1st July, 1451, James II., with consent of the Three Estates of the Realm in Parliament, grants to his consort Mary, *inter alia*, Stirling Castle, the great customs and burgh dues of Stirling, with office of Sheriff; also Aldpark, Raplauch, Quenis-halch, Sergandlande, &c. Mr Ronald mentions an interesting connection between Queenshaugh and the birth of James III. at Stirling, and we refer to the matter for the purpose of showing that the authorities Mr Ronald quotes—usually the best of all authorities—have not succeeded in proving satisfactorily that the historians have all been wrong with regard to the year in which King James was born.

The late Mr George Burnett, who edited the Exchequer Rolls, says in a note to his Preface to vol. v. page lxxxviii.—"1452 is generally said to have been the year of the birth of James III., but as pointed out by Mr Dickson in his preface to the Accounts of the Lord High Treasurer of Scotland, vol. i., p. xxxvii., his parliamentary revocation, on 10th July, 1476, of Acts prejudicial to the Crown, shows that he had then, and probably on that very day, attained the age of twenty-five." Dr Dickson, in addition to some other evidence that the date of the King's birth was 10th July,

1451, cites the charters of 20th July, 1451, and 1st June, 1452, by which the lands of Queenshalch and the Ward of Gudy were granted to Robert Nory by James II. for bringing the news of the birth of his son and heir. It is only the latter charter, however, that contains any reference to the interesting event. It sets forth that the King, with consent of his Queen, grants to Robert Nory, his faithful servant, and to his heirs, for the joyous news brought first by him to the King of the birth of Prince James, the lands of the Ward of Gudy in the lordship of Menteith, and lands of Quenys-halch on the banks of the water of Forth, the reddendo being a red rose at the Feast of St John the Baptist at Quenyshalch. This charter was sealed with the Queen's seal. It may be noted that Tytler gives as the date of the Prince's birth the 1st June, 1452, the very date of the charter in question, and if we can suppose that Nory arriyed at Holyrood with the news on the day of the Queen's delivery at Stirling (no very extravagant supposition) and that the King in his joy at once intimated his gift to the messenger, a *prima facie* case in favour of 1452 being the right year may be said to be set up. But apart from this coincidence, there are certain facts which go to show that Tytler and the older historians, Lesley, Buchanan, Pitscottie, and others, were right, at least as far as the year is concerned. The charter of 20th July, 1451, fixes the reddendo of Queenshaugh at £3 6s 8d, and for the Ward of Gudy Nory paid 40s for the year 1452, whereas the charter of 1st June, 1452, gives a grant of these lands *blench* a proof, we think, that the event mentioned in the second charter as being the cause of the grant, took place in the interval between the dates of the respective charters. Nory's reward for bringing the gratifying tidings of the Prince's birth was, therefore, the quittance of the "fermes" he had paid for lands previously in his possession. Another bit of evidence in support of the historians' statement is supplied by a work of some authority on Scottish affairs, viz., "Extracta ex Cronicis Scocie," one of the Abbotsford Club books. The original MS. of this work is said by the editor, Mr Turnbull, to be in a hand of the close of the fifteenth or the commencement of the sixteenth century, and it is suggested that the writer may have been Alexander Myln, Abbot of Cambuskenneth, author of the "Lives of the Bishops of Dunkeld." On folio 288 of this MS. is the following entry:—"Jacobus primogenitus regis, regni princeps, nascitur ex regina Maria, anno Domini M°iiii°lii." With such a respectable authority for 1452, it is remarkable how such works as Anderson's "Scottish Nation" and Chambers' Encyclopedia give the year of the third James's birth as 1453. Mr Burnett's reference to "Saint Margarete's sark" may apply to a second premature confinement of the Queen in 1451, or, which is more likely, to the accouchement of 19th May, 1450. It is noticeable also that the Exchequer Rolls show the christening of Prince James to have taken place between April, 1452, and June, 1453. The former date would mark a longish period for a child born in July, 1451, although not perhaps unusual in the royal family, but the interval more naturally applies to a child born in 1452. We admit the force of Dr Dickson's arguments from the dates of the Parliamentary revocation, and Maundy alms, but we think they are scarcely conclusive, and at any rate we have shown that they are not strengthened by the grants of Queenshaugh to Robert Nory.

After Nory's death, Queenshaugh reverted to the Crown, but again came into the possession of the Nory family. In 1526 James V. grants to George Douglas, brother of the Earl of Angus, the barony of Keir, along with *inter alia* the lands of Queenshall [? Queenshaugh] in the county of Stirling. In 1533 the King confirms a charter of Robert Nory of Boquhapple, who sold to Sir John Stirling of Keir the superiority of the lands of Queenishalch, with fishings, &c., also whatever of the said lands belonged to him, the reddendo being still a red rose in name of blench ferme. Nory signs this charter with his hand at the pen of a notary because he could not write. In 1516 Queen Mary confirms a charter of James Stirling of Keir selling to his relative, Duncan Forrester, and Isabella, his spouse, the lands of Queenshauch, with fishings on the Forth. This Duncan Forrester, who was probably a brother of Alexander Forrester of Garden, took the designation of Queenishauch. The retours show that a certain John Guthrie succeeded his father John, indweller of Stirling, in an annualrent of 40 merks from the lands of Queenshauch. It is a surmise on our part that Queenshaugh eventually passed into the hands of the Murrays of Polmaise, and was sold by that family to the predecessors of the present proprietor.

THE STANDING STONES OF STIRLING DISTRICT.*

BY MR A. F. HUTCHISON, M.A., RECTOR OF THE HIGH SCHOOL, STIRLING.

Before describing in detail the Standing Stones of the district—of the greater number of which Mr Kidston has prepared photographs to be shown by the lime-light—it may be proper to make a few remarks of a somewhat general character.

DISTRIBUTION.

Mr Kidston has kindly prepared a map of the district showing the geographical distribution of these ancient monuments. A very cursory examination of it shows that they follow very much the hill-contour of the country. The greater number of them keep along the hill-slopes; the others are scattered over minor rising grounds, often surrounded by higher summits. It is well, however, to be cautious in drawing an inference from this with too great certainty. The stones that still remain are in positions which have afforded the best chances of preservation. The lower grounds have been under cultivation for many centuries, and if Standing Stones ever did, in any numbers, exist on them, they are not unlikely to have been destroyed or removed as obstacles to the cultivation of the soil. Very few of those to be described are situated on arable ground, and one of these—the Harperston Circle—has been irretrievably ruined by the operations of the farmer. The very small fragments of it which remain would probably by this time have entirely disappeared, had not the field been allowed to go out of cultivation. The majority are distributed over hillsides and uncultivated moorlands.

ORIENTATION.

All the stones examined show of a sort of Orientation. Wherever there was anything like an alignment, or where there was any indication of a diametrical direction—as in the Circle at Aberfoyle—and, in the case of single stones, where any peculiarity of setting gave them the appearance of pointing to a particular quarter, the direction has been carefully taken with an azimuth compass, with the result that all have been found to point nearly in the same direction. That direction is North of East. They all look as nearly as possible to the quarter of sunrise at the summer

*Paper read to the Stirling Natural History and Archæological Society, 19th April, 1893.

solstice. Such a general uniformity of direction can scarcely be accidental. It seems to point to their erection by a race of nature-worshippers, who set up their rude altars or memorial stones to catch the first beams of the rising sun. That the direction is not invariably exact to a point or two of the compass seems rather a confirmation of this idea than otherwise. There were no magnetic compasses in those days. The worshippers of the sun-god would have to watch for his appearance. And according to the nature of the bounding horizon—whether sea, or plain, or hill—the point from which his first rays struck the sacred place would be a little more to the North or a little nearer the East.

BURIALS.

There can be no doubt that many—I should say most—of these stones mark places of interment of the unknown great of early times. Burial and worship may have been conjoined at the same place. The practice of burying in sacred places has come down through the ages to the present day. But even when stones were set up simply to mark interment, it is natural to suppose that they would be set to face the sacred quarter. As a matter of fact, cists that have been dug up in stone circles and beside Standing Stones have been found generally—so far as my own knowledge goes, invariably—lying in this same north-easterly direction. The only stone in the list I am about to submit that varies from this general direction is the incised stone in Alloa Park, which faces east and west. This, however, does not affect the statement. The Alloa stone bears marks of an early Christian origin, and so is oriented in conformity with Christian custom, while the earlier Pagan monuments face the rising sun.

COMMEMORATION STONES.

Some stones are said to have been erected to commemorate battles and other historical events. It was no doubt a widely prevalent custom to set up memorial stones of that kind, although I do not know to what extent it ever prevailed in this country. In our own neighbourhoood there are at least two sets of stones usually said to be connected with battle sites. This identification, in the one case (Randolphfield) rests entirely on tradition, and of the existence of that tradition we have no written evidence that goes back much beyond a hundred years. In the other case (Airthrey) it has no other foundation than a guess of the historian of Stirlingshire.

BOUNDARY STONES.

Some stones undoubtedly have been erected to mark the boundaries of properties or the limits of sanctuary rights. These—especially the latter kind—would acquire a character of sanctity; but they are, of course, of comparatively recent origin.

AGE.

In regard to the periods of erection of the rude stone monuments, the general agreements among experts may be summarised as follows. The unhewn and uninscribed stones are assigned to Pagan times. Stones incised with rude crosses and symbols belong to the early Christian ages. The more elaborately sculptured stones, of course, are of a later period. Stone Circles and Dolmens have been found to contain burials of the Bronze Age, with both cremated and unburned remains. Triangular and rectangular groups of Standing Stones are held to belong to the Iron Age.

CUP-MARKS.

The cup-marks are still a puzzle to archæologists. It was once supposed that they might have been intended for containing liquid-milk, or fat, or even blood—for the gods. As they are shallow—and their contents therefore would be soon exhaled or dried up by the sun, and so apparently be accepted by the god, the idea was thought not to be without probability. But, in the case of Standing Stones at least, the cups are found quite as often on the side as on the top of the stone, and, in other cases, more often than not, the surface on which they appear is sloping and not flat. By far the most numerous and elaborate cup-markings are on rock-surfaces or great boulders. It is on these that the encircling grooves, the radial ducts, the connecting lines, the spirals and other characteristic markings appear. The most that can be said of their meaning as yet is, that they appear to belong to some still undeciphered religious symbolism of early man. I should not be surprised if it should be found that they have some preference to the appearance of the heavens and possibly to the movements of the celestial bodies. But that is a mere conjecture of my own, which may prove to be quite as unfounded as other theories.

GEOLOGY.

The geological character of the Standing Stones is varied. Some are pieces of the local rock, but a much larger number are of a geological formation, different from that of the district. On Sheriffmuir for instance, we find Standing Stones of a kind of a rock which is not found *in situ* nearer than the hills of Balquhidder. It is not necessary, however, to suppose that great blocks of stone like these were quarried and brought from a distance. When a stone differs from the rock of the district, it was no doubt brought thither and dropped by the glacial flow. The men who set up the Standing Stones looked to those most suitable for their purpose. If slabs of the native rock were handy, they would set them up. If not, over every hill side were strewn boulders brought down by ice from the higher Grampian summits, and from these they could select those that suited their purpose. Stones of columnar shape were specially suitable. We need not therefore be surprised to find that the dolerite pillars of the Castle Rock and the Abbey Craig have furnished the Standing Stones of the immediate neighbourhood. There is no violence in the supposition that these may have been carried from their native positions to the sites at Randolphfield and Airthrey Park.

RANDOLPHFIELD STONES.

In the grounds of Randolphfield, in front of the house, are two stones standing in a line from S.W. to N.E.—the line of direction making an angle of 235° with the magnetic north. The south-west stone stands 4 ft. above ground. The portion underground measures 2 ft. 5 in.; so that in all it measures 6 ft. 5 in. Its girth is 6 ft. 6 in. It is four sided in shape—nearly square—three of the faces measuring each 21 inches, and the fourth 15 inches. The north-east stone is smaller, and less regular in form. Its height above ground is 3 ft. 6 in., and its girth 4 ft. 6 in. Both stones are pillars of dolerite, of the same material as the pillar stones of the Castle rock, from which place they have apparently been brought. The larger stone shows some marks on it, which have been supposed to be artificial. They are, however, merely the natural joints characteristic of these blocks, such as may be seen on their fellows at the Back Walk. The local tradition as to the origin and meaning of these stones is well-known. It is thus stated by Nimmo in his History of Stirlingshire, p. 84 (first edition, 1777):—"Two stones stand to this day in the field near Stirling, where Randolph, Earl of Murray, and Lord Clifford, the English general, had a sharp rencounter, the evening before the great battle of Bannockburn." Again, p. 193:—"To perpetuate the memory of this victory" (the skirmish above referred to) "two stones were reared up in that field and are still to be seen there. They stand in a spot *which has been lately enclosed for a garden*, at the north end of the village of Newhouse, about a quarter of a mile from the south port of Stirling." The Old Statistical Account of St Ninians (Rev. Mr Sheriff, 1796), makes the same statement, pp. 406-8:—"In a garden at Newhouse, two large stones still standing were erected in memory of the battle fought on the evening before the battle of Bannockburn, between Randolph and Clifford. . . . *The place has lately received the name of Randolphfield.*" The New Statistical Account tells the same story more concisely. The statists evidently follow Nimmo. I can find no earlier mention of these stones. Barbour, the principal ancient authority for the battle of Bannockburn, is silent regarding them. Nimmo's appears to be the traditional account of the meaning of the stones, although it seems that the name of Randolphfield dates no further back than about or somewhat later than the period at which he wrote. In fact, both names — Randolphfield and Clifford Hall — are obviously artificial. They did not arise spontaneously out of the popular recollection, but were stuck on at the end of last century. For all that, they may serve to preserve to us the locality which tradition has identified with the skirmish, and tradition may well enough be correct. As to the stones themselves, it is not impossible that they may be much older than the period of Bannockburn. The direction in which they stand to each other seems to indicate an alignment of the ancient type, and they stand upon just such a summit of rising ground as the old groups of standing stones usually occupy.

AIRTHREY PARK STONES.

Two stones stand in the grounds of Airthrey Castle. The more westerly one is near the boundary wall at Blalowan. The other is about a quarter of a mile further east, near the stone which has been put up to mark the meeting-place of the counties. The west stone stands 9 ft. 4 in. in height above the ground, and has a basal circumference of 9 ft. 2½ in. Looked at from the north it has a rudely cruciform shape. This striking appearance, however, is not due to art. It is quite natural. The east stone—the more massive of the two—is 9 ft. 1 in. in height. Its greatest breadth is 4 ft. 10 in., and its circumference 14 ft. Both are dolerite columns, similar to the blocks of the Abbey Craig. No tradition regarding the origin of these stones exists, but Nimmo makes the following suggestion (History of Stirling, 1st edition, sec. v., p.p. 83 and 84); "Near the Parish Church of Logie, two miles north from the town of Stirling, are *several* large stones standing erect. Of what event these stones are monuments can not with certainty be determined. In the ninth century, Kenneth II. assembled the Scottish army in the neighbourhood of Stirling, in order to avenge the death of Alpin his father, taken prisoner and murdered by the Picts. Before they had time to march from the place of rendezvous they were attacked by the Picts, aided by some auxiliaries from England: the combat was fierce and bloody; but the victory at last fell to Kenneth, who pursued the flying enemy with great slaughter, and drove many of them into the Forth (Boethius, lib. 10). As the Castle and town of Stirling were at that date in the hands of the Picts, the rendezvous of Kenneth's army and the battle must have been on the north side of the river; and as every circumstance of that action leads us to conclude that it happened near the spot where these stones stand, we are strongly inclined to consider them as monuments of it. The conjecture, too, is further confirmed from a tract of ground in the neighbourhood which, from time immemorial, hath gone by the name of Cambuskenneth, that is, the the field or Creek of Kenneth, upon which the noble monastery of the same name stood." The new Statistical Account (published 1845) makes the cautious statement that the stones are "intended probably to commemorate some battle or event long since forgotten." This account, which bears evidence of personal and careful examination, gives the measurement of the stones, and makes them *two* as against Nimmo's *several*. It is, of course, quite possible that one or more stones had disappeared in the course of the seventy years that elapsed between the two accounts, but it is more probable that Nimmo's statement is merely a loose one. Forty years later Nimmo's conjecture has hardened—in the hands of the bookmakers—into a *popular belief*:—"Two standing stones are in the Park (Airthrey) without inscription, emblem, or any historical identification, yet popularly believed to be commemorative of the total defeat of the Picts by the Scots in 839." (Ordnance Gazetter, 1885).

ALLOA PARK INCISED STONE.

This stone is situated in a field on the south side of the road from Alloa to Clackmannan, about half a mile east from Alloa, and not very far from the east lodge of Alloa Park. If stands, facing as nearly as possible, due east and west (285° magnetic), on the crest of a long and not very high ridge. The highest point of the ridge has been immediately to the west of the present position of the stone, which looks as if it had been moved from its original site. Round the base it is built in with stones, one of which, on the west side, bears the date 1305, evidently recently cut, perhaps when the stone was interfered with. The stone is a hard sandstone, it stands 8 ft. in height above ground, is 2 ft. 6 in. in width near the base, and 2 ft. 1 in. at top, and from 7 to 9 in. thick. On either side is an incised cross. That on the eastern side is 6 ft. 5 in. in height; the lower limb being 52 inches long, the centre 10 inches, and the upper limb 16 inches. The arms are each a foot long, and the centre is 10 inches across. The whole cross is thus 6 ft. 5 in. high by 2 ft. 10 in. across. At the intersection of the arms with the body of the cross are four circular cup-like hollows. The cross on the west side is placed about 15 in. lower on the stone than that on the east side, and is more deeply incised. Either the lines have originally been cut deeper, or, as is not unlikely, this side has been less weathered than that exposed on the east. The earlier statistical writer, in his reference to the stone, mentions that he had been told by old people that it once had carvings of men on horseback. He adds that there were no traces of these carvings in his day. Probably they never did exist except in the imagination of the "old people." He mentions, however, that when the adjacent farm was being enclosed twenty years before (about 1770) a ditch was made close to the stone, when many human bones were discovered. Another and still more interesting discovery was made in 1829. This is narrated in Dr John Stuart's *Sculptured Stones of Scotland* (appendix to preface of second volume). "A very interesting example," he says, "of burial of what seems a transition character was found near to the town of Alloa. About half a mile east from it upon the ridge of a swelling ground immediately adjoining the alluvial banks of the river Forth, and with the river in view, stands a stone pillar, having a cross of a very primitive type cut on either face. An examination of the site in the year 1829 led to the discovery of many human bones, much decayed, close to the stone; and at about 9 feet north of its base, of a cist 3 feet in length, formed of sandstone flags, which also contained human bones much decayed. The cist was covered with a flag, at each end of which, on the inside, was incised a small cross of the simplest form, but evidently cut with care." The inference he draws is that the cist represents an early Christian interment, of the period when the Pagan custom of doubling up the body in a short cist had not yet disappeared. Dr P. Miller, who investigated the stone and read a paper on the subject some years ago to the Society of Antiquaries of Scotland, makes the statement—from his personal knowledge of the fact—that the stone actually was taken down and re-set in the year 1829. He makes no allusion, however, to the date at the base, 1365. His measurements agree very nearly with those I obtained. He makes the height 8 ft. 3 in., breadth 2 ft. 7½ in., and thickness about 9 inches. "Taking Dr Stuart's views as a foundation, that the stone cist with its cover, with the two incised crosses on its under side, and the Pictish cross within a few feet of the cist, mark the last resting-place of some eminent or illustrious personage at the time that the Pagan form of burial had passed or was passing away, and another mode more in harmony with the new gospel of peace was supplanting it." Dr Miller arrives at the conclusion, which he supports by an investigation of the place-names in the immediate neighbourhood, that "this standing-stone marks the spot where was buried in Pictish times the remains of some person known as *Brath*, *Breidhi*, or *Brude*."

CLACKMANNAN STONE.

The famous stone at Clackmannan, which is supposed to give name to the place—*Clackmanach*, (spelling in old charters, Clackmaneck), "The Monks' Stones"—is not properly a standing stone. It now occupies the summit of a tall natural pillar of dolerite brought from the Abbey Craig. It was placed there in 1833 by Mr Bruce of Kennet, father of the present Lord Balfour of Burleigh, and the Rev. Mr Fleming (afterwards Professor Fleming of the New College, Edinburgh), at that time minister of the parish of Clackmannan. Previously, and from time immemorial, it lay on the ground beside the old jail and Court-house, near the Town Cross. The ancient stone, like the pillar which now supports it, is of dolerite. It is over 3 feet in length, 2 feet broad, and about the same in thickness. The two pieces of which it consists are clasped together with iron. This stone was associated with some sort of religious rites in Pagan times. The character of sanctity thus attaching to it would be utilised —as was frequently the case in like circumstances—by the monks for purposes of worship. Before the erection of a Court-house, the Sheriff—as is learned from an old Act of Parliament—used to hold his courts in the open air at the Cross, and it is a reasonable conjecture that prior to the erection of the Cross, courts were held and binding bargains made at this stone, whose tradition of sanctity had come down from pre-historic times.

[For the information in this note regarding the Clackmannan stone, I am indebted to the paper by Dr. Miller already referred to.]

THE GATHERING STONE ON THE FIELD OF SHERIFFMOOR.

This Battle Stone (as it is locally called) is a block of fine Highland grit, travelled possibly from Balquhidder. In 1840 it was enclosed by an iron grating, which bears the following inscription:—"The Gathering Stone of the Highland army on the day of the memorable battle of Sheriffmuir, fought in November, 1715. This grating has been erected to preserve the stone by John Stirling, Esq., of Kippendavie, Principal Heritor in the parish of Dunblane." I have been told that this battle stone used formerly to be known as the Beltane Stane. If that is the case, it has probably a much older interest than the battle of Sheriffmoor. It certainly has the appearance, so far as it can now be seen, of an overthrown standing stone.

THE WALLACE STONES.

On the east side of the Sheriffmoor road stands what is known as the Wallace Stone. Although only one great stone is now standing, five others are to be found at intervals prostrate amid the heath. Several fragments of the same material (dolerite) as that of the most of the stones is scattered about, especially towards the north-east end of the line. One small stone, which stands by itself at a considerable distance from the others, close to the road, a little distance below the hotel, makes a line with the great standing stone of 260°. This stone is altogether different in size and appearance from the others. It does not seem to belong to the alignment, but may, perhaps, have been set up as a boundary stone. It measures 2 ft. 9 in. above ground, and is 9 ft. in circumference at the base. The other six seem to have formed a series running in a direction south-west to north east, 253°. The first prostrate stone in this line is 7 feet in length, 8 feet in circumference at the base or thicker end, and 6 feet at the top. In shape it roughly resembles a square pyramid. On the exposed side—which, when the stone was erect, would be the south-east—appear over 20 cup-marks, of from 1½ inches to 2 inches in diameter. About 75 yards distant, and in the same line (253°) with the standing stone, lies a roughly rectangular stone of dolerite, not so shapely as the first one, measuring 6 ft. 6 in. in length, and about 10 feet in circumference. The next in the series is a flat stone 5 ft. 6 in. in length, and 4 feet 6 inch broad. It is sunk in the ground, so that the peripheral measurement could not be ascertained. It is slightly out of line, with the others. But, near it, and in more exact line is a small stone, 4 feet in length. These may be fragments of a single original stone. The interval between this and the great standing stone is about 150 yards, which gives rise to the suspicion that there is a stone amissing in the series. This great stone, the only one now erect, and specially denominated the Wallace Stone, stands 6 feet above the ground, and measures 14 feet in circumference. It is four-sided—the faces measuring respectively, west, 3 ft. 6 in.; north, 2 feet 10 inch; east, 2 feet 8 inch; and south, 5 feet. Beyond this, still in the same line, and at the usual distance of about 75 yards, lies another great stone—a sort of flattened pyramid in shape, 10 feet in length and from 16 to 18 feet in girth. In a paper read to this Association about three years ago, I described these stones in a general way, and discussed the question of the name by which they are now known. I do not go over that ground again. The incident in the life of Wallace, which connects that hero with the Sheriffmoor stones, will be found narrated by Blind Harry in book v., lines 284-301.

STONE AT WHITTIESTON—(MACGREGOR STONE.)

Almost straight north from the Wallace Stones, on the lower northern slope of the Ochils, stands the Whittieston Stone. It is in a field on the south side of the road from Dunblane to Greenloaning and just in front of the farm-house of Upper Whittieston. A tall slab of Highland grit (fine micaceous), it measures 9 ft. 4 inches at its greatest (south-west) and 8 ft. 10 inches at its least (north-east) height. In width it is 6 ft. 10 inches, and its thickness varies from 1 to 2 feet. On the east side it is marked with one large and seven smaller cups. The direction along its length is 225°. This is an interesting stone, evidently of high antiquity. I have not been able to ascertain whether any interment has ever been found near. Its only legend is of quite recent date. In the district the stone is known as the Macgregor Stone, and the tradition accounting for the name is to the effect that here a countryman was sacrificed by the followers of Rob Roy, when forming for the engagement on Sheriffmuir, in order to satisfy the ancient highland superstition that first-blood was an infallible omen of success. As Sir Walter Scott phrases it in the Lady of the Lake—

> Who spills the foremost foeman's life
> His party conquers in the strife.

The tradition is precise enough to state that a man of the name of Dawson was seized in the adjoining hamlet of Whiteheadston (for such is the original name) as a whig, and therefore a foeman and proper victim. Dawson, however, suspecting the intentions of the captors, vehemently professed himself a supporter of King James, and was let off. But another inhabitant of the hamlet not so accute or not so hypocritical, was immolated at the stone. Such is the story. It occurs to me, however, to suggest that the stone may have taken its present name simply enough from the Macgregors of Balhaldies, on whose lands it stood. Notwithstanding, it is of much earlier date than the Macgregors of Balhaldie or any other sept of the Children of the Mist.

GREENLOANING INSCRIBED STONE.

Keeping eastward along the Ochil slope for about a couple of miles, we come to the standing stone at Greenloaning, which I formerly described with measurements. I have nothing to add to what I then said regarding the stone. It is mentioned again because Mr Kidston has made some photographs which show the stone and its noteworthy surroundings. The inscription still awaits decipherment.

HARPERSTONE CIRCLE.

About two miles south of Greenloaning, up the northern face of the Ochils, 900 feet above sea level, lies the farm-house of Harperston. Here, as formerly stated, I imagined I had found the ruins of an ancient stone circle. A later visit along with Mr Kidston has confirmed the impression, and I now give th edimensions of the circle, so far as we could make them out in the excessively ruinous condition in which it now is. The Harper Stone lies a little north-east of the farmhouse. It is 9 feet long by 6 feet across on the top, is 3 feet thick, and measures 26 feet round. This appears to have been a centre stone, and a surrounding circle is traceable more or less distinctly—more so to the west and north, less so to the east and south. The radius of the circle is about 15 yards, and a similar distance separates each of the larger stones yet traceable in the circle. The ground beside the great central stone appears to have been excavated. This excavation is on the north-east side of the stone, just where an interment, if there was one, might be expected to be found. This supposition is confirmed by an article in the *Stirling Journal* of May 5th, 1830, to which Mrs Hogg has drawn my attention. I think the whole article refers to this circle, but the localisation is so loose as to render the identification somewhat uncertain. "About eight miles from Stirling," says the writer, "by the Sheriffmuir Road, near a place called Harperstone, there is a remarkable circle of stones, supposed to have been a Druidical place of worship of old. The site of this circle is rather uncommon in this country—being on the back summit of a high hill, one of the Ochils, called the Black Hill, and exposed to every wind that blows. It is about two English miles south of the present roadway. Tradition records two remarkable circumstances connected with this Druidical circle, which may perhaps be worthy of being preserved. About the middle of last century there were dug up at the foot of the larger stones three vessels of clay of antique shapes, containing coins of very ancient date, which were long preserved by Monteath of Park, but are now, we regret to say, lost. So late as 1770, these coins were, it is said, to be seen at Park House, all of gold. About the year 1715, some stones on which had been engraved inscriptions were dug up at the same place; and at a previous period specimens of ancient Pictish (*sic*) armour were dug up from the bowels of this hill, which had been carefully deposited of yore some feet below the surface in crypts of curious description."

STIRLING AT THE DISRUPTION.

Before 1843.

Our narrative begins about the middle of the Ten Years' Conflict, when a vacancy in one of the Stirling charges afforded the Voluntaries an opportunity of showing their hostility to the Established Churches. While there were only two churches belonging to the Establishment, there were three charges, the minister of the third charge officiating alternately in the East and West Churches. The Rev. Mr Bennie having been translated to Edinburgh, the first charge became vacant, and the Town Council, which was composed for the most part of political "Reformers," made an attempt to suppress one of the charges. Opinion of counsel was taken relative to the stipends of the second and third charges, the lawyers applied to being Mr Alexander Dunlop, Sir John Hope, Dean of Faculty, and Mr Andrew Rutherfurd. The opinions received gave the Council little hope of being able to suppress either of the charges, and at the October meeting a deputation appeared from the East Church asking the promotion of the Rev Mr Cupples from the second to the first charge. The Voluntary party, however, led by Bailie Smith, father of Mr R. Smith of Brentham Park, refused to discuss the request of the petitioners until the constituency had expressed their opinion on the matter at the November election, and by a majority they resolved to pay the stipends of the second and third charges under protest. At this meeting of the Council, Mr Ebenezer Johnstone, who founded the *Observer* in the following year, declared that he would not hesitate to go to the House of Lords with the question, and others were as strongly in favour of litigation. One Councillor, a Mr Henderson, who took the same view, caused much laughter by saying that the Council would be "perjured villains" if they paid the stipend, and declaring that he "stood upon his own bottom and paid no respect to the opinion of any one of them."

The Municipal Election of 1835.

The municipal election of that year accordingly turned upon the church question. The Voluntaries joined with the East Church people, who wanted that Church declared the first charge, and desired Mr Cupples as their minister. They were supposed by the Voluntaries to be in favour of the suppression of one of the other two charges, or at least of a reduction of the stipend. On the other side was the West Church people, who claimed that the first charge belonged to them, because Mr Bennie, their minister, was the former incumbent of the first charge. The contest therefore assumed much of the character of a struggle between the friends of the Establishment and its opponents. There were eight vacancies in the Council and both parties nominated candidates for each seat, the late Provost Rankin having the fortune to be nominated by both sides. The result was a complete victory for the West Church party, Bailie Smith, the late ex-Bailie Yellowlees, and Mr Henderson being amongst the defeated candidates. On account of this decided expression of opinion, the minute anent paying the ministers' stipends under protest was rescinded at the first Council meeting after the election, and Mr Cupples did not get the East Church, the vacancy being filled the following year by the appointment of the Rev. Julius Wood, Newton-on-Ayr. But litigation over the stipend question was not averted but only postponed.

The Ministers' Widows' Fund Case.

A vacancy of over six months having occurred in the third charge, after the translation of the Rev. Mr Macfarlane to Edinburgh in 1832, the Trustees of the Ministers' Widows' Fund made a claim for the six months' stipend, and the Town Council presented a bill of suspension and interdict, contending that the statutory provision founded on by the trustees did not apply to the provision made by them for the third minister. The third charge, they pleaded, was merely a pastoral charge, erected by the authority of the Church Courts alone, and was not a benefice recognised or erected by the Court of Teinds. Here, again, the Voluntaries failed, the Court of Session deciding, in 1837, that the third charge being permanently endowed by the Town Council, with the consent and under the authority of the Presbytery of Stirling, was to be held as a benefice under the statute, and the Widows' Fund was adjudged the £100 of half-yearly stipend. The town was, of course, mulct in the whole of the expenses.

Church Extension.

These successive defeats of the Voluntaries seem to have encouraged the supporters of the Establishment to proceed with the work of Church extension, which was then being strongly advocated by the Rev. Dr Chalmers. The Church Extension Committee had obtained returns of the population, number of communicants, number of sittings, &c., in the various districts of the town. We have before us the replies to the Committee's queries in regard to the district comprising Queen Street, Irvine Place, and the lower part of St Mary's Wynd, from the houses of Robert Laing and Peter Comrie, to the head of Upper Bridge Street, including the Barn Road. Out of a population of 353, the Established Church claimed 212; and the number of sittings rented or otherwise held in the East and West Churches, was 228. The other districts did not show such a large proportion of sittings to the population. The Church Commission met at Stirling on the 2nd March, 1838, to receive the reports which had been drawn up by the different clergymen in the town. The whole of the sittings in the two parish churches were reported to amount to 2364, and those in the dissenting churches to 4477—a total of 6841, for a population of 8364. It may be interesting to note the attendance at the various churches. The seats in the parish churches were all filled; indeed, there was not sitting room for those who did attend. The attendance at what was then called the First United Secession Congregation Church, (now the Erskine Church), amounted to 1176; Second do.; (Viewfield Church), 363; Episcopal Chapel, 90; Associate Burgher, 260; Cameronian, 100; Independent, 120; Baptist meeting in Guildhall, 35; do. in Trades Hall, 35; Roman Catholic, 350—total, 2269. It has been generally supposed that the movement for the erection of the North Church was initiated by the late Rev. Dr Beith, although he himself declared that it had been a favourite object in the town for twenty years before he came to Stirling, but that every proposal in prosecution of the object had failed. One of these proposals was made in September, 1838, and there can be little doubt that the scheme would have gone on whoever had been called to succeed Dr Wood, who was translated to Edinburgh in 1839. The circular issued in 1838 lies before us as we write, and we find that not only was the whole plan arranged for the erection of a third church in the lower part of the town, but that trustees had been appointed for the new church, and their duties defined, and a committee formed to procure donations and subscriptions along with the trustees. To Dr Beith, however, belongs the credit of having pushed on the scheme—or rather an amended one—to a speedier completion than would otherwise have been the case. The Presbytery of Stirling, having had the subject of an ecclesiastical division of the Parish of Stirling brought under their notice, appointed a committee of their number to consider the whole subject and to report. This having been done, the Presbytery finally resolved, on 14th May, 1840, on an arrangement for uncollegiating the three charges, and dividing the parish into four districts, the fourth district being assigned to the minister of the Spittal Square Church, now the Free South Church, and at that time a mission charge. The number of families of all denominations in each district, according to the census of 1831, was as follows:—First District, 501½; Second do., 487½; Third do., 501; Fourth do., 481. Each district was to have its own Kirk Session, which was to report every half-year to the General Session. The latter body was to meet, as usual, on the first Monday of every month for the management of the affairs of the poor. The following were the members of Session:—Revs. Alex. Beith, George Cupples, and Alex. Leitch; Provost Thomson, Captain Forrester, Dr Muschet, Messrs P. M'Dougal, J. Weir, J. M'Millan, J. Grant,

R. Hill, T. Balfour, R. Henderson, P. Drummond, A. Hutton, J. Aikman, W. Oatt, and P. Fisher.

The Building of the North Church.

In a pamphlet by the Rev. Dr. Beith, published in 1872, and entitled "Statement for the Surviving Managers of the North Church," an account is given of the steps which preceded the erection of the Church in Murray Place, and this account may be accepted as fairly accurate. Five gentlemen from each of the East and West Churches, associated themselves with Dr. Beith as a body of managers of the new church. These were—From the East Church—Sir John Hay, Bart., Sheriff Substitute; Messrs William Turnbull of Forthbank; Robert Gillies of Gormire, Linlithgow; John Sawers, Procurator-Fiscal, and James Drummond, draper; from the West Church—Dr. Andrew Beath, Messrs Thomas Colville, Annfield; Thomas M'Micking of Miltonise; William Galbraith, Town Clerk; Dr. Andrew Beath, and Alexander Boyd, Registrar of Sasines. "It was intended," says Dr. Beith, "that the new erection should be a Parish Church, as the West and East Churches were. . . . A Chapel of Ease, or an Extension Chapel, in the usual acceptation, or a *quoad sacra* Church, it was not to be." It is important to bear in mind the provision thus emphatically stated by Dr. Beith, because it explains much of what he calls the "painful history" of the North Church, and because there is reason to believe that Dr. Beith himself sometimes forgot, or at least did not give sufficient weight to the fact, that it was a Parish Church he was dealing with in the great controversy which followed the Disruption.

After some negotiations with the Town Council, a bond was signed by the managers, the conditions of which Dr. Beith has correctly summarised as follows:—The first provided that the managers should at their own expense, and of themselves, obtain the "sanction of the Church" to the uncollegiating of the ministerial charges, and the transferring of one of the present ministers to the new church, as proposed—no right remaining to them, or any of their successors, to claim a colleague. The second provided that the town and heritors of the parish were not to be exposed to any additional expense for communion elements, salaries of precentors, &c., &c., during the period the arrangement should be in force. The third provided that during the period the managers retained the management of the new church, they should "maintain it," and at the expiry of the period, "leave it in good condition." The fourth provided "that it shall be in the power of the Magistrates and Town Council to demand that the Church shall be disponed to them free of debt, at the end of thirty years. Yet it shall not be obligatory on them to accept of such disposition at the time, but it shall be entirely optional on their part to insist on such conveyance being granted, or to postpone the same indefinitely, or to such period as they may see fit"; but "during such postponed period, if any such shall be, all the obligations hereby incumbent on the applicants and their successors shall continue to be of equal force as they are during the said thirty years, and the Magistrates and Town Council for the time shall, at any time thereafter they may see cause, be entitled to require, and the parties vested in the property of the church shall be bound on such requisition being made to grant, a conveyance to the Magistrates and Town Council of the said church, free of debt and in good condition, in the manner before specified." The fifth provided that the sum to be expended in erecting the new church should not be less than £2,600. The sixth provided that the Town Council and heritors should be freed from all expense which might arise in obtaining the uncollegiating of the charges and the new arrangement generally.

The site originally secured for the North Church was the ground belonging to the Bank of Scotland, upon which the Free North Church now stands. Mrs Burd, of Forthside, having offered a donation of £500 to the building fund if an infant school was provided along with the Church, the managers unfortunately accepted the offer, which necessitated a change of site to Spring Gardens, and an additional expense of £1000 in building. There was thus a clear loss of £500, and the worst of it was that as the infant school was placed under separate management, it afterwards became a very undesirable adjunct to the Church proper, and gave rise to much contention. As it has all along been claimed that it was the people who left the Establishment with Dr. Beith that built the North Church, it may be as well to give here what the rev. Doctor discreetly kept in the back ground—a list of subscriptions to the building fund from persons who never were members of the Free North congregation. The list is taken from the *Stirling Journal* of 18th August, 1843, and we have reason to believe was supplied to that paper by the late Mr James Lucas, writer, to whose collection of local documents we are chiefly indebted for the materials for these articles.

Lord Abercromby, ...	£50	0	0
Wm. Murray, Esq., of Polmaise,	50	0	0
Robert Bruce, Esq., of Kennet	20	0	0
Two Ladies in Glasgow, (not certain)	15	0	0
Wm. Campbell, Esq., Glasgow,	50	0	0
A. Stirling, Esq., of Keir, ...	50	0	0
Lord Dalmeny, ...	20	0	0
Colonel Graham of Meiklewood,	10	0	0
W. R. Ramsay, Esq., of Barnton,	26	5	0
Wm. Forbes, Esq., of Callendar,	50	0	0
Rev. Mr Laurie, ...	10	10	0
Miss Hadaway, ...	10	0	0
Robert Tennent. Esq., ...	20	0	0
Mrs Edmond, ...	21	0	0
Miss Dees, (not certain), ...	10	0	0
Eben. Bow, Esq., ...	10	0	0
Twenty-four Gentlemen in Glasgow,	49	19	6
Three Subscriptions in Edinburgh,	30	0	0
Thirty-two Subscribers in Stirling and Neighbourhood, ...	102	11	6
	£605	6	0
Add Mrs Burd's donation, ...	500	0	0
Also subscriptions of those who remained in the North Church,	130	0	0
Total,	£1235	6	0

According to Dr. Beith's own statement, the total subscriptions obtained amounted to £1816 13s, so that all his Free Church congregation could claim credit for was £581 7s. We have anticipated the course of events a little for the purpose of making clear the exact extent of the interest which the Free Church can truthfully be said to have in the North Parish Church.

The subscriptions, however, did not nearly meet the cost of the building, which amounted to £4000, and the balance was met by advances on the personal security of the managers, who looked forward to their being repaid by the seat rents they were entitled to charge. The idea of a church bazaar had not yet occurred to anybody, and strangely enough, no attempt was made until too late to get a loan by means of a bond over the property. The loose manner in which the financial business was conducted, and for which Dr. Beith was, of course, equally responsible with his colleagues, gave rise to serious misunderstanding and much heart-burning after the Disruption. On the 29th May, 1842, the North Church was opened for worship, Mr Beith, first minister, having been selected as the future pastor, and before the close of the year nearly all the sittings were let.

The Eve of the Disruption.

Owing to the erection of a new parish church, the situation of Stirling during the six months preceding the Disruption was a very peculiar one, and tended to increase the popular excitement—materially stirred up by Dr. Beith—over the non-intrusion controversy. On this question, the lay managers of the North Church were equally divided, but the non-intrusionists, having the minister on their side, had the voting power. When, therefore, the majority of the congregation pledged themselves to quit the Establishment along with their minister, Mr Beith was able to carry a resolution that the managers should apply to the Town Council for the use of the church for the intending seceders from the Establishment until the expiry of the thirty years stipulated in the bond. Looking at this proposal now, it strikes one as being either exceedingly simple or exceedingly cool. The intending seceders must have known it was not within the power of the Town Council, however willing they might be, to grant such an absurd request, and even if their consent had been obtained, there were the Ecclesiastical Courts to reckon with. The fact that one of the majority of the managers was also Town Clerk, may have suggested the proposal, especially as it was well known that the friends of the Established Church were in a minority in the Council, but the wonder remains that the idea should ever have been entertained, and that such a ridiculous document as the "Memorial" contained in Dr. Beith's "Statement" should have actually been drawn up. Mr Lucas, writing a week or two before the Disruption, showed the illegality of the proposed procedure, and on the minority of the managers threatening to take legal steps to defend their rights, the "Memorial" was withdrawn, and was never in fact presented to the Town Council. Matters accordingly remained as they were, but only for a very short time.

The Disruption.

On the 18th May, 1843, occurred the great secession from the Church of Scotland, and all the Stirling ministers joined the seceders. For months there had been preparations for the event, and when we are asked to admire the heroism of the ministers who left their benefices—"went out into the desert" is a phrase often used in this connection—we temper our admiration with the reflection that the desert was not quite so bare as we are asked to believe, the Sustentation

Fund collected before the Disruption amounting to over £72,000, and the building fund to upwards of £150,000. There was plenty of manna in the wilderness, and in view of this fact the heroism of the so-called "sacrifice" rather decreases in its quality and proportions. When, on the other hand, we consider the exaltation of public feeling, the certainty of the seceders that they were the elect, and that the "Erastians" or "Residuaries," were doomed to everlasting perdition—an idea, by the way, that has not altogether died out in our own time—the breaking-up of society and domestic discord that were caused by the secession, the taunts and the sneers levelled at those who were not carried away with the crowd, the bitter animosity which existed for years towards the old Church and its members—when we think of all these things, we confess that our sympathies are entirely with those who remained in the Establishment, whose heads were not turned by the cant of "spiritual independence," so miserably misunderstood by the ignorant, and who were strong-minded enough to hold their own course despite all the efforts of well-meaning but mistaken and hasty clerical zealots.

The Local Press of the Period.

As we shall have occasion to quote from the Stirling newspapers of the time, it may be well to insert here a note on the position of the local press. During the political agitation of 1831-32, the *Journal* advocated the cause of Reform, but gradually became more Conservative, and the appearance of the *Observer* in 1836 as an advanced Liberal paper, necessarily made the *Journal* the organ of the Tory party. At the first meeting of the Free Presbytery of Stirling, which was held in the Court-Room in Broad Street, "most considerately and kindly granted for the purpose by our Liberal Town Council," (says the *Observer*) reference was made to the fact that the *Stirling Observer* had recently supported the Free Church in an able manner; and it was stated that there was every reason to believe it would continue to do so, and would become a representative of the adherents of the Free Church in this part of the country. The Editor takes occasion in the same report to remark—"All this is the more gratifying to us, that the recent articles which have appeared in our columns were written without suggestion or solicitation on the part of any individual connected with the Free Church." According to the oldest local printer, Mr Leslie Neilson, the Disruption came just in time to save the *Observer*, which was in a languishing condition, and would have collapsed if it had not been taken up by the Free Church party. At all events, it was entirely controlled by that party, and the hand of Dr. Beith can be traced in several of its leading articles in 1843, the *Journal*, which championed the Establishment, frequently referring to him as the "intermeddling editor" of its rival.

After the Disruption.

The great event of the 18th May, 1843, made no difference in the Stirling Churches on the following Sunday, the pulpits being supplied as usual, but on Sunday, 28th May, there was no service in the North Church. The doors were opened, and a few people attended, but no minister appearing, they dispersed. In the East Church, Mr Cupples preached, and announced that the afternoon services would be held in the Court House. Mr Leitch occupied the West Church pulpit both forenoon and afternoon, but stated that on the following Sunday he would preach in the Guild Hall. Dr. Beith preached to large crowds in the Corn Exchange. On the first Sunday of June, in the East and West Churches, the services were conducted by the Rev. Mr Robertson of Logie, the Rev. Mr Anderson, assistant at St Ninians, and Mr Murdoch, licentiate. According to the *Observer*, the attendance at the East Church at one of the services was 109, and at the other 83; the West, 210 and 226; "but it is said, with respect to the West Church, that the attendance was somewhat increased for the want of room to accommodate those who wished to hear Mr Leitch." These numbers were taken by persons who said they counted the people as they came out, and by a curious kind of arithmetic, the *Observer* made out that the 648 attendances represented only 335 individuals. "This was the first turn out of these congregations, which before the 18th of last month produced an average attendance of from 2000 to 2400 assembling in their Churches.

"In the Free Church [of course] the aspect of things was very different. Mr Leitch's congregation in the Upper Guild Hall [which had then two floors] amounted to between 400 and 500, which was all the place could hold, either sitting or standing. Mr Cupples' congregation in the Justiciary Court-house was uncomfortably crowded, and the Corn Exchange was as crowded as it had been the previous Sabbath, notwithstanding the people from St Ninians (many of whom were present then) had their time occupied at their own Parish Church. Thus, from present appearances, our townsmen have almost wholly left the Church, and if the number of ministers who have turned out is great, the number of people we consider as still greater; nor did we expect such a result from the comparative calmness with which the agitation was conducted here, during the period it was carried on within the bosom of the Church."

With regard to the North Church, round which a fierce battle was soon to rage, a meeting of the seatholders who adhered to the Establishment was held on Wednesday, 31st May, to consider the steps necessary to be taken in consequence of the secession of the Rev. Mr. Beith. At this meeting it was resolved that it was highly necessary that during the vacancy in the North Church the pulpit should be regularly supplied, and that all proper steps should be taken to attain that object. At the request of a committee appointed at the meeting of seatholders, and two of the elders of the North Church, the Rev. Mr Robertson of Logie, and Mr Murdoch, Cornton, agreed to preach on the 4th June. This arrangement was highly objectionable to the seceding managers, who were determined to keep the church shut unless they got it for Mr Beith's Free Church congregation. On the following Saturday, therefore, the managers met for the first time after the Disruption, when there were present the Rev. Mr Beith (preses), Sir John Hay, Messrs M'Micking, Colville, Turnbull, Drummond, Boyd, Sawers, and Dr A. Beath. Mr M'Micking, one of the seceders, moved that the managers resolve to prevent any person irregularly officiating in the North Church on Sabbath next of whatever denomination. The reasons given for this motion were that the managers were the legal custodiers of the church during any vacancy, and that they had no power of themselves to appoint supplies to the pulpit. This was certainly a most extraordinary proposition. Sir John Hay, seconded by Mr Turnbull, moved that in view of the resolution of the seatholders and the sanction given by the Presbytery, "any steps to prevent the preaching of the Gospel to-morrow, such as is now attempted by the motion on the table, is unjust to the seatholders and highly expedient." There voted for the first motion—Mr M'Micking, Mr Colville, Mr Drummond, and Dr. Beath; and for the second motion—Sir John Hay, Mr Turnbull, Mr Sawers, and Mr Boyd. The votes being equal, the Rev. Mr Beith gave his vote for the first motion. There was accordingly no service in the North Church on the Sunday. The *Edinburgh Advertiser* having commented on the Rev. Mr. Beith giving his casting vote against the preaching of the Gospel, the *Observer* maintained that as there were nine managers present there could be no casting vote, but the *Journal*, by publishing the minute of the meeting, which we have summarised above, clearly proved that it was by the rev. gentleman's vote the North Church was closed. This was the beginning of a most extraordinary and exciting struggle between the seceding managers, backed by the Town Council, and their colleagues, backed by the Presbytery of Stirling. The chief events of this memorable fight will be described in the course of our narrative.

Barricading the North Church.

The attenuated Presbytery of Stirling, at a meeting on the 6th June, appointed supplies for the vacant pulpits, but they were not allowed to do so without a protest by the seceding managers of the North Church, who submitted a petition setting forth that it was *ultra vires* of the Presbytery to make such appointment in respect that the North Church was neither a Parish Church nor a Chapel of Ease connected with the Establishment. "It is true," the petition proceeded to state, "that by a resolution of the Presbytery of Stirling, in the month of March last year, the said Church was declared one of the Parish Churches of Stirling; but it is quite apparent, from the decision of the Court of Session in the case of Stewarton, that this was beyond their powers as a Church Court, even had they been a legally constituted Presbytery. And that they were not so, the rev. Presbytery are bound to hold, by the resolution of the late General Assembly of the Established Church, seeing that certain of the constituent members of the Presbytery were ministers of *quoad sacra* parishes." On these grounds, the Presbytery were asked to refrain from interfering with the administration of religious ordinances in the said North Church, or in any other manner or way. This document was signed by the Rev. Mr Beith, who, if the creation of the North Church as a parish church was illegal in consequence of ministers of *quoad sacra* churches having a seat in the Presbytery, was himself never legally parish minister, because he was inducted by a Presbytery similarly constituted, and had a *quoad sacra* minister presiding at his induction. It was therefore very pertinently asked if he was prepared to hand back to the heritors the stipend unlawfully exacted from them. In later years, as we have seen from his "Statement," Dr Beith abandoned his untenable position, which, indeed, was a mere legal quirk—one of many emanating from the same quarter at that time.

The Presbytery, ignoring the extraordinary petition of the seceding managers, appointed the Rev. Mr Brown, of Alva, to preach in the North Church on the following Sunday, and to demand the keys of the church. The Rev. Mr Beith and his friends had, however, no intention of submitting to the "Residuary" Presbytery, and they formed the bold design of locking out the minister appointed to preach—a somewhat novel application of the principle of "spiritual" independence. It will be the fairest way to give the two accounts published at the time of this remarkable display of physical force. In a newspaper article, evidently penned by the Rev. Mr Beith, the writer says:—"Between that time [the Presbytery meeting] and the Sabbath, those who are friendly to the Kirk had got possession of the keys, but as it should seem, without the consent of the majority of the managers. When this fact became known to the majority of the managers, a meeting was called late on Saturday night, at which it was resolved, seeing the keys had been obtained, the workmen should enter the house in another way and barricade the doors in the inside, which was accordingly done, but lest even this should not be found sufficient to prevent intrusion, a watch was placed on the outside all night. When the hour for public worship arrived, the watch was still there, and the clergyman found that, although he was in possession of the keys, the doors would not open. At this moment a good many people were collected, more for the purpose of seeing what was going on, than with, as it appeared, the intention of forming a congregation. When the minister approached, the people drew near, but he was received without any external expression of satisfaction or dissatisfaction, and when he went away he was allowed to depart in the same peaceable manner." The rev. writer seems surprised and disappointed the minister was not hooted or assaulted, for he adds, "So thoroughly are the principles of religious liberty understood and acted upon in Stirling, that we verily believe any form of worship would be tolerated; and its followers left unmolested, provided they only kept the public peace."

The other version of the story is as follows:—"It is no stretch of charity [this is, of course, not the meaning of the writer] to say that the late hour of meeting was adopted because it precluded the minority from resorting to such means as might be deemed legal or advisable for securing the rights of the congregation and maintaining the authority of the Presbytery. We wish this were all we had to say of the spirit evinced by the non-intrusionists; but we are sorry to add that their hostility has shown itself in a still more unseemly manner. Without going into details, we may shortly state that, to prevent worship as intended by the Presbytery, tradesmen were set to work to barricade and nail up the doors, and we believe were engaged in this operation till the indecent hour of twelve o'clock at least. It may be proper to state that Mr Brown, of Alva, appeared at the Church at the usual time for worship in the forenoon. On finding that entrance could not be effected, he directed the church-officer, who was in attendance, to make the requisite proclamation of marriages at the Church door, and thereupon withdrew." The real object of all this opposition was, as the *Journal* pointed out, to keep the Church shut as long as possible in the hope that the congregation would be dispersed, and the incident shows how bitter the seceders were, and, with all their pride of superior righteousness, how utterly they were oblivious of the great principle of Christian love and charity. At the meeting of Presbytery on the following Tuesday, the Rev. Mr Brown reported what had taken place, and laid the keys of the North Church on the table. A deputation from the congregation, headed by the late Sheriff Sconce, an able and steadfast friend of the Established Church in her hour of trial, appeared before the Presbytery, asking regular supplies for the pulpit, and the Presbytery resolved to ask the advice of the General Assembly's Law Committee in the case, the seceding managers again protesting.

The Town Council and the Parish Churches.

The Disruption afforded too good an opportunity for reviving the question of the suppression of the second or third charges, or both, to be overlooked by the Town Council of the time, which was said to be mainly composed of Leaguers, Chartists, and Voluntaries. On the 13th June, after adopting a motion to admit the public to all meetings of the Council for the consideration of Town and Hospital business, the members adjourned from the Council Chamber (the present Parochial Board-room) to the Sheriff Court-room, the doors of which were thrown open to the public, but only a limited number attended. Bailie Smith, after repeating his former statement as to the origin of the second and third charges, moved a series of resolutions which need not be given in full. They were founded on the legal quibble that the Council had had no official intimation of the uncollegiating of the three charges by any competent authority, and it was maintained that as the agreed on conditions had never been complied with, and the three incumbents had withdrawn from the Establishment, to present to the three ministerial charges would be a misapplication of the funds of the town, by making sinecure offices for such ministers as would, in the altered circumstances, have no congregation. It was therefore proposed that the minister paid from the funds of the parish should be presented to the East or West Church, and a committee was moved to intimate this resolution to the managers of the North Church, and with instructions to make all necessary inquiry as to the best means of legally getting the second and third charges suppressed. The Establishment had only a handful of supporters in the Council, and while objecting to any interference with the North Church, they weakly agreed to the resolution to suppress the second and third charges. The *Journal* expressed its surprise that there was no friend of the Church in the Council to tell its enemies that the blow which they had in such breathless indecent haste levelled at the venerable institution, was beyond their power, and it republished the opinions of counsel in the case of 1835, and the decision of the Court of Session in the Ministers' Widows' Fund case, which we have already dealt with. In the same article we get a glimpse of the seceding ministers' attempts to seduce the members of the Church of Scotland. Every day of the week, Sabbath not excepted, an organised system of proselytising was kept up, the ministers of the Establishment being held up as incapable of preaching the gospel, as men placed beyond the pale of saving grace, "whose prayers can never reach the throne of mercy." "Is it," asks the *Journal*, "in such a state of things we are called upon to pronounce an opinion as to the number and conditions of particular congregations? Surely not. As everything will be done to maintain the vigour of the existing crusade against the church, it may be long before the present feverish excitement expires, and the people in a condition to inform themselves and judge calmly and without prejudice. But we are satisfied that when this fair and desirable period arrives, a prodigious change will take place in public opinion, and that many will look back with shame and confusion on the revilings and bitter scoffings which they aided in heaping on the heads of their fellow-citizens." This contemporary testimony is valuable as showing the spirit of the seceders towards those who remained loyal to the Church of their fathers.

Signs of Reaction.

It was not long before the Established Church gave evidence of recovery from the staggering blow she had received by the Disruption. It seems that certain members of the Town Council, with the view of strengthening their position, undertook the task of personally counting the people who attended the East and West Churches (the North Church still being shut) on Sunday, 25th June. The Free Church organ said there was only a skeleton congregation—a "miserable turnout," whereas the *Journal* maintained that in the afternoon the West Church was crowded, and that many abstained from attending from resentment against the counting process, while others refrained from appearing, for fear of tresspassing on the kindness of friends, or incommoding the seatholders. But the *Observer* itself afterwards supplied the best evidence of the reaction which had thus early begun. It acknowledged that the number of communicants at the first sacrament was 350, while, according to the same authority. the skeleton congregation, a month after the Disruption, only numbered 380. There must therefore have been great progress in the interval, as the number of communicants would represent a congregation of nearly a thousand.

The Town Council Checkmated.

There can be little doubt that but for the fact of the Town Clerk having joined the Free Church, the Council would not have committed the blunder of adopting the illegal resolutions previously mentioned. The Glasgow Town Council, having taken opinion of counsel as to whether it was imperative upon them to fill every vacant pulpit and pay the full amount of the stipends, were informed that they must fill and pay. Of course, the same thing was found to apply to Stirling, and the Council's heroic resolutions became null and void. Their resolution with regard to the North Church was rescinded by a later

Council, as it was found to be contrary to both law and fact. The Rev. Mr Beith was in sore distress over the expenditure of £1000 annually for the religious instruction of about 500 people, including men, women and children, "merely because it pleased them to remain in the Kirk," and he advised the Town Council not to fill up the vacancies, but to allow the Presbytery to exercise the *jus devolutum*, and meanwhile petition the Legislature to alter the law. This advice the Council did not accept, but at the instigation of their own legal adviser, they began a series of strategic movements, which, firmly met by the Presbytery and the local supporters of the Establishment, ended in failure and disgrace Under the power of a Court of Session interdict against the seceding managers taking illegal possession of the North Church, that place of worship was re-opened on Sunday, 6th August, and on the following Tuesday the defeated and disappointed minister of the Free North met with his congregation, and it was decided to build a new church behind the present site of the Baptist Chapel. "Popery, in her palmiest days," (wrote the Rev. Mr Beith in the bitterness of his spirit), "never exceeded conduct like this." The analogy, however, is not quite clear.

The East Church Vacancy.

Actuated by Free Church hostility to the Establishment, the Town Council refused to give the East Church congregation the choice of a minister, thereby earning an unenviable distinction among Scottish Corporations. As the majority of the Council were great advocates of "spiritual independence," the outward and visible sign of which was freedom to choose a minister, their inconsistency excited as much ridicule as their rancour did disgust among the sober-minded of the community. Strangely enough, Bailie M'Alley and other members of the Established Church played into the hands of the enemy. It was the Bailie who moved a presentation to the Rev. Dr Wilson of Irvine, and this was agreed to by a Council most of whose members had left the Establishment on account of patronage, and who knew that the presentation was opposed to the wishes of the congregation. The Presbytery were bound to moderate in a call to Dr Wilson, but they showed their sense of the situation by sending two Commissioners to the Presbytery of Irvine, instead of transmitting the call and other documents in the usual way. The call was signed by only 14 members of the congregation, exactly double the number of signatures appended to the call to that great apostle of non-intrusion, the Rev. Mr Beith! At the next meeting of the Presbytery of Stirling, the Commissioners reported that they had requested to be heard in explanation of some of the papers, but this the Presbytery of Irvine had refused, and had agreed to the translation of Dr Wilson. Counsel appeared for the presentee, and also for a number of objectors to Dr Wilson, and the Presbytery resolving to receive the objections, Dr Wilson's advocate protested and appealed to the Synod of Perth and Stirling. The case was referred by the Synod to the Assembly, which, by a small majority, decided in favour of Dr Wilson, and remitted to the Presbytery to proceed with all convenient speed with his settlement. Dr Wilson was accordingly inducted on the 22d August, 1844. He was said to be in delicate health at the time, but he survived till 1853.

The West Church Vacancy.

Finding they were bound by law to present to all the three charges, the Town Council determined to perform this duty in as disagreeable a manner as possible to the remanent members of the Establishment. Being patrons, they threw all their non-intrusion principles to the winds, and resolved to exercise their patronage with as little regard for the wishes of the people as any private patron had shown previous to the Disruption. In the case of the West Church, a petition was presented to the Council signed by no fewer than 211 members of the congregation, nearly all communicants, praying the Council to present the Rev. William Findlay to the second charge. Treasurer (afterwards Bailie) Menteath, writer, one of the Free Church members of the Council, took up the position that as they had refused to give the East Church people their choice of a minister, they must also refuse the West and every other, or else sacrifice their constituency. Mr Monteath evidently thought nothing of his own inconsistency as a non-intrusionist in refusing the people their choice. At a later stage of the same Council meeting, (16th October, 1843) this Free Churchman rose and said that when he entered the Council that evening he did not intend to propose anyone to fill the second charge, but he would now move that the Rev. Robert Watson, Chaplain of the Castle, should be presented to the second charge and West Church. He had met Mr Watson at dinner and elsewhere, and could bear testimony to his being an excellent man. Mr Monteath's extraordinary conduct did not escape public notice and condemnation. He was reminded that he entered the Council in 1835, on the express and sole condition that he would vote for the West Church congregation being allowed to choose Dr Bennie's successor, and that at an entertainment given to him and other successful candidates, he said "his sole consideration in soliciting their suffrages was his anxiety for the interests of the West Church." Mr Monteath was also chaffed about his reference to meeting Mr Watson at dinner, and was asked what were these dinner-table qualifications of the rev. gentleman which had called forth his admiration? Was it his carving, or his carnivorous and potatory capacities, or his enlivening talk? Provost Galbraith also incurred some censure by an ill-considered speech he delivered at the same meeting of the Town Council. He said that "at one time he did not intend to take any part in Church matters, but he had since altered his opinion. As a non-intrusionist, he held the principle that the people should have their choice of a minister, but that was not the law of the Church of Scotland, nor was it the law of the land, under the enactments of which they administered the right of patronage with which they had been invested by virtue of their office. He knew he would give offence to many individuals in town by the rigorous exercise of this right, but that was unavoidable, and therefore the less to be regretted." The *morale* of the Council was, it appears, seriously deteriorated by the Disruption. By a majority of 13 to 5, they decided in favour of Mr Watson, and Mr Lucas, in a letter signed "Justus," forcibly expressed what must have been the opinion of every person who was capable of judging impartially. "It must fill every honourable mind with indignation and sorrow (he writes) to see such a spectacle of pitiable inconsistency as is displayed by these members of the Town Council who profess to have left the Church because patronage is sinful and the Establishment is in bondage to the civil power, and yet exercise that patronage themselves, and exert their ingenuity to tighten the bonds which they imagine are now imposed upon the Church. If they act thus to accomplish what they may reckon a good, namely, the ruin of the Church, they are committing a sin which the Word of God most emphatically condemns; they are doing evil that good may come, they are acting on the most detestable of all principles, that the end sanctifies the means. Or if they act thus merely to show their brief authority, then, if they have escaped, by their secession, the character of the slave, they have earned the far more hateful character of the tyrant." The lapse of half-a-century has not deprived those words of of their weight, and in the cool light of to-day they stand forth as a well-merited condemnation of the Free Church policy of 1843.

A Lower Deep.

While the Town Council were thus engaged in harassing the section of the community who chose to adhere to the Church of Scotland, one of the seceding ministers was descending to the grossest libels upon the members of what he called the "Residuary" Presbytery of Stirling. In a scurrilous work emanating from Dundee, and entitled "The Wheat and the Chaff Gathered into Bundles," the author gave pen-and-ink portraits of the "old Moderates" and their "new allies." The Rev. Mr M'Culloch, who had been presented to Denny, was pourtrayed as "a very high and ardent professor of non-intrusion and spiritual independence, and a thorough-going supporter of the Evangelical side up to the era of the Convocation." This was republished in the local Free Church organ, which prided itself upon being a "religious paper," with the following note:—"What an appendix could we write to this short notice of the parish minister of Denny—but we forbear, as we would refrain touching, even with our stick, an unclean reptile settled in its lair." The Rev. Mr Beith being openly taxed with the authorship of this libel, was unable to deny it, and again Mr Lucas was ready with his lash. "Can the man (he asks in a letter signed "Philagathos") who deliberately avows that he nourishes the utmost loathing and abhorrence of a fellow-creature be a follower of the Lamb? Can the heart which, by his own confession, is full of enmity, be also at the same time full of grace?" The Disruption may have been all the jubilee speakers claim for it, but unquestionably, in its local aspect, it was the cause of much evil-speaking on the part of the seceders, ministers as well as laymen.

Another Check.

The manifest unfairness and harshness of the majority of the Town Council towards the Established Church congregations occasioned a revulsion of public feeling in their favour, and the Council found they had opponents of their high-handed and oppressive policy to reckon with upon whom they had not counted. The Seven Incorporated Trades stepped in and demanded to have a vote in the presentation of ministers to the second and third charges. Mr Chrystal, writer, father of the late Mr James Chrystal, and clerk to the Incorporation, appeared before the Presbytery and objected to the presentation to the Rev. Mr Watson, on the ground that it had been issued in disregard of the rights which belonged to the Incorporated Trades. Mr Galbraith, Town Clerk, contended that the Town Council were the sole patrons, and that all the Trades could claim was a vote in the calling of the minister after he had been presented. The Presbytery, nothing loth to encourage opposition to the Town Council, appointed a committee to search the records of the Presbytery and draw up a memorial for the purpose of obtaining the advice of the Procurator of the Church. The situation was afterwards complicated by a similar objection to the presentation of the Rev. Mr Findlay to the North Church, but the Trades, in view of the fact that in this latter case the congregation had made choice of Mr Findlay, did not insist on their alleged right of co-patronage. Mr Lucas, in a letter signed "Civis," explained how the matter stood. In choosing the first minister, the Town Council, the heritors of the parish, and the elders met and formed one body and elected the minister. No presentation was issued but an extract of the minute of the meeting was laid on the Presbytery table and upon it the Presbytery proceeded. The second minister was elected by the Town Council, along with delegates from each of the Seven Incorporated trades, the Tolerated Communities, and the Guildry. In 1818 the majority of the Council were opposed to Mr Small, but he was elected by a majority of the combined body and settled in opposition to the Town Council, whose nominee, the Rev. Archibald Bruce, was presented to the third charge by the same body. It was contended that the right of the Incorporated Trades, &c., although not exercised in subsequent elections of ministers to the second and third charges, continued to exist, and after much discussion, both in the Council and Presbytery, an action of interdict and reduction was entered in the Court of Session by the Incorporated Trades, but was departed from, and the settlement of Mr Watson in the West Church was proceeded with on the 19th September 1844. All these troubles, the Rev. Mr Beith affected to believe, came from internal dissension among the members of the Established

Church, but as we have seen, they really proceeded from the determination of the non-intrusion majority of the Town Council to exercise the right of patronage in a tryannical manner. This fact will become more apparent when we come to deal with the vacancy in the North Church.

A Bell-Ringing Episode.

The first Sacrament in the Established Church after the Disruption was celebrated on the second last Sunday of November, 1843, and, as usual, the town bells were rung on the fast-day and Saturday preceding, and on the Monday following. This roused the jealousy of the Free Church members of the Town Council, and at a meeting on the Monday, Councillor Parlane stated that the Sacrament of the Free Church was to be held on the first Sunday of December, and he moved that the bells of the Athenæum (now the Burgh Chambers) and the Town-house in Broad Street should be rung at the usual hours of worship on the fast-day preceding, and also on the Saturday and Monday. Mr Jaffrey, who seconded the motion, said he considered it highly proper that the bells belonging to the town should be rung to accommodate the congregations belonging to the church of the majority. He went further, and said that the bells should not be rung on the fast-days and other occasions of public worship in the Establishment. It was a perfect annoyance to the inhabitants in their shops to be dinned with the noisy jingle of bells while engaged in business. Mr Sawers considered Mr Parlane's proposition altogether a piece of silly vanity, but it was agreed to by the Council, and instructions given accordingly. It appeared, however, that the Council, in their anxiety to please the Free Church people, went beyond their powers, the Court of Session having decided in 1835 that the town bells of Paisley could not be rung except for service in the Established Churches, and that the Magistrates being bound to support the rights of the Established Church, had no power to authorise the burgh bell to be rung at the meeting of any dissenting congregation whatever, whether of the Secession, of Papists, Espiscopalian, or any other denomination whatever. According to the strict letter of the law, the Free Church folk had no right to ring a bell even in their own churches, and it was only by toleration they could use one. Councillor Jaffrey, therefore, found that his "liberal" ideas were contrary to the law of the land, and although the town bells were rung at the first Sacrament of the Free Church, the innovation was not continued. The incident is a small one, but it shows the virulent spirit of the seceders of 1843.

The North Church Vacancy.

The faithful few left in the North Church, having waived their claim to the services of the first minister, and been denied those of the second minister by the Free Church patrons, were left without a settled pastorate for some time. It was suggested to the Town Council, in a letter signed "Lud," (another *alias* of Mr Lucas') that having passed over the Rev. Mr Findlay for the second charge, notwithstanding the feeling of the congregation in his favour, they might present him to the third charge in the event of the North Church people showing a similar preference. This was too good advice to recommend itself to the Council, and taking advantage of the threatened action of the Incorporated Trades, they maintained that the only course was delay until it was seen what came out of the Glasgow case. At their meeting on the 20th November, 1843, Bailie Steel proposed that the Rev. Mr Jaffrey, assistant at Bothkennar, should be presented to the third charge, but this was met by a motion for delay, proposed by Bailie Smith. Bailie M'Alley said he suspected that a desire to keep the parish without a minister lurked under the motion for delay, and he could not refrain from expressing a conscientious opinion, that by their dilatoriness they had already inflicted a blow on the Establishment in Stirling, which they were only striving to render more severe by urging for unreasonable delay. To this well-founded charge the Free Church party could make no answer. During the discussion it was pointed out that if the Council did not present a minister to the third charge, the Presbytery could exercise the *jus devolutum* on the 24th November, the Rev. Mr Beith having vacated his church on the 24th May. The Town Clerk stated this was a mistake, as the Presbytery had not declared the third charge vacant until the 20th July. But here, as in all his rulings in connection with Church matters, the Town Clerk was proved to be wrong. The motion for delay was carried in the Council by 11 to 9, a notable circumstance being that the old seceders voted with the friends of the Establishment. Indeed, throughout the Council's ecclesiastical debates, the honourable way in which the old dissenters behaved was in marked contrast to the sectarian bitterness shown by the red-hot Free Churchmen.

Between the 20th and the 24th November, the Town Clerk had come to be of opinion that the safest way to prevent the Presbytery taking the presentation of a minister to the third charge out of the Council's hands, was to meet on the 24th and issue a presentation themselves. The North Church managers were made acquainted with this wheelabout, and a requisition in favour of Mr Findlay, although only got up in the course of the day, was signed by 106 members of the North Church. When the Council met in the evening, Provost Galbraith moved that Mr Findlay should be presented to the North Church, adding that he believed Mr Findlay to be a most excellent man, and one who, he was happy to think, would prove very acceptable to the congregation. Mr Grant remarked that he was not a little astonished at the sudden change that had occurred in the opinions of certain members of Council, but he was not more astonished than happy at the circumstance, as they would thereby be doing an act of tardy justice to the congregation. No opposition being offered to Mr Findlay, the presentation was signed by those present in order that it might be transmitted to the Moderator of the Presbytery that night.

The glaring inconsistency of the Council did not escape the notice of the critics. "They have (said the *Journal*) not only filled the very charge which eight days before they had resolved to suppress, if possible, but they have appointed the very man whom they formerly rejected. Nor is this all—they appoint him, knowing him to be recommended by the congregation—although they had previously declared that to be consistent, they must exercise their right as patrons in the case of the third charge, without regard to the wishes of the people, in the same way as they had done in those of the first and second charges." The Rev. Mr Beith, on the other hand, patted the Council on the back through the medium of the Free Church organ. "We cannot (he wrote) too much praise this justly popular body for their consistent conduct in the exercise of their rights as patrons," an observation which gained for him for the first and only time in his life a character as a humourist. But the most amusing part of the proceedings was still to come.

At the Presbytery meeting on the 11th December, Provost Galbraith and the Town Clerk appeared on behalf of the patrons, and acquiesced in the sustaining of the presentation to Mr Findlay, but immediately thereafter the Town

Clerk protested against the Presbytery proceeding farther in the matter till the decision of the Incorporated Trades' action in the Court of Session. The late Sheriff Sconce, who appeared for the presentee, Mr Findlay, exposed the absurdity of this protest, as the mandate from the Council simply empowered their representatives to lay the presentation on the table, and "to take all farther necessary steps in order that it might be sustained." The scene that followed the reading of the mandate must be given from the newspaper report of the proceedings:—

Mr SCONCE (to the Town Clerk)—That is your commission, and there your power ends. You are no party here.

Mr GALBRAITH (to the Clerk)—Show me that mandate. Does it not expressly say that—(reading the paper)—we are empowered to take all necessary steps—(here he stopped short)—

Mr SCONCE—To do what? To sustain the presentation (Applause.) That has been done, and your subsequent proceedings are incompetent.

Mr GALBRAITH—But I consider that the Provost is entitled, when he finds his rights endangered, to protest in order to protect these rights.

Mr SCONCE—Neither the Provost nor Mr Galbraith have any right to appear here without authority from the Council. The Presbytery ought not to allow it.

And the Presbytery did not allow it, and the Town Clerk took a protest in the hands of a notary public. Mr P. G. Morrison, writer, then said he appeared for the managers of the North Church, but was called in question by Mr Sawers, one of the managers, and asked to produce his mandate. This document bore to be signed by the six managers who had seceded, and Mr Sawers thereupon remarked that the mandate was of no more value than as much waste paper. Mr Morrison, on being asked what he wanted, said he wanted to protest against the deliverance of the Presbytery regarding the settlement of Mr Findlay in the North Church, inasmuch as that might interfere with the rights of the managers, and because the constitution of that Court was vitiated by the presence of *quoad sacra* members. This statement was received with loud laughter and hissing, and the Rev. Mr Brown replied that the Presbytery were all perfectly aware of their right to the North Church, in which they, unchallenged, preached and performed public work. But neither the Town Clerk nor Mr Morrison were easily put down, and a great hubbub arose over their attempts to get their protests recorded. Amid the confusion, Mr Morrison dictated his protest to the Presbytery Clerk, and Mr Galbraith, chuckling, remarked that he had managed it well. The Rev. Mr

Brown, however, proved more than a match for the two lawyers, and pointed out that no protest could be recorded without the leave of the Presbytery. To do justice to what followed, we must again have recourse to the *verbatim* report :—

Mr GALBRAITH—I say no (hear, hear, oh' and loud hissing)—that is not the fact (renewed disapprobation, to suppress which the Moderator interfered.)

Mr BROWN—I repeat a party who comes here to appeal must first ask leave. (Applause).

Mr M'CULLOCH, Denny—I am indeed happy to observe that Mr Brown has given such an intimation for the benefit of certain parties who either really are or pretend to be ignorant, (Much applause.) Mr Brown is quite correct.

Mr GALBRAITH—I have attended far more church courts than ever Mr Brown or Mr M'Culloch has done—(oh, oh ! and hissing)—and have seen much more of church law than either. I have taken protests and appeals hundreds of times and I never asked leave to do so, (renewed hissing.)

Mr M'CULLOCH—If you did not, you ought to have done so. And though I do not say that you are ignorant of that law which belongs to your own peculiar sphere and vocation, yet you will find you can get a lesson in church law here. (Great applause.)

Mr GALBRAITH (much excited)—This is the authority of a person who has been about six months a parish minister—formerly a *quoad sacra* mi——. The conclusion of the sentence was drowned in a perfect hurricane of hissing, loud cries of "disgraceful !" "shame ! shame !" and other strong expressions of disapprobation amidst which Mr Galbraith resumed his seat.

Mr M'CULLOCH—I despise as much as I disdain to answer that personal attack of Mr Galbraith. He has been sufficiently answered by the audience. But I may tell him, that not only may he here be instructed in what is church law ; but we can also give him a lesson in courtesy—the courtesy which is due to a church court and its members. *(Much applause.)*

The Town Clerk, baffled on this point, attempted to appear as a manager of the North Church, but was informed by Mr Brown that, as the managers appeared by an agent, he, as an individual manager, could not be heard. What is remarkable in these proceedings is the fact that the legal adviser of the Town Council should have made so many blunders, and that the sympathies of the public should have been so unmistakably with the "unpopular" Establishment.

On the 28th December, Mr P. G. Morrison appeared at the Presbytery meeting for the seceding managers of the North Church and took a notarial protest against the Presbytery moderating in the call, or settling Mr Findlay in the church. The Presbytery, however, took no notice of this protest, and adjourned to the Church, where the Rev. Mr Brotherston, of Alloa, preached, and the call was read and signed by about 70 members, no objections being offered. On Thursday, 18th January 1844, when the Presbytery met for Mr Findlay's induction, a protest on the part of Mr

Bruce of Kennet, as an heritor of the parish, was taken in the hands of a notary public, the reason assigned being that Mr Bruce held the North Church was not a parish church. It was stated for the Presbytery, in answer to the protest, that they found the North Church was admitted and already held to be a parish church by the Presbytery, and that, moreover, Mr Bruce was a member of the Presbytery at the time the North Church was so declared a parish church and agreed to its being made such, and therefore no objections could now be made by him to its being a parish church. The induction of Mr Findlay was then proceeded with.

The Parish Church Question again.

The troubles of the North Church did not end with the induction of Mr Findlay. The first and second ministers, for some reason or other, considered that the minister of the third charge ought to assist them in the East and West Churches, and at the Presbytery on 10th December 1844, Mr Monteath, writer, presented a petition signed by fifteen persons asking that the Rev. Mr Findlay be ordained to officiate regularly in the Parish Church. Dr. Wilson, in supporting the petition, held that the North Church was merely a preaching station, and was supported by his colleague in the West Church. At the next meeting of the Presbytery, on the last day of the year, Mr Sconce presented a petition signed by no fewer than 605 hearers in the different Established Churches in Stirling (showing the growth of the Establishment since the Disruption) including 13 elders, praying that no alteration be made in the ecclesiastical arrangements of the town and parish. An animated discussion ensued, in which Dr. Wilson and Mr Watson were opposed by nearly all the other members of the Presbytery. Mr Johnstone of Alva, in moving the continuance of the *status quo*, remarked that it was with pain and sorrow he perceived gentlemen holding high positions in the church lending themselves eagerly to break up existing arrangements highly beneficial to the interests of the church and its adherents. The two heritors that had signed the first petition, Mr Bruce of Kennet (father of Lord Balfour of Burleigh), and Mrs Burd of Forthside, Mr Johnstone considered were excluded from appearing because Mr Bruce was a consenting party to the arrangement, and Mrs Burd was one of the largest subscribers to the North Church. Mr Robert Sawers, another of the 15 petitioners, was, he said, a seatholder with an imaginary grievance, and of the remaining dozen, six were cobblers living in a garret, while the remainder had eluded all search. It was evident that Mr Johnstone felt, what is now quite apparent, that the whole thing was a Free Church plot, and that the two ministers, and the two heritors, were either the victims or the aiders and abettors of the conspirators. Dr Wilson spoke so strongly from his point of view that he incurred the rebuke of the Presbytery, Mr Balfour of Clackmannan (father of Mr J. B. Balfour, M.P., Lord Advocate), finding it necessary to instruct him in Church law. In the division eight voted for Mr Johnstone's motion, and only the mover and seconder for Dr. Wilson's, Mr Stark Gargunnock, declining to vote. An appeal was taken to the Synod, but nothing came of it, and the Rev. Mr Beith's last efforts to destroy the North Parish Church proved as abortive as its predecessors.

After the lapse of half-a-century, it is clear that the Disruption, so far as Stirling is concerned, was a deplorable mistake, and that the Town Council, if they had been allowed to suppress the second and third charges, would have committed an irremediable injustice and inflicted irreparable loss on the community. The flourishing condition of the Establishment in Stirling to-day is the best answer to the sneers and the slanders of the Rev. Dr. Beith and his supporters, and it is pleasing to think the ill-feeling they created has now almost entirely disappeared. The North Parish Church, served by a succession of able ministers, is the most prosperous of all, having a larger membership than the Free North itself, and doing, it may fairly be claimed, quite as much good. When the thirty years elapsed, the Rev. Dr. Beith, while disclaiming any "mercantile" motives, had the assurance to claim interest at the rate of 5 per cent. per annum on the money the managers had to advance at the time of the erection of the Church. The sum, amounting for his own share to £300, would have been a very nice return in a transaction in which, according to his own statement, "no profit could under any circumstances accrue." The rev. gentleman got his own money back, and in view of his attempts in 1843 and 1844 to wreck the congregation and render the Church useless for the purposes of the bond, this was more than he deserved or had any right to expect. Under an agreement with the Council in 1873, the North Church congregation paid over to the Rev. Dr. Beith and the other surviving managers, the sum of £425, the latter disponing the Church to the

Town Council, who accepted it in full implement of the obligations in the bond of 1843, and handed it over to the congregation for fifteen years. This period expired in 1888, but the arrangement continues to subsist by tacit relocation, as the lawyers say. There is, no doubt, however, that if the congregation liked, they could oblige the Town Council to take over the fabric and maintain it in precisely the same way as the other two parish churches in the town. But perhaps things are better as they are.

June, 1893. ED.

STIRLING ANCIENT 30.

AN INTERESTING OLD MANUSCRIPT.

W. J. Hughan writes as follows to *The Freemason:*—It is again my privilege and pleasure to announce the discovery, or recognition, of another MS. of the "Old Charges." It is owned by the Ancient Stirling Lodge, No. 30, Stirling, Scotland, and in its style is different to all the others known, being some two feet wide and 20 inches long, the writing running across the full width of the parchment. The document is mounted on cardboard and kept framed in the lodge, but by vote of the lodge the precious transcript of these regulations and history of the olden time was taken out of its surroundings and sent me for examination and report, through the kind services of the R.W.M., Bro. Thomas Allison.

Owing doubtless to its appearance, this copy of the "Old Charges" has for long been looked upon by the members as a Charter, and the meetings would not be deemed legal unless it was exhibited in the lodge room. Possibly owing to this circumstance the real character of the treasure has been overlooked, and thus has remained unknown and unrecognised for many years.

A letter has been preserved from the Clerk of the Grand Lodge of Scotland (Bro. Woodman), dated July 18th, 1854, to whom it was sent, to the effect that "the old and curious document, purporting to be the Charter of the Ancient Lodge, Stirling," could scarcely be so termed, as "it was more like a history or lecture upon Masonry, and contains many of the Charges well-known among Masons of the present day. It has been written, I should say, about the middle of the seventeenth century." It was the sight of this communication which led me to believe that another copy of the "Old Charges" was about to be traced, and so it has proved to be.

The text is similar to that of the "Grand Lodge MS., No. 1," to which "Family" it belongs, and in many respects agrees with the "Kilwinning MS.," but not uniformally so, for sometimes it more closely follows the former roll. There is, therefore, nothing new to report in regard to its recital, save a few funny errors, which, more or less, distinguish most of the scrolls.

The lodge is very old and of uncertain origin, the year 1706 ascribed to it, being, in my opinion, much too late. It is likely to be the same lodge that was represented on the junior of the two charters granted to the St. Clair family, as protectors of the Craft, which, according to the estimate of Bro. D. Murray Lyon, was written in 1628 *(circa.)* This copy of the "Old Charges" was evidently used by the lodge at the reception of candidates soon after that period, and, possibly, then it was either wholly, or mainly operative in character.

That this was so, is practically established by two forms of certificates which are written at the foot of the document. These are quite new to me, and I do not believe any such have hitherto been made known.

The one on the left hand reads—

Wee the Gentelmen Bayliffes and other undersubscribers withine the Toune and Shire of Stirling do by this p'nts testifie and declair that ——— Maister Maissone of Stirling heath lab'od witine the said Brugh of Stirling since his infancie, during which speace he heath beheaved himself honestlie to our knowledge ffrie of any offence, and heath ffinished all the works and buildings that ever he took in hand within or about this Sheire, as we know no impedement why the ——— may not be accepted to work as Maister Maissone within any part of this ———. He always beheaving himself as offoir, whereof we testifie to between us, as witnesseth our handes———

The other form, to the right, is to the following effect—

We the nobelmen barons knights Gentelmen Tutors of minors and others under wrot subscribers do by these p'nts declair that ——— heath ffinished Completed and fullie endit all the mainers of Ouses, Castells, Abays, and buildings, that he did tak in hand most deutiefullie ffaithfullie and honestlie to our contentment and so may be admitted to work as Maister Maissone in any place off this Statione when he can heave occaisione. In testimoney whereof subscribit as ffolowes.

Many portions of the caligraphy are most difficult to decipher, both of the MS. proper and the two forms of certificate, but I believe my transcript will be found to be as correct as possible, under the circumstances. A few of the peculiar readings of this "Old Charge" will be given in a separate issue of the reproduction; and I quite agree with the opinion of the late Bro. Woodman, Grand Clerk, that the period of its transcription may be fixed for 1650 *circa*. It does not appear to me to be a copy of the "Kilwinning MS." or at least, not of the one known by that title, but of an older, and in some respects, different document. The Lodge was sometimes called "Stirling Kilwinin" (or Kilwinning), so early as 1745, in the records preserved; but there is no evidence of such an origin, neither is it at all likely; only it was the fashion last century to describe old lodges as pendicles of "Mother Kilwinning."

TENT PREACHING IN NORRIESTON.

The gospel tents of various Evangelistic Associations, moving from place to place, have made us familiar with tent preaching. But the tent preaching of the past generation was an entirely different institution. The tent was simply an erection to shield the preacher from wind and rain. Now it is capacious enough to hold both preacher and people, and is made, as far as possible, both wind and water proof. The Norrieston tent was square, with a sloping roof, and was raised by four feet somewhat above the ground. It was painted and was neither unhandsome to the audience nor inconvenient to the occupant.

Some part of the churchyard, or more usually a field near the church, was selected as the site.

Open air preaching, or conventicles, as such services were called, was declared to be illegal during the troublous times of the seventeenth century, yet the ousted ministers continued to proclaim the gospel as opportunity offered. Rev. John King, chaplain to Lord Cardross and minister of the Port of Monteith, who afterwards was beheaded, made himself obnoxious to the authorities by holding field services. Soldiers were despatched from Stirling and apprehended him at Cardross. "Some country people," however, "who had profited much by his ministry," rose in his defence and rescued him from the soldiers. In this encounter, which took place in 1675, "in the moss beneath Boquhapple," one of the Norries of Norrieston was slain. At this stirring time William, the eighth Earl of Menteith, was residing in his house on Inch Talla, Port of Monteith, and being related to "the bloody Claverhouse" and "Bonnie Dundee," he sought with a high hand to put down the field preachings. In a letter of thanks sent him by the Chancellor of Scotland (in the Red Book of Menteith) it is stated "that your Lordship has taken great care and been at extraordinary paines in searching for conventicles and apprehending rebells and other disorderlie persones who frequented the same."

John Balfour, known as "Burley," visited Ure of Shirgarton, and the Earl of Menteith was anxious to apprehend him. In this he failed, but handed over two notable prisoners, Arthur Dougall, whose refuge in Kippen is still pointed out, and Harie Dow of Polder, of whom "wee doe impower you to sett him at libertie, &c., and in your prosecution of his Majesty's service your Lordship may expect all due encouragement from us."

With so powerful and active a neighbour, our ancestors would not dare lightly to hold open air services. The battle of Bothwell Bridge, so disastrous to the persecuted Covenanters, was fought in 1679. There is a well-grounded tradition that three brothers of the name of Marjoribanks, fled after the defeat and settled in this neighbourhood. There is a gravestone in Norrieston Churchyard thus inscribed, "Heir lyes Samuel Marjoribanks, who departed this life the 14 day of March and of his age 28, 1690." [In a former article in the *Sentinel*, this was stated by mistake as the grave of Samuel Macgregor.] If the above Samuel was one of the three fugitives, he was a lad of 18 years when Bothwell Bridge was fought.

The first minute of the Church of Bridge of Teith contains an interesting notice of open air services in our neighbourhood. It was on the 17th July, 1740, that Ebenezer Erskine, minister of Stirling, preached at Cessintully, at the east end of Thornhill, in a field near Burnhead, and formed the seceders into a church, which immediately proceeded to an election of elders and the formation of a Kirk Session.

The communion of the Lord's Supper is no longer the elaborate and lengthy service it used to be. Worshippers are not detained from dinner much longer on the communion Sunday than by the ordinary services. No extra staff of assistants is essential any longer. In olden times ministers were wont to secure the help of neighbouring ministers for the services of the fast day, of the preparation Saturday, of the Sabbath, and of the

Thanksgiving Monday. On the Sabbath great crowds of worshippers would convene, and, in order to supplement the pulpit supply, the tent was called into requisition. Sometimes they would walk long distances to hear a favourite preacher. On one occasion, an esteemed clergyman, still alive, observed a restless movement among the hearers around the tent, and, taking in the situation, he announced to his audience, "It seems this is to be a walking sermon; be it so; I shall walk, too," and leaving the tent he discoursed in peripatetic fashion. When a popular speaker ascended the steps of the tent, the people crowded around him, but when a "dry stick" appeared there, they would suddenly recollect that they had somewhere else to go. The tent was used while "the tables" were being served within the Church.

Although there was a large gathering of strangers, yet they did not usually go forward to the table. They contented themselves with hearing, and seeing, and singing. The communion tokens of Norrieston Church, dated 1776, are numbered up to 9, indicating that there might have been nine tables served during the day.

It is told that at one of the diets of catechising in the Port of Monteith parish, the question was asked, "How many sacraments are there?" The parishioners replied, "Five—the Kippen ane, the Callander ane, the Norrieston ane—that's three; Kincardine's four, and yer ain ane, sir, that mak's five." Hospitality was always readily extended to strangers from other parishes on the occasion of a communion. It is said that if the day were fine about 40 would go to Kippen communion from the Norrieston district, and "an awfu' lot of strangers," said an aged informant, "used to come to Norrieston from Kippen, the Port, Callander, and a' roun' an' roun'." The leader of the praise had a chair near the tent, and if he was well supported, the effect of this part of the worship would be more telling under the open sky than inside the sacred building.

Tent preaching was discontinued in this district a year or two after the Disruption.

THE NORRIE MONUMENT IN THE CHURCHYARD OF NORRIESTON.

As this interesting monument in the north wall of the churchyard is fast becoming illegible in several places, it will not be amiss to give the inscription in the *Sentinel*:—

"The righteous shall be in | everlasting remembrance | The underneath | TOMBSTONES | were discovered in digging | the foundation of the new chapel of Norriestown | in the year 1812 and are | placed here at the expense of the public in token | of respect and to perpetuate the memory of G. Norrie | of Norriestown the original donor of the site of the chapel | and churchyard—erected A.D. 1827.

Heir lyes Gabriel | Norrie of Norriestoun | who [ended] this lif | the 13 Septr 81 and of his age 47 |
He ever wys and prudent was
At hom abrood as wys men knaws
G. N. & M. F
Memento mori—with the emblems of mortality.
After death remains [ ]
Heir lyes Margaret Forrester,
Lady Norrie, who depairted this lif
the 22 of Jany. 83 of her age 41.

The knot of soul and body death untyed
Heir ly my bones, my soul which death defy'd
The earthly pairt which dropt in dust heir lyes
Like Phoenix from the ashes shall arise
Pure and resplendant thus restored to me.
My sweet companion we shall joyntly see.

From Kincardine Churchyard we take the following:—

ASHENTREE
A.D. A.C.
(With shield charged with plough and other agricultural implements.)

Just at an age when youthful minds are full
Of transitory vanities and pride
He felt religion, by it formed a rule
Nor did his after actions it deride.
Death called him sudden tho' advanced in years
Obedient to the message he resigned
While strong his hopes increased and few his fears
Noble sincere simplicity combined.
Indifferent about sublunary fame
Even *dust to dust* his latest word proclaim.

Died, 3rd May, MDCCCVIII., aged 81 years.
[" Dust to dust " is cut in German characters.]

AN OLD CERTIFICATE OF CHURCH MEMBERSHIP.

Norriestown, May 29, 1798.

That the bearer, John M'Culloch, left the perambulated bounds in March 1797, having resided therein two years and upwards preceding that date, always behaving soberly and devoutly, and left this free of public scandal or ground of church censure known to me; and might thus be admitted into any christian congregation or society wherever Providence might cast his lot, is attested by JAMES HUGHES, Minister.

Thornhill. G. W.

THE STANDING STONES OF STIRLING DISTRICT.

(Continued.)

BLACKFORD STONES.

(1) On the south side of the road from Blackford to Auchterarder, about 50 yards west from Loaninghead, where the line of the road is crossed by that from Gleneagles to Crieff, stands a fine stone of Highland grit. It measures 4 ft. 10 in. in height above ground, 10½ ft. in girth at the base, and 6 ft. 9 in. in circumference at top. It shows four sides of nearly equal measurement:—that facing noth being 2 ft 4 in., south 2 ft. 8 in., west 2 ft. 8 in., and east 3 ft. On the north is an incised figure in the form of an parallelogram, 10 in. broad by 9 in. high, divided into three equal portions by two horizontal lines. (2) About 300 yards in a westerly direction from this is another stone standing in a field. This is roughly columnar in shape, but wider at the base than above. Its height is 3 ft. above ground; circumference at base 6 ft. 5 in., diminishing to 4 ft. 2 in at the top. It is of metamorphic schist. The line of direction between these two gives a horizontal angle of 260°.

AUCHTERARDER STONES.

Less than a mile to the west of the town, at the point where the roads from Gleneagles and from Auchterarder for Kinkell meet, is a fine group of stones, two only of which are now standing. These stand on the summit of what has been a well-defined mound, and the stones now lying where the roads unite seem to have stood originally at the same height. The road has been driven through the group at a lower level than the summit of the mound, and the stones have been thrown down and laid in the waste space at the point of junction. The small mercy to be thankful for is that they have not been broken up altogether and used for road metal. This has probably been due to the circumstances that one of these stones has a curious encircling groove running round it, which perhaps impressed even the vandal roadmakers with the idea that it might be worthy of preservation. It would be interesting to know whether, when the circle or group of stones was cut through, any cist or interment was found. One would expect such to be the case, but I have not yet got any information on the point. There are several stones lying on the spot which may or may not be pieces of the original standing stones. Two considerable bits of old red sandstone, at least, look as if they were fragments of an original whole. Two great stones, however, are unmistakeably prostrate standing-stones; and from the positions in which they lie, it seems to me as if the persons who had uprooted them had laid them down as nearly as possible on the sites they had occupied (at the original higher level, of course) when standing. The direction in which both of the standing stones point is 235°, and a line taken from each of the prostrate stones to the opposite standing one gives very nearly the same angle (240°). The prostrate stones are of metamorphic schist. The northerly one measures 7 feet in length by 3 feet in width, and is from 12 to 18 inches thick. A grove or furrow, 2 inches deep at its greatest depth, and from 2 to 4 inches wide, appears to run right round it, at a distance of 2 feet 10 inches from the end, which may have been about the middle height of the stone when erect. The lower side of the stone cannot be seen, but the appearance at the edges indicates that the furrow is carried all the way round. It looks just such a hollow as might be worn in stone by the long-continued attrition of an iron chain. The more southerly prostrate stone is 6 feet in length, 4 feet wide, and has an average thickness of 18 inches. The two stones still standing are on the high bank above the road, just inside the hedge. These are both of old red sandstone, thinnish slabs, facing in the direction already mentioned. That to the south is 4 feet 10 inches in height, 2 feet 8 inch broad at the base, and 10 inches thick. The other is 5 ft. 3 in. at its greatest height, 3 feet 10 inches wide, and from 13 to 15 inches thick. On its northern face it shows a number of depressions or indentations curiously resembling prints of human feet. These Mr Kidston considers to be due to natural weathering.

CAMP STONES—BRAES OF DOUNE.

This, and the stone to be immediately after referred to, I notice in passing, not because I consider them in the same category with the others, but simply because their names seem to indicate some obscure historical or traditional connection which may yet be cleared up. What is called the Camp Stone lies high up on the Braes of Doune, on an eminence in a plantation on the left hand of the Annat, just where that stream leaves the moorland and leaps over a waterfall to take its way through the more cultivated ground below. It is a large split block of conglomerate, such as are scattered plenteously enough over the braes that slope down from Uamvar, and does not seem to me ever to have been a standing stone. Its length is 9 feet 9 inches, breadth at base 3 feet, and height 2 feet. As to the reason of the name, I have not been able to learn much. It has been suggested that it is connected with the names Cambus and Cambus-Wallace—places further down the Annat.

GORDON STONE—BRAES OF FEDDAL.

The Gordon stone lies on the south bank of the Bullie burn, about 300 yards west of where it is joined by the Tochie burn. It is a huge block of conglomerate, similar in most respects to the Camp stone on the Braes of Doune, but much larger. It measures, at its greatest length—south-west to north-east—14½ ft. It has a height of 7 ft., almost uniform throughout, and is 7 ft. across at the south-west end. A line taken through its long axis makes an angle of 255°. The north side is the natural bed of the rock, inclined to the horizon at an angle of 70°. It is not a standing stone, in the usual sense of the term, but merely, like the Camp stone, a great boulder dropped from the glacial drift. No one in the neighbourhood, so far as my enquiries went, could explain the origin of the name. I have a vague remembrance of having read somewhere that there were once proprietors of Feddal of the name of Gordon.

THE GLENHEAD STONES.

1. These stones have also been referred to in my previous paper, but for the sake of completeness and as the measurements have been verified by additional visits, they are included here. They occupy a site about equi-distant from Dunblane, Bridge of Allan, and Doune, on the farm of Glenhead, close to the boundary line between the parishes of Lecropt and Kilmadock, but within the confines of the latter, and about 100 yards north of the line of road between Bridge of Allan and Doune. Three stones are still standing in a line which takes a direction of 235°. Another lies beside the most northerly of three. One is inclined at first sight to take this for a portion broken off from the stone beside which it lies. But the way in which the bed-markings run seems to be rather against this supposition. It may have formed a fourth in the original group, which had been overthrown and moved to beside the other in order to be out of the way of agricultural operations. The most southerly stone is irregularly pyramidal in shape. It stands 6 ft. 8 in. above ground. The

converging sides are each 3 ft. 6 in., and the third 2 ft. in breadth. The circumference is therefore 9 ft. The second in the series is interesting from the cup-marks which cover the flat top. Of these there are 24 in all, one near the centre larger than the others—although it has obviously and recently been tampered with. This stone, though not so high, is more massive than the others. It has four sides which run almost straight up from base to top. The two greater sides are each 3½ ft., and the two smaller each 2½ ft. across. The circumference is 12 ft., the height 4 ft. 6 in. The third stone is 6 ft. in height, 2 ft. 6 in. in breadth, and 1 ft. 6 in. thick. The fourth, which lies beside it, measures 7 ft. in length, is 4 ft. 6 in. at its greatest breadth, and 1 ft. 10 in. thick. All the stones are of Highland grit. 2. To the north of this alignment, about a quarter of a mile distant, and a little to the east of the farm buildings of Glenhead, stands another tall stone in the line of a wall that bounds a strip of plantation. It is seven feet in height above the level of the field to the east, is 5 ft. 6 in. in width, and varies in thickness from 15 in. to 2 ft. It is a large slab of the native rough sandstone of the district, and is set in a line of 253°.

BLAIR DRUMMOND STONE.

There is a very fine boulder of Highland grit, stranded on a gravel mound, near the official residences on the Blair Drummond estate. The knoll is wooded, leaving a clear space in the centre for the stone. It would thus appear to have been thought worthy of preservation for some reason or other. It has no appearance, however, of having been erected as a standing stone. It measures 6 feet in height and 12 feet at its widest circumference. In the new Statistical Account of Kincardine-in-Menteith it is thus referred to:—"We may take notice of a large stone which stands on the summit of Borland Hill. It is 5 feet above the ground and 12 feet in circumference, but more flat than round, and of a conical form near the top. It is apparently in a native state, bearing no marks of the hammer or the chisel, and is a very large boulder of slate *(sic)*." A very vague tradition represents it as having been a place of religious worship in superstitious times. There are no other remains near to confirm this opinion; but whether it be correct or not, it is evident that its site is a very important one, and may have been useful as a signal station, as it commands a view not only of the road across the Moss of Kincardine, but also of the line of the Roman stations along the Forth and Teith in the direction of the Camp at Ardoch.

MALLING CUP-MARKED STONE—LAKE OF MENTEITH.

On the west side of the Lake of Menteith, about half a mile south from the farm-house of Malling, this stone is to be found, lying at the boundary of the arable land. The ground at the place rises into a slight eminence, on the top of which the stone lay till some seven or eight years ago, when a labourer took it into his head that a stone on which so much labour had evidently been spent must have been intended to cover something valuable. He proceeded to excavate the earth at the side with the intention of getting at the buried treasure, with the result that the stone slipped down into the hole which he had made, where it now lies. It is quite possible, however, that an interment, if no treasure. might be found beside it on further research. The stone is roughly circular on the surface, measuring about 4 feet in diameter. It is entirely covered with with cup and ring marks—22 cups in all—varying in size from an inch to two inches in diameter. The cups and rings are very symmetrically formed. Nearly in the centre is a fine one surrounded by four circular grooves. Others have incomplete triple and quadruple circles, with radial duct dividing them. There are other curious curves that sometimes interlace, and near the lower side of the stone are five or six cups with straight channels running out from them over the edge. This is an extremely interesting stone. It is unique in our neighbourhood, so far as I know, in showing these symmetrical carvings. They are now, however, much weather-worn.

ABERFOYLE STONE CIRCLES.

To the south-west of the Manse of Aberfoyle, and just outside its policy wall, there is a sort of plateau not of great extent. Just to the north of this plateau, it may be mentioned, used to stand the change-house and the old Clachan, some ruins of which may still be seen. The edge of this eminence is a large arc of a circle, and from it the ground dips to a marshy hollow. Here stands a small stone circle, about 20 feet in diameter. It has unfortunately been dug into, and the stones consequently somewhat displaced. The present ruin consists of 12 or 14 stones, set pretty close together and surrounding a central one. At one or two points the appearance suggests an original double circle, but the outer one is not now nearly complete. From the circumference a straight line of stones runs outwards to a distance of 55 feet in a direction 45° west of magnetic north. In this line there are six stones, arranged at nearly equal distances from each other, the largest being a nearly rectangular slab 16½ feet by 4 feet. None of these are now standing. This line is a radius of the circle produced; and if we take a diametrical line through the circle at right angles to this radius, we get a direction of 251°. Another line, nearly a tangent to this circle, runs from circumference a distance of about 50 feet in a direction 5° to the east of magnetic south. The stones in this line are more irregularly placed, and there is a considerable blank about the middle. Both lines run down the sloping edge of the plateau—the latter more directly. At the extremity of this there is a circular mound of about 28 feet radius, not very high. This appears to be of a gravelly nature. A boulder on the top is about 4 feet from the centre. Round the circumference are several blocks showing above ground—not standing up. The mound is close to the edge of the previously mentioned marsh. The first circle has been dug into, the other has no appearance of having been touched.

FINTRY STONES.

1. *The Knockcraich Stone.*—This stone stands on the north side of the Water of Endrick, about a mile below the bridge at the village of Fintry, and two or three hundred yards below the farm-house of Knockcraich. It is placed on the bank rising up from the river. In shape it is approximately square—the two sides facing nearly east and west, measuring each 1 ft. 7 in., the north face 1 ft. 6 in., and the south 1 ft. 3 in. These dimensions are uniform from top to bottom. The total girth is therefore 5 ft. 11 in., while the height is 3 ft. 8 in. Orientation, 225°. There are a number of cupmarks both on the top and side, as well as several incised lines and other markings, some of which, however, give evidence of recent sculpture. The stone seems to have brought down through the ages a tradition of sanctity in connection with it, as there is a legend to the effect that any attempt to move it is attended by convulsions of nature and evil consequences to the rash disturber.

2. *The Machar Stones.*—The name by which these stones are locally known merely indicates the position they occupy in a plain (Gaelic *magh*) or comparatively level among the hills. It has

come down, of course, from the time when Gaelic was the language of the district. They are situated on the summit of a low mound which rises in the upper valley of the Carron, not far from the source of that stream, and close to its junction with the Bin Burn. This secluded valley is enclosed on the south by the Meikle Bin and the Campsie Fells, on the north by Duncarron Hill, which separates it from the glen of the Endrick, on the west by Holehead and the hills which give rise to Carron Water, while it is open to the east in the direction of the vale of Carron, although, even in this direction, the view is cut off by the hills of Dundaff. The rising ground, overshadowed by the Meikle Bin, on which the stones stand, is so regularly shaped on the top as to raise a suspicion that it has been formed, or at any rate, assisted by art. Geological authority, however, pronounces it to be quite a natural formation. Two stones are standing in a line pointing to 220°. The more northerly one is the taller of the two, measuring 8 feet in total height. The width, from north to south, is 3 feet, the breadth of the north side is 2 feet 6 inches, and of the south side 1 foot 2 inches. The other stone stands 5 feet 7 inches in height. In width from north to south it measures 3 feet 9 inches. It has a nearly uniform breadth of 1 foot 9 inches, and its girth at the widest part is 10 feet.

BROADGATES STONE.

Crosing the Campsie Fells, we find a very pretty standing stone on the farm of Broadgates, in the parish of Strathblane. It stands in a field immediately adjoining the farm buildidings, on the east, between Broadgates and Ballagan House. It is a few yards north of the roadway leading from Strathblane to Campsie. It is a nearly circular pillar of Highland grit, 4 feet 6 inches above ground, and 7 feet in circumference. The local tradition, as told us on the spot, is that it was erected to mark the burial place of "Sir James the Rose," the hero of the well-known Scottish ballad. This, however, is not the only place in Scotland which claims that distinction. In the account of the parish of Strathblane (*New Statistical Account of Stirling*, 1841), occurs the following note:—"An erect stone, on the north of the turnpike road to Campsie, marks the spot where, two centuries ago, Mr Stirling of Ballagan was killed by a miller of the name of Abernethy." This seems to refer to the Broadgates Stone.

THE AULD WIVES' LIFT.

This famous dolmen stands nearly at the summit of Craigmaddie moor, in the parish of Baldernock—a position which commands an extensive prospect in both directions along the low-lying isthmus that separates the Firths of Forth and Clyde. The stones, however, really stand in a hollow of nearly circular form. This hollow is enclosed all round by a cliff-face of rough sandstone, except to the south, where the wall of rock sinks down and permits a wide view. The older statist affirms that the cromlech formerly was surrounded by a grove of oak trees, of which the stumps were still visible in his day. The name he thinks has affinity to the *pierres levées* of Brittany. The country legends are well known. The first affirms that the stones were brought thither by three *carlines* of the olden times in their laps. The other instructs every visitor who finds himself beside the stones to pass through the opening between them if he does not wish to die childless. The monument consists of two supporting stones, capped by a third. The two supporting stones are prismatic in shape, so that between them a triangular opening (referred to in the legend) is left. This opening looks south-west and north-east. A line taken through the longest axis of the capstone gives a direction of 250° magnetic. This may be taken also as the line of direction of the opening. Between the north-west stone and the capstone are two smaller pieces—either to fill up a chink, or broken off by the great pressure. The under stone facing the south-east is 12 feet in length, 14 feet in width at the base, and 7 feet high. That looking to the north-west is 19 feet long, 7 feet at base, and 7 feet high. The top stone, laid flat on the edges of these two, is nearly rectangular in surface shape, 18 feet long, 12 feet wide, and 6 feet in thickness. The stones have not been brought from a distance. They are blocks of the rough sandstone of which the hill is composed.

HERBERTSHIRE CASTLE STONE.

In the *Stirling Journal* of 12th June, 1828, appears a notice of two stone monuments in the neighbourhood of Denny. One, which was known by the name of *Hornbean*, is described as a standing stone within the private grounds of "Herbertshire Castle, which had, at that time, some unintelligible characters engraved on it." The name Hornbean is now utterly lost. There is, however, still in Herbertshire Castle grounds a small stone which has certainly some defaced carvings on it. Whether this be Hornbean, I cannot, of course, say.

It stands about 200 yards to the east of the Castle, upon the edge of a steep bank overlooking the Carron. This bank is an old sea-beach, which is here very beautifully marked. The stone is of coarse sandstone with grit. It stands—slightly off the perpendicular—2 ft. 2 in. in height above ground, is 2 feet broad, and 7 inches thick. On the front or north side a band, bounded by two horizontal lines, run across the top. Beneath this is something like a rude panel, measuring a foot wide at top, 3 inches at the bottom, and 20 inches along the sloping side. At the top of this panel, just under the horizontal band, are some incised marks, which may once have been characters of an alphabetical nature, but they are now so worn as to be practically obliterated.

THE DRUIDS' STONES—DUCHLAGE MOOR.

The second reference in the article above mentioned is to a stone on Duchlage Moor, called the Druids' stone, and said at that time to be a "rocking stone." This is an interesting example in several respects. It is situated high up on the hills, on the edge of a small ravine about midway between the farms of Duchlage and Wester Barnego, nearer the latter, but on the ground of the former. There is quite a group of great stones of dolerite. Mr Kidston thinks their formation and grouping is on the whole the work of nature; but they bear such a close resemblane to an artificially constructed cromlech, that they may have been utilised by the early inhabitants for the purpose for which such grouups of stones were reared by them. In front is an immense mass, consisting of one stone resting on two others. These two appear to have been originally one split into parts. The height of the whole taken at the front is about 9 feet, at the middle, 8 feet, and the length of the mass is 15 feet. A line taken along the length gives a direction of 220° magnetic. The lower stone is 25 feet in circumference. The cap stone, or rocking stone, measures 15 feet in circumference. It seems to have been naturally weathered from the lower stone, and to have originally rested upon it. When thus balanced it may have rocked. It has now, however slipped back, and rocks no more. Accounts are conflicting as to when it ceased to rock. According to the note in the *Journal*, it was rocking 65 years ago. Other information is to the effect that it was rockable less than 30 years ago; but this statement wants verification. Behind the front mass with its capstone is a group of six or seven large stones standing together. I have been told that less than twenty years ago there was a circle of standing stones surrounding the whole group. That is a very interesting statement, and on the authority of a native of the immediate neighbourhood. Unfortunately the circle is not now traceable.

COWANE'S KETTLE.

At a meeting of Stirling Guildry, held in 1892, Dean Millar stated that the Guildry were asked to accept an article that belonged to the founder of Cowane's Hospital, who flourished between 1580 and 1633. Cowane's kettle had been in the possession of the Forresters of Craigannet and Braes for four generations. Captain Gabriel Forrester gave it to his daughter, who married a Mr Glas, Dean of the Stirling Guildry in 1817, and she handed it over to her brother, Captain John Napier Forrester, whose daughters now presented it to the Guildry. The meeting unanimously agreed to accept the welcome gift, and instructed their Clerk to thank the donors. The kettle is of handsome design in brass, and the Guildry intend preserving it in the Guild Hall, so that visitors may have an opportunity of inspecting the interesting relic.

A KING'S BIRTHDAY RIOT IN THE DAYS OF GEORGE II.

(Continued from page 83.)

The action of the Court Party was met by a petition by the Magistrates to the High Court of Justiciary, setting forth the facts of the case from their point of view, and in much the same terms as those of the letter signed "A Burgess of Stirling," who is supposed to have been none other than the Rev. Ebenezer Erskine. In March 1735, the Court of Justiciary disposed of the criminal libel at the instance of the Court Party. The jury returned a verdict of not guilty, and the Court assoilzied the whole of the 19 pannels and dismissed them from the bar. It was observed from the bench that John Don, younger, merchant in Stirling, one of the pursuers, had by his disorder and imprudence, upon the night of the King's birthday, in invading and disturbing the Town Guard, been the occasion and instrument of the whole riot, tumult, and injury committed upon any of the parties, either pursuers or pannels, and also the cause of the whole expenses laid out on the several prosecutions on account of the riots of that evening. The diet of trial of the Magistrates of Stirling, with that of the libel at the magistrates' instance against Sir James Campbell, and the other pursuers in the above case, as also another libel pursued by Sir James Campbell and others against John Watson of Thirty-Acres, and others, merchants and inhabitants of Stirling, was continued till the second Monday of June.

There was afterwards a further adjournment of the trials, and ultimately the whole proceedings were dropped, the action for reduction of the election of magistrates at the previous Michaelmas, which was the original cause of all the disturbance in the burgh, being withdrawn. Mr James Erskine of Grange, whose election as Member of Parliament for the Stirling Burgh had been the burning question in the municipal contest, acted as counsel for the Magistrates in the civil and criminal processes which followed the riot, and in recognition of his services, which were given without fee or reward, he was admitted to the freedom of the burgh on the 4th August, 1735. Mr Erskine's grandson, John Francis, succeeded to the peerage in the family, as seventh Earl of Mar.

END OF VOL. I.